THE TEN COMMANDMENTS IN HISTORY

EMORY UNIVERSITY STUDIES IN LAW AND RELIGION

John Witte Jr., General Editor

BOOKS IN THE SERIES

THE TEN COMMANDMENTS
IN HISTORY

Mosaic Paradigms for a Well-Ordered Society

Paul Grimley Kuntz

Edited by

Thomas D'Evelyn

With a Foreword by

Marion Leathers Kuntz

William B. Eerdmans Publishing Company
Grand Rapids, Michigan / Cambridge, U.K.

Wm. B. Eerdmans Publishing Co.
255 Jefferson Ave. S.E., Grand Rapids, Michigan 49503 /
P.O. Box 163, Cambridge CB3 9PU U.K.

Printed in the United States of America

09 08 07 06 05 04   7 6 5 4 3 2 1

Library of Congress Cataloging-in-Publication Data

Kuntz, Paul Grimley, 1915-2000
The ten commandments in history: Mosaic paradigms for a well-ordered society /
Paul Grimley Kuntz; edited by Thomas D'Evelyn;
with a foreword by Marion Leathers Kuntz.
p.   cm.
Includes bibliographical references and index.
ISBN 0-8028-2660-1 (pbk.: alk. paper)
1. Ten commandments — Criticism, interpretation, etc. — History.
I. D'Evelyn, Thomas.   II. Title.

BV4655.K86   2004
222'.1606 — dc22

2003064205

www.eerdmans.com

Contents

III. Modern

Foreword

My husband, Paul Grimley Kuntz, was a passionate man — passionate
about ideas, passionate about life and living. As a metaphysician, he
was constantly thinking of possibilities and solutions to intellectual problems. He was a Platonist with a deep commitment to the concept of harmony. In fact, our first conversation in March 1970 was about harmony. I
was preparing Jean Bodin's *Colloquium Heptaplomeres* for publication, and I
suggested to my future husband this work as an outstanding example of
various concepts of harmony. We married six months after our initial discussion, and we never ceased discussing harmony. I used to tease Paul by
saying he wanted to marry me because I knew something about harmony
that he did not.

From his early philosophic studies he was fascinated by concepts of
order. This interest was correlative to his intellectual pursuit of harmony.
From his numerous publications about order and from his speculations
about order and chaos, the seed for his final work on the Decalogue was
nourished.[1] Paul also gleaned ideas about the universality of the Decalogue
and its place in an ordered society from Jean Bodin's *Colloquium
Heptaplomeres*,[2] which I was translating and annotating in the early days of
our marriage. Bodin's use of the Decalogue figures prominently in Paul's final work.

When the Supreme Court of the United States ruled in 1980 that the

1. See especially *The Concept of Order*, ed. Paul G. Kuntz (Seattle: University of
Washington Press, 1968).
2. *Colloquium of the Seven about Secrets of the Sublime of Jean Bodin*, translation,
annotations, and critical readings by Marion Leathers Kuntz (Princeton: Princeton University Press, 1975).

1978 Kentucky statute "mandating the display of the Ten Commandments in every classroom of the state" was unconstitutional, my husband wrote in an important article that Kentucky's Ten Commandments statute "is most instructive in the crisis of moral education in the United States."[3] My husband was constantly concerned with the moral decline in American education and society, and the Supreme Court's negative ruling on the Ten Commandments was the catalyst for almost ten years of research and thought about the Decalogue and its role in American life. He noted: "There has come into being a new body of legal knowledge that shows how the Ten Commandments traditionally were used to teach the moral restraint that undergirds obedience to the law." In a carefully analyzed article my husband spelled out the legal propositions involved and the pursuant ethical concerns. He spent more than a year writing to legal experts and speaking to legal scholars about the Decalogue, and he enjoyed especially his conversations with Professor Harold J. Berman of Emory University School of Law, Dr. John J. Hayes of Emory University Candler School of Theology, and also many others. The legal aspects were only a starting point for Paul Kuntz's investigations and reflections about the Decalogue.

He left no stone unturned as he began to prepare his magnum opus on the Decalogue. He considered its history and its use throughout the ages until the present. Every conceivable aspect of the Ten Commandments and the number ten as an ordering principle was explored with extensive research and numerous conversations with biblical scholars, historians, art historians, philosophers, and others who had a knowledge of the subject. His study of the number ten as a paradigm for ordering led him to study the zodiac, and he published a significant article on this subject.[4] He studied the Ten Commandments in art, and his extensive research in this area alone provided enough material for a separate book. He preferred, however, to include this aspect of the Decalogue in the body of his work. He was interested in the movie versions of the Ten Commandments and corresponded with the heirs of Cecil B. DeMille. The earliest black-and-white version of the Decalogue was especially important to him, since it emphasized the moral aspects of the Decalogue in an explicit manner.

3. See "The Ten Commandments on Schoolroom Walls? Why Did the Supreme Court Reject the 1978 Kentucky Statute (Stone v. Graham)? Could Such a Law Succeed?" *Journal of Law and Public Policy* (University of Florida) 9, no. 1 (fall 1997): 2-36, note esp. p. 3.

4. See the article "Zodiac," in the *Encyclopaedia of Iconography*, ed. Helene Roberts.

He traveled to the slide library of the Fogg Art Museum and to the J. Pierpont Morgan collection. I remember the joy he expressed when we went to the Museo Correr in Venezia to see Titian's *Procession of Christ,* a *xilografia* in which the ark of the covenant and the ten tables of God's law are prominently displayed. He loved to go to the Chiesa di San Moisè in Venezia, where behind the central altar is a huge stone sculpture of Moses bringing God's law down from Mount Sinai. He was also thrilled when we viewed the first column in the colonnade of the Palazzo Ducale, on whose capital is sculpted God handing down the Decalogue to Moses. On this capital, which is dedicated to justice, Moses and the law are represented on two sides of the column. On the side which faces the main entry to the Palazzo Ducale, one sees Moses receiving the law from God on Mount Sinai; on the side facing the colonnade Moses is depicted as the lawgiver to the Israelites.

My husband spent the last years of his life researching and writing his great work on the Decalogue. Throughout the long labors of research he was always joyful, and he completed his book two years before his death. Paul Kuntz was a deeply religious man who not only found religious profundity in the Decalogue, but he was convinced that the Decalogue offered the most reasonable paradigm for a well-ordered society. He decried the loss of the true meaning of the Decalogue. His research proved what he had suspected: that in modern usage a decalogue had become only a paradigm for the number ten. For example, he found that Benito Mussolini had a decalogue of principles for his socialist program.[5] Hollywood brought out a movie entitled *Ten,* starring a glamorous actress as the epitome of sexual desire — hence she was a "ten." Paul hoped his book would be a catalyst for a more profound understanding of the meaning of the Decalogue and its appropriate application in the modern world. He longed for the time when the Decalogue would reassume its true significance.

My husband's work on the Decalogue led him to begin a study of Thomas Jefferson and his concept of rights and responsibilities, and on this topic he was working when he was stricken in Venezia with a massive stroke which resulted in his untimely death seven months later in Atlanta.

I am deeply grateful for those who have worked diligently for the publication of this book. Colonel Nimrod McNair was impressed with my husband's book when he read it while still in manuscript, and it was he

5. Don Bruno Bertoli, director, Archivio Patriarcale, Venezia, first brought this to my husband's attention.

who secured the funds for the editing of Paul's opus. Although the book had been completed two years prior to his death, my husband chose not to make his syntax more felicitous. This task was completed by Tom D'Evelyn, who shortened the book and smoothed out the grammar. His editing of Paul's two-thousand-page text is deeply appreciated. I am also grateful to Professor John Witte, Jr., of the Emory University School of Law for his interest in the book and his help in its publication. To these and to many others who have provided valuable information for this undertaking, I am deeply grateful.

In regard to my husband's work on the Decalogue, I think a citation from the Roman poet Horace is appropriate:

Exegi monumentum aere perennius. (*Odes* 3.30.1, "I have built a monument more lasting than bronze")

MARION LEATHERS KUNTZ
Fuller E. Callaway Professor
Regents Professor
Research Professor
Georgia State University
Atlanta, Georgia

Editor's Preface

Paul Kuntz worked on this book for the last decade of his life. It was his last project in a retirement that saw him writing and publishing in a way not possible during his career as a teacher. It is the work of a teacher-scholar at the height of his powers.

It was incomplete at his death. When it came to me for editing, it contained twice as many chapters and ten times as many words. Some of the chapters were polished; indeed, some had been published in journals. But the mass of it was rough. In a majority of cases the documentation of bibliographical sources was incomplete or nonexistent.

Paul had envisioned a large, indeed an encyclopedic work. His research had been prodigious. His plans for the book changed and expanded as he discovered new facets of the topic. Throughout the 1990s I watched with amusement, enthusiasm, and the horror that only a developmental editor can feel at such moments. The work was ongoing and luminous. Each chapter was a self-standing essay, and he was planning new chapters as if he were a young man with a lifetime ahead of him.

The process of bringing it to the publisher involved some hard decisions. It was simply too large to publish as is. Editing it into what Paul would have himself expected was impossible: Paul alone could have done that. In the end, complexity had to be sacrificed in favor of what seemed the remarkable thing about it: a continuous, almost seamless discourse about the tradition of the Ten Commandments. The result is a set of readings that engages the reader in the very experience about which Paul had devoted his study of the Decalogue: the act of interpreting principles in terms of changing circumstances.

So Paul's impetus was not solely scholarly. Indeed, it was in part political. Paul was concerned about a decline of civil order in the United States. As a philosopher, Paul believed in conversation; in this and other ways he was Socratic. I believe he wrote these chapters in the spirit of dialogue. He believed his essays on the varieties of decalogues would inspire a new reverence for the Ten Commandments and thus help bring order out of what seemed to verge on chaos.

This spirit informs his view of the Decalogue itself. Paul believed the commandments were principles of universal adaptability. The reader will note his use of the word "paradigm." His essays focus on how great minds adapted the Ten Commandments to the needs of their peculiar circumstances.

This question of interpretation is relevant in several areas today. In *Natural and Divine Law: Reclaiming the Tradition for Christian Ethics*, Jean Porter writes in terms familiar to the reader of this book:

> How do we move from the first principles of practical reason, or the immediate conclusion expressed in the Decalogue, to more specific moral judgements? The summary answer to this question would be that these more specific moral judgements are derived through rational reflection, starting from first principles and taking account of the intelligible ordering of human nature and the needs of human life. However, it would be a mistake to attempt to translate this into a formula for arriving at moral conclusions in any and all circumstances. The kind of reflection that is needed, and the generality and certainty of the conclusions, will legitimately reflect the kind of issue being addressed.[1]

The tension between the closed letter and open or revisable significance is a hermeneutic principle. In Michael Fishbane's words, it is essential to the activity carried on by "the sages." "[J]ust as the closing of Scripture in later times meant that 'all' is 'in it' (as an old epigram put it) and nowhere else, so too is 'everything' already on the tablets. In this sense, divine instruction was virtually complete at Sinai. Ongoing interpretations (of those or other words) do not therefore add to God's original voice, but rather give it historical and human expressions. This is an essential postulate of the sages, and it is fundamental to the work of Midrash."[2]

---

1. Jean Porter, *Natural and Divine Law: Reclaiming the Tradition for Christian Ethics* (Grand Rapids: Eerdmans, 1995), p. 95.
2. Michael Fishbane, *The Exegetical Imagination* (Cambridge, Mass., and London: Harvard University Press, 1998), pp. 10-11.

Paul Kuntz was, as it were, a "sage." His profound commitment to the word is matched by his commitment to its changing senses, as the reader can see on every page of this book. Personally, he was inspired by Eric Voegelin's writings on Moses and the Decalogue. Voegelin writes: "While the Decalogue, to be sure, has something to do with 'morality,' just as the thornbush episode had with 'philosophy,' it is not a moral catechism but the body of fundamental rules which constitute a people under God."

Interpretation is then constitutive of the people of God. Voegelin writes: "The commands are not general rules of conduct but the substance of divine order to be absorbed by the souls of those who listen to the call. Only to the degree to which the divine substance of the proclamation has entered the human substance will the people indeed have been transformed into the royal domain under God."

Paul was a patriot. I think he longed to see the United States of America as a "people of God." But he was also, as a philosopher and, equally important, as a man, a citizen of the world.

I write this on July 4, 2002: Independence Day. A discussion on National Public Radio focuses attention on the flexibility of the Constitution. The issue: rewrite the Constitution through amendments or reinterpret it though court cases and ongoing debate? On the whole, the latter approach has prevailed. Why? The principles of the Constitution seem to both prevent rewriting and encourage reinterpretation. Could it be that the United States of America is a "nation under God" in this sense, among others: that the very enduringness of the nation depends upon an ethos of interpretation rooted in the Mosaic Decalogue? I see Paul as he cocks his shining eye at my proposal and begins talking.

Acknowledgments

I t is a special privilege to publish this, the last great work of my late colleague Professor Paul Grimley Kuntz. Paul Kuntz was a distinguished member of the Emory philosophy faculty and an ardent supporter of the Law and Religion Program. He was also an avid reader and reviewer of several earlier titles in our Emory University Studies in Law and Religion series. His two favorite titles in this series were Harold J. Berman's *Faith and Order: The Reconciliation of Law and Religion* (1993) and Brian Tierney's *The Idea of Natural Rights* (1997). This title is very much like those earlier series titles that Paul so much admired — broad in ken, bold in vision, and balanced in wit, wisdom, and *Wissenschaft*.

On behalf of my colleagues in the Law and Religion Program, I would like to express my appreciation to a number of persons who have generously supported the preparation of this title. Special thanks are due to Professor Marion L. Kuntz, Paul's widow and coworker on many projects, for supporting the preparation of this text and for establishing, in Paul's memory, the Decalogue Lecture Series and Decalogue Scholars Program under the auspices of our Law and Religion Program at Emory University.

I would like to thank Colonel Nimrod McNair and other members of the Executive Leadership Foundation in Atlanta for their gracious and unstinting support of the publication of this book. I also wish to thank Dr. Thomas D'Evelyn for working so effectively to transform Paul's unfinished manuscript into such a learned, lithe, and lively text, and Ms. Amy Wheeler, Assistant Editor of this series, for overseeing the production of this manuscript.

JOHN WITTE, JR.
General Editor

∽ I ∽

CLASSICAL AND MEDIEVAL

◡ 1 ◡

The Ten Commandments,
Ancient and Modern

It is easy to be talked out of the old Mosaic "Thou shalt not's." They are so frustrating to what comes naturally. The ancient Old Testament God of wrath, whose fear was taken to mean fright rather than awe, needed, says modernism, to be replaced. Moses lived in a world of Oriental despots and could not avoid using the model of a pharaoh of Egypt or king of Babylonia in summoning Israel to serve the Lord. Christians rejoiced that Jesus gave a "new commandment, to love one another," and Jews coupled Hillel to Jesus in summarizing the law: "Thou shalt love the Lord thy God . . . and thy neighbor as thyself." So modern revision was following the noblest reformulation of Judaism and of Christianity. Encourage virtue rather than rebuke vice. Show how people considered equal can build democracy, freed from subjection to the harsh overlord and judge whose prohibitions damn sinners, which, viewed with prophetic stringency, means all of us.

Let us look at the two parallel accounts of the tables brought down from Sinai and surmise in the King James Version what various moderns have sought to supplant. We have here a double purpose. The problem is to see the difficulties the modernists have with the tablets of stone, and then to appreciate the task of apologetics from a small sampling of Jewish, Catholic, and Protestant thinkers.

EXODUS
Chapter 20
And God spake all these words, saying,

I am the LORD thy God, which have brought thee out of the land of Egypt, out of the house of bondage.

Thou shalt have no other gods before me.

Thou shalt not make unto thee any graven image, or any likeness of any thing that is in heaven above, or that is in the earth beneath, or that is in the water under the earth:

Thou shalt not bow down thyself to them, nor serve them: for I the LORD thy God am a jealous God, visiting the iniquity of the fathers upon the children unto the third and fourth generation of them that hate me;

And shewing mercy unto thousands of them that love me, and keep my commandments.

Thou shalt not take the name of the LORD thy God in vain; for the LORD will not hold him guiltless that taketh his name in vain.

Remember the sabbath day, to keep it holy.

Six days shalt thou labour, and do all thy work:

But the seventh day is the sabbath of the LORD thy God: in it thou shalt not do any work, thou, nor thy son, nor thy daughter, thy manservant, nor thy maidservant, nor thy cattle, nor thy stranger that is within thy gates:

For in six days the LORD made heaven and earth, the sea, and all that in them is, and rested the seventh day: wherefore the LORD blessed the sabbath day, and hallowed it.

Honour thy father and thy mother: that thy days may be long upon the land which the LORD thy God giveth thee.

Thou shalt not kill.

Thou shalt not commit adultery.

Thou shalt not steal.

Thou shalt not bear false witness against thy neighbour.

Thou shalt not covet thy neighbour's house, thou shalt not covet thy neighbour's wife, nor his manservant, nor his maidservant, nor his ox, nor his ass, nor any thing that is thy neighbour's.

DEUTERONOMY

Chapter 5

And Moses called all Israel, and said unto them, Hear, O Israel, the statutes and judgments which I speak in your ears this day, that ye may learn them, and keep, and do them.

The LORD our God made a covenant with us in Horeb.

The LORD made not this covenant with our fathers, but with us, even us, who are all of us here alive this day.

The LORD talked with you face to face in the mount out of the midst of the fire,

(I stood between the LORD and you at that time, to shew you the word of the LORD: for ye were afraid by reason of the fire, and went not up into the mount;) saying,

I am the LORD thy God, which brought thee out of the land of Egypt, from the house of bondage.

Thou shalt have none other gods before me.

Thou shalt not make thee any graven image, or any likeness of any thing that is in heaven above, or that is in the earth beneath, or that is in the waters beneath the earth:

Thou shalt not bow down thyself unto them, nor serve them: for I the LORD thy God am a jealous God, visiting the iniquity of the fathers upon the children unto the third and fourth generation of them that hate me,

And shewing mercy unto thousands of them that love me and keep my commandments.

Thou shalt not take the name of the LORD thy God in vain: for the LORD will not hold him guiltless that taketh his name in vain.

Keep the sabbath day to sanctify it, as the LORD thy God hath commanded thee.

Six days thou shalt labour, and do all thy work:

But the seventh day is the sabbath of the LORD thy God: in it thou shalt not do any work, thou, nor thy son, nor thy daughter, nor thy manservant, nor thy maidservant, nor thine ox, nor thine ass, nor any of thy cattle, nor thy stranger that is within thy gates; that thy manservant and thy maidservant may rest as well as thou.

And remember that thou wast a servant in the land of Egypt, and that the LORD thy God brought thee out thence through a mighty hand and by a stretched out arm: therefore the LORD thy God commanded thee to keep the sabbath day.

Honour thy father and thy mother, as the LORD thy God hath commanded thee; that thy days may be prolonged, and that it may go well with thee, in the land which the LORD thy God giveth thee.

Thou shalt not kill.

Neither shalt thou commit adultery.

Neither shalt thou steal.

Neither shalt thou bear false witness against thy neighbour.

Neither shalt thou desire thy neighbour's wife, neither shalt thou covet thy neighbour's house, his field, or his manservant, or his maidservant, his ox, or his ass, or any thing that is thy neighbour's.

When we study the Decalogue through modern and modernistic eyes, there emerge problems which may most appropriately be stated as "Ten Difficulties" confronting modernists (I shall not trouble to define "modernistic," which is a losing battle, like trying to define any -ism).

Ten Difficulties Modernists Have with Moses' Decalogues

1. How could anyone think that any code or abstract formula could prescribe the good life? Can any creed succeed in stating the ultimate truth? Are there not so many variations in both thought and conduct that a code must fail?

2. To reduce the good life to ten precepts is doubly illusory. Ten has come to suggest completeness, and each precept carries the appearance of clarity. As to the first difficulty, the Sabbath is prescribed, but not other festivals that are also obligatory; and as a sign of the covenant, circumcision of males is not included. Similarly, just as ten fails to signify completeness, and the 613 laws of the Torah presented in the Pentateuch come closer to completeness, so the simplicity of each of the ten fails. They are really "ten ambiguities," for "thou shalt not take the name of the Lord in vain" may mean to proscribe magical imprecations, or cursing one's enemies in God's name, or general blasphemy.

3. The force of moral law stated as imperative comes from allowing no exception or change. In words appropriate to Kant, famous in moral philosophy for his versions of the categorical imperative ("so act that the rule of thy act is law universal"), the principle must be universal and eternal. But the Mosaic Decalogue is far from necessary. It is particularly Near Eastern geographically, from pastoral and patriarchal stages of culture, and characteristically the covenant of the Hebrew people with the particular God of Abraham, Isaac, and Jacob. Four leading assumptions of the first or pious tablet are exclusive monotheism (or henotheism), aniconism, antiblasphemy or anti-incantation, and Sabbatarianism. These have become so common to those of us who grew up in a puritanical Anglo-American culture that we sometimes overlook how peculiar is the adoption of these Israelitic taboos as our very own. Why should we presume to think that all cultures at all times must conform to these standards? Why should we further assume that we are obliged to convert all peoples

to conformity to these commandments, and like us, to believe that unless they have these taboos they cannot honor parents, and know the basis for prohibiting murder, adultery, theft, and covetousness of property? A minimal knowledge of Chinese ethical teaching, of Confucius or of Mencius, shows us important moral precepts independent of our peculiar religious heritage.

4. The Mosaic law is partly a matter of cult or religious practice, partly a matter of civil law, partly moral law. It is very mixed by our standard, because we have clarified these aspects of culture. It may well satisfy our nostalgia for a unified culture to read the magnificent account of the mediation of the awesome god of Sinai and the people at the foot of the mountain. But we cannot make Sabbath observance a matter of law as we do murder and theft. Crimes differ from pious observances and pious avoidances. To do otherwise is to try to punish blasphemy, for example, which for orthodox Christians includes denying that God is in three persons. The Christian meaning of "taking the Lord's name in vain" would condemn Moses himself. It is rather difficult for the state to fix an *A* upon the breast of an adulteress, and most would say that violation of the marriage vow of faithfulness was primarily a sin, and also a vice, but not as such a crime. Certainly the attitude of lust, desire of another's wife, and envy of another's property leading to covetousness are properly sins. It is indeed a merit of Moses' formula to cover thought, word, and deed. But we cannot at our stage of culture accept without much clarification such a mixed bag of cult, civil law, and moral teaching. Civil law proscribes deeds only. It is piety and morality that concern thought and word. For us to adopt Mosaic law proves our confusion and perpetuates it.

5. We cannot take as the sole basis of civil law and morality such a peculiar conception of divinity, or even of any theology. That is, the Decalogue says who is to be the God of Israel and what he requires of his people, what he approves, what he condemns. The assumption is of a "jealous" God who rewards the faithful with long life in the promised land and punishes the faithless to the third and fourth generation. Sometimes it is said that the model here is of an Oriental tyrant who loves his favorites and despises those who do not serve him. How can we rest our judgment of right and wrong on this peculiar conception of divinity, or on any theology? We can formulate voluntary contractual relations between persons, and on a human basis deduce what is wrong about murder, adultery, theft, lust, and covetous-

ness, and we may assume that honoring of parents is a relation within the family, as is the reciprocal care of children, which is required for education in a harmonious atmosphere.

6. Then there is the ambiguity in the numbering. Does the Decalogue begin with one taboo, the worship of other gods and the prohibition of idols, as in Deuteronomy, or with two taboos, as conventionally numbered in Exodus? On this hinges whether there is one prohibition of coveting a neighbor's house, wife, etc., or two prohibitions, of "desir[ing] thy neighbour's wife" and of "covet[ing] thy neighbour's house, his field," etc. Coming out with ten seems forced upon the series. Much arbitrariness enters upon what is supposedly necessary.

7. Sometimes, widely accepted rules seem only suggested by particular prohibitions. If the Ten Words are to be primarily moral rather than statements of cult or law, then it would be appropriate to condemn lying and deceit. "Thou shalt not tell falsehoods" would be a general or universal prohibition. Then the prohibition of false testimony would be a specific falling under the general and an application covered by law against slander, libel, and perjury. Or the command might be, as in Kantian morality, "Always tell the truth," and we could deduce "Thou shalt not lie."

8. We have now opened up a frequent objection against the Mosaic code. This is the negative form of the injunction, "Thou shalt not." Negativity rouses rebellion, and is often a frustrating technique, now disapproved of in education. The proper attitude of worship is set by the early positive commands "Keep the Sabbath" and "Honour thy father and thy mother." But why the concluding set of "Thou shalt not's"? Fit for a legal code, in which crimes must be prohibited, but not for issues we may leave up to the free person. The confusion of moral and legal is then this: if the Ten Words are to direct thought, word, and deed, they should be stated positively to guide and instruct, particularly in training the youth, but if the Ten Words are to proscribe crimes, then all should be negative. What we now have, because it is both moral and legal, as well as cultic, is a mixture that is never defended in the texts.

9. Besides negativity, another common objection to the Mosaic code is that it is concerned with protecting private property and that women are, at least in the earlier version of Exodus, classified as property of husbands. Or this: from the perspective of shared or common property, the documents seem to be bourgeois, a defense of the property of

those who possess much, and aimed to prevent class war by the have-nots. Persons of socialist persuasion would prefer to represent the divine as concerned with the poor, and therefore to find spiritually higher the prophets such as Amos and the New Testament Beatitudes of Jesus. Feminist ire is directed against the patriarchal attitudes of the conclusion of the Mosaic Decalogue. It is often noted that "wife" is second to "house," and classified with manservant, maidservant, ox and ass, etc. The command "thou shalt not covet" is directed to the male lord, and the female is a thing, slave, or animal! Not to distinguish person from thing or animal is only slightly corrected in Deuteronomy, which at least distinguishes the lust leading to adultery ("Neither shalt thou desire thy neighbour's wife") from the envy that leads to theft ("Neither shalt thou covet thy neighbor's house, his field, or his manservant, or his maidservant, his ox, or his ass, or any thing . . ."). Some modern critics who revise morality would rather see a decalogue that inculcated protection of public property and equal respect for all persons (and, it is often added, if sexual discrimination is condemned, then any and all discrimination based on color, ancestry, language, age, would also be condemned).

10. The tenth difficulty with the Ten Commandments of Moses is that grounding cult, law, and morals on divine imperative makes the whole set of taboos, crimes, virtues, and vices *a matter of faith*. The whole way of life is protected by the faith as sacrosanct, and discussion, let alone criticism and revision, is rendered impossible. What is dogmatically asserted is protected from rational argumentation; it has been made undiscussable and undebatable. What God so commanded, what is given on authority of Moses, what is ratified by Christ and all the prophets and scholars of synagogue and church — the only appropriate response is to obey.

This book participates in a millennia-long conversation about the Ten Commandments. Modern objections are just that — contemporary responses to an idea of order that has always been challenged. Regarding the tenth objection, we may note here that the modern conception of "beyond debate" does not square with what the scribes of Exodus and of Deuteronomy themselves did. Faced with a new situation, they interpreted the law. Interpretations or versions of the law have come down to us. One version, the earlier, reasons that since God the Creator rested on the seventh day after six days, so man should rest after six days of work. There is a cosmic myth used to justify human worship. The later version uses the history of Israel's bondage in Egypt to justify the rest of Sabbath.

This book is a selective history of and a contribution to a process begun in the Pentateuch itself — a process of interpretation. Contrary to the assumption of the modernists, the original Ten Commandments are not innocent of the facts of changing circumstances. Indeed, they are originally presented in an interpretive context. First, the legal text is embedded in a narrative, the story of the covenant, which backdates all the laws to the time of Moses, thus making them essential to the continuity of the existence of the emerging Jewish commonwealth. The laws look back, but they also look forward to the life of Israel, and so will be reinterpreted in successive frameworks of understanding. Second, there is a distinction between the ten, which are command laws, and the balance of the laws in Exodus, and those found in Numbers, Leviticus, and Deuteronomy, which are primarily "case" laws — extensions of the ten based on new circumstances and pronounced by the judges. From Moses and Solomon to Daniel, interpretation of law is the sign of wisdom and leadership.

The law is a living thing. It is no wonder, then, that it has been said there are seventy different ways of interpreting the Torah. This book is a contribution to the ongoing life of the Ten Commandments.

∽ 2 ∽

Philo Judaeus:
A Decalogue in Balance

P hilo of Alexandria, known as Philo Judaeus (30 B.C.E.–50 C.E.), a contemporary of Paul the apostle, was a leading member of the Jewish
community in Alexandria. In about 40 C.E. he headed a deputation to the
mad emperor Claudius in Rome to plead on behalf of Jews who refused to
worship the emperor. A prolific author, Philo worked on a synthesis of
Greek philosophy and Jewish Scripture. He presents the Ten Commandments of Moses as the best moral guide for all mankind. His universalistic
interpretation helped shape Christian theology.

Philo formulated his Mosaic philosophy in the Greek language, using
Greek philosophical concepts to show that the Jew lived by the most intelligible and loftiest morality possible. In his remarkable treatise *De
Decalogo*, known by its Latin title, he speaks as a rational man addressing
rational men. It deserves close study, particularly by those who accuse Judaism of remaining tribal, as did Arnold Toynbee, and those who consider
Jewish law little but eccentric taboos. (Another important conception of
the purpose of Judaic faithfulness to Torah is seen in Moses Maimonides'
Guide for the Perplexed.) The good Jew is guided by examples of all the virtues known to the Greek philosophers, especially temperance, courage,
prudence, and justice; and this ideal, revealed by Moses and the prophets,
as the perfection of humanity, surpasses the Hellenic model in judgment,
righteousness, and loving-kindness. *De Decalogo* was often quoted by the
fathers of the Christian church — sometimes without acknowledgment, as
by Clement of Alexandria.

Philo brings an array of philosophical methods to the text of the
Decalogue, as presented in the Greek of the seventy translators, the Septua-
gint Bible. Now the seventy certainly used grammar, logic, and epistemol-

ogy, but they had not developed them as theoretical disciplines. Philo used these techniques to make explicit what the text of Moses means. Thus he created his "Mosaic philosophy." After we have examined the methods Philo used, we shall state some of the results of reinterpreting the particular commandments of the Decalogue as parts of a logical whole. (All quotes are from *De Decalogo*.)

Philo begins with the method of allegory, which takes one beyond the literal to the hidden meaning. Philo speaks of men who found a nation and are "in themselves unwritten laws." For Philo, Abraham was symbolic of faithfulness, and his life could be read as the injunction "Be faithful!" Similarly we could justly say that Samson means "Be strong!"; that Deborah means "Lead your people against their enemies!"; that Nathan means "Face the King and tell him he is a murderer and adulterer!"

The laws were given not in a city but in the wilderness. Cities are full of evils, "impiety towards God and wrongdoing between man and man." God's world is turned upside down by a pride which "brings divine things into utter contempt, even though they are supposed to receive the highest honours." The pagan worships "idols of stone and wood" and seeks to make himself happy with "gold crowns and purple robes." The allegorical meaning of Israel in the wilderness, after the exodus from Egypt, is that one should withdraw from wickedness to "cleanse his soul and purge away the . . . stains." Only then can one receive the holy laws.

Philo often provides a third and fourth meaning: so he does for the law given in the wilderness. The third is that men setting out on a long voyage need rules, and life needs "principles of justice" which foster "harmony and fellowship of spirit [by] rendering to every man his due." The allegorical meaning of the giving of the law through Moses is that we should look to a prophet, here one judged "best suited to be the revealer of verities," to get the main points, the "heads summarizing the particular laws." Such a principle as justice is not invented, but lies "ready for . . . use."

Rational man wants to know and abhors being deceived. The Ten Commandments command motives, words, and acts that are *good* because they *are* good and can be *known* to be good. And what is forbidden is forbidden because certain motives, words, and acts are evil and can be known to be evil. God commands what he commands because these are good, and he forbids what he forbids because these are evil. The reason for this is that he is good, perfect good, and reveals himself in a creation, nature, that is "very good." How can we know good? By knowing God, for he is the standard by which we judge all good things. Moreover, we can know our conscience, the inner voice of God. "For every soul has for its birth-fellow and house-mate a monitor whose way is to admit nothing that calls for censure, whose nature is ever to hate evil and love virtue, who is its accuser and its judge in one."

The one bit of classical myth used in *De Decalogo* is: "desire entails the punishment of Tantalus; . . . he missed everything that he wished for just when he was about to touch it." (In Greek mythology Tantalus was a king who killed his father Pelops and was punished by being incapable of reaching fruit and water placed before him. His name is the origin of the word "tantalize.")

Human nature can be known through society and politics. We can know which motives, words, and acts produce harmony, such as friendship, and we can know what produces war and know its miseries. We can know that either the rule of a few or the rule of a mob is an evil constitution, and that the principle of equality before the law is essential to a good constitution.

But if these arguments were all we knew of Philo, we would miss the heart of his Mosaic philosophy. The heart of the system is that all depends upon One, the Eternal, the Creator, the Judge; that there is a heaven of perfect order, and man's soul is akin to the higher level, he is of all creatures the most intelligent and civilized; and that he is dependent upon mother nature and needs to respect nature's limits. "A man should not forget what he is." Philo's theism is *also* deeply humanistic and naturalistic.

The result of Philo's methods is a philosophy holding the cosmic meaning of the first table of the law in balance with the moral meaning of the second table. "The transcendent source of all that exists is God, [and] piety is the source of the virtues." Among the attributes of God, many expressed by metaphor, the ones most relevant to the moral commandments are: "Father and Maker of all [whose nature] parents copy by begetting particular persons." Honoring parents is analogical to honoring God. God is "the primal and most perfect good, from whom as from a fountain is showered the water of each particular good upon the world and them that dwell therein." Creation is here expressed as emanation.

To ignore or to neglect God is to fail to recognize the principle of goodness, and consequently atheism leads to immorality. "Atheism is the source of all iniquities." To turn to idols, particularly idols of the pagan gods about whom myths tell of much immorality, is perverse. It is to turn from the one to the many; from Creator to creatures; from the Eternal, without beginning or end, to the temporal and transient; from the unchanging to the ever changing; from the perfect to the imperfect.

Thus Philo moves from the first to the second commandment. Idolatry is turning from knowledge to fancy. For Philo, to philosophize is to pose pure pieties against polytheistic idolatry. Not surprisingly, to use the arts, painting and sculpture, to represent gods is mischievous: "for these idolaters cut away the most excellent support of the soul, the rightful conception of the Ever-living God."

The first and second commandments lead logically to the third: "not to take God's name in vain." "The name always stands second to the thing which it represents as the shadow which follows the body." After the "existence of the Ever-existent and the honour due to Him as such, He follows it at once in orderly sequence by giving a commandment on the proper use of His title."

The generalization of the third commandment is "swear not at all," which was a teaching of Jesus, who gave a theological reason. Philo gives a philosophical reason: "To swear not at all is the best course and most profitable to life, well suited to a rational nature which has been taught to speak the truth so well on each occasion that its words are regarded as oaths." Since swearing is unnecessary, to take an oath "casts suspicion on the trustworthiness of the man." Philo would thoroughly approve the saying: "Let your yea be yea, and your nay, nay."

Philo includes two arguments, more logical than psychological, why perjury involves self-contradiction. The absurdity of "appeal[ing] to God as a witness . . . to a lie" is evident. God knows the truth and is the Truth; swearing is tantamount to saying that a falsehood is true and not a falsehood. Philo is trying to awaken the conscience and shame the perjurer. Similar is the appeal to friendship: to "work iniquity, transgress the law, join me in impiety." In the appeal to a virtuous relation, the tempter is trying to attract others to vice. Philo hopes the friend will "rush away," keeping his virtue unspoiled by the so-called friend.

Philo adds a more theological analysis. If there is divine providence, then the "height of impiety" is to think that lying can have good result. Would God "disguise the truth" to maintain "my good name with men"? The absurdity here is rather metaphysical, asking the superior, "the Divine, the best of all" to be wicked for the sake of dishonest men.

In short, Philo's argument against perjury is that, as with all evil thoughts, words, and deeds, there are consequences. He never warns of outer darkness of a future life, nor of hellfire and damnation, nor of any devil to pay. He states the bad consequence argument in terms of *Dikē,* Greek for "Justice": "For justice, who surveys human affairs, is inflexible and implacable towards such grave misdeeds, and when she thinks well to refrain from immediate chastisement, be sure that she does but put out her penalties to loan at high interest, only to exact them when the time comes to the common benefit of all."

There are in Philo two quite different accounts of the Sabbath. The second states that the seventh day is "nothing less than a gathering under one head of the feasts and the purifications" of the Jewish year. The conclusion of Philo's second account celebrates the application to nature — to allow fields to lie fallow every seventh year — and recommends the Year of Jubilee every fiftieth year, restoring inheritances to original families, "a very necessary procedure abounding in humanity and justice."

Philo's first version is dependent on the second biblical version in Deuteronomy which reminds Israelites that they had once been slaves in Egypt and should show mercy to the stranger. The first account of the Sabbath gives the justification from Exodus that God ceased from creation after six days, to contemplate his works, and therefore we citizens should "work for six days but rest on the seventh." So much is simply paraphrase. But Philo specifies, as Scripture does not, exactly how to keep the Sabbath holy: to study wisdom and to "contemplate the truths of nature." By "wisdom" apparently is meant critical knowledge arrived at by thinking in detail of all we have done during the preceding six days and to think of what we have "neglected and to take precaution against repetition of any sin." The injunction is to study "every virtue and piety most of all." The coupling of mental work and leisure fulfills the injunction to follow "this great archetype of the two best lives, the practical and the contemplative."

To study "wisdom" is not only moral but intellectual. (Here Philo recalls Plato's *Timaeus.*) We learn "lessons of nature" by turning our minds from the world of change toward the One and the archetypical "incorporeal heaven which is the pattern of the visible." The highest heaven is one of "undeviating revolution" and of "uniformity unbroken and . . . admitting no swerving or alteration." In perfect spheres is best revealed what the Maker has shared with us, a "vision of God." This model of the cosmos was amplified in the cosmic vision of Dante.

But there is a difference between keeping the holy days of the Jewish calendar and using contemplation to gain moral and natural wisdom. We might think the ritual practices need some further justification, such as the cycle of the seasons, to be assimilated to the philosophic justification. But within the system of concepts of order there is alternation between work and leisure and between day and night; and there's the principle of balance between opposite aspects of life; and such observations might justify the combination of ritual practices and the mystical quest of the beatific vision.

The first table of the law, which reminds us about the creation of the world and mankind by the Father, ends with the earthly father begetting and the mother bearing children. The table is unified because the lower, secondary order is a "copy of His nature." As we honor God in the mode of worship, which is proper to the highest cause, so we ought to honor parents in the mode of respect, which is owed to the secondary causes of our being. There is a reference to "pieties," and Philo could justify cosmic piety balanced by familial piety. The fifth commandment is on "the border-line" between the first set, including cosmic and familial piety; we might subsume the five prohibitions as the vices to be avoided by the man of civic piety. Philo's "border-line" is "between the mortal and the immortal side of existence." Father and mother participate in both sides of this division, "the mortal because of the kinship with men and other animals through the perishableness of the body; the immortal because the act of generation assimilates them to God, the generator of the All."

In the fourth commandment there are two sides, both necessary — work and rest; and there are two sides of the Sabbath itself, ritual and contemplation. Underlying all we see a crucial mode of order, the thought of polarity and balance.

> Now we have known some who associate themselves with one of the two sides and are seen to neglect the other. They have drunk of the unmixed wine of pious aspirations and turning their backs upon all other concerns devoted their personal life wholly to the service of God. Others concerning the idea that there is no good outside doing justice to men have no heart for anything else. . . . These may be justly called lovers of men, the former lovers of God. Both come but halfway in virtue; they have it whole who win honours in both departments.

The analysis of the two necessary sides may be compared to the passage in Plato's *Republic* on the good man as devoted to both *mousikē* and *gymnastikē*. The vice attendant on exclusive devotion to the fine arts is weakness, the vice attendant on exclusive devotion to athletics is crudeness. "But all who neither take their fit place in dealings with men by sharing the joy of others at the common good and their grief at the reverse, nor cling to piety and holiness, would seem to have been transformed into the nature of wild beasts. The directions of the fully human life are both towards God and toward fellow humans." Philo's arguments in support of honoring parents are partly theological but largely philosophical. The theological aspect is that parents imitate God (a form of mimesis) in creating children; not to honor parents is to dishonor God, for "he who dishonours the servants of God . . . dishonours also the Lord." Parents are as gods to children, and they deserve gratitude. The "human court" judges those who dishonour parents to be inhuman, foes of mankind, as they are foes of God. Through parents we come "forth from non-existence to existence." The debt is such that it can never be repaid, and strictly speaking justice cannot be secured, for we can only do *something* in return for *everything*. There can be no rate of exchange, but "because they are unable to make a complete return [there can be only indignation for those who] refuse to make even the slightest."

The commandment is tagged to the general maxim, *show proper respect to persons of different status.* There are many other instructions given: to the young in courtesy to the old, to the old on taking care of the young, to subjects on obeying their rulers, to rulers on promoting the welfare of their subjects, to recipients of benefits on requiting them with gratitude, to those who have given of their own initiative not seeking to get repayment as though it were a debt, to servants on rendering an affectionate loyalty to their masters, to masters on showing the gentleness and kindness by which inequality is equalized.

The second table is a set of five enactments which are "all . . . prohibitions, namely adultery, murder, theft, false witness, covetousness or lust." Philo, quite unlike modern interpreters, makes no apology for the negatives in the Decalogue, and does not soften the rebuke to our practices by logical transformation into affirmatives. There are very many vices.

Under the "first head . . . against adultery . . . [are] enactments against seducers and pederasty, against dissolute living and indulgence in lawless and licentious forms of intercourse." Moses describes these "not to show the multiform varieties which incontinence assures, but to bring to shame those who live a disreputable life.

"The second head forbids murder, and . . . violence, insult, outrage, wounding and mutilation.

"The third is that against stealing under which are . . . defaulting debtors, repudiations of deposits, partnerships which are not true to their name, shameless robberies and in general covetous feelings which urge men openly or secretly to appropriate the possessions of others.

"The fourth against bearing false witness embraces many prohibitions. It forbids deceit, false accusation, cooperation with evil doers and using honesty as a screen for dishonesty. . . .

"The fifth blocks that fount of injustice, desire, from which flow the
most iniquitous actions, public and private, small and great, dealing with
things sacred or things profane, affecting bodies and souls and what are
called external things. Nothing escapes desire, and . . . like a flame in the
forest, it spreads abroad and consumes and destroys everything."

Moses' five is expanded to Philo's twenty-five by his subsuming the
more particular prohibitions under the five of the second table, and by his
following the method of reading Moses' five as species whose genera are
suggested. Philo's Decalogue illustrates the fruitfulness of the paradigm
when applied to circumstances by a first-class analytic mind. Ambiguities
and questions lead to further differentiation of goods and bads, virtues and
vices.

Are these vices all evil, and how can we be sure they should be prohibited
most generally by Moses' very firm "thou shalt not"? Are there no exceptions? Is there no gradation between right and wrong? Are not circumstances and alternatives to be considered and judged in particular cases?

Philo's second table begins not with murder but with adultery. Commentators commonly judge the sixth to be the worst, and so our author
also: adultery is the "greatest of crimes." Adultery outranks the seventh,
murder. The corruption of souls is worse than the destruction of the body.
The argument is based on a corrupting motive, a sinful act with another,
and bad results for three: families, children, and the state.

The motive is not the honorable "duty to fellow-men" but "the love
of pleasure which enervates the bodies" of those who indulge in it and so
waste their substance.

The act is not merely the adulterer's but the partner's also, and one
"teach[es] another to share the wrong." The relationship based upon licen-
tiousness cannot be "a true partnership." What Philo may mean by this can
be suggested by the idea that friendship, to be a virtue, must be based on
ends that are honorable. As in partnership of thieves, so in partnership of
adultery, deceit is involved in keeping the secret.

The consequences are many. Does Philo assume the fault to lie with
the woman? The adulteress is estranged from her husband; hatred is
masked by affection. "Indeed it makes havoc of three families: of that of the
husband who suffers from the breach of faith . . . and of two others, those of

the adulterer and the woman, for the infection of the outrage and dishonor and disgrace of the deepest kind extends to the families of both."

Theology is kept to a minimum by concluding that the worst of wrongdoing is also "naturally the abominable God-detested sin of adultery." Murder, by Philo's count the topic of the seventh commandment, takes far less space than his argument against adultery. He appeals to a principle of nature and to a principle of God's possession. First the metaphysical, then the theological argument.

Murder is contrary to nature. Nature, which created man, has equipped him for fellowship by endowing him with reason, the exercise of which leads to harmony and reciprocity of feeling. To murder is to subvert the natural order principle of the well-being of all. At this point Philo's ground is the same law of nature to which a Stoic might appeal.

The biblical argument is that murder is sacrilege and robbery "from its sanctuary of the most sacred of God's possessions." If votive offerings of silver and gold in a building are sacred, how much more the soul in a body? Man is the highest creature because his "soul, . . . most nearly akin to heaven, the purest thing in all that exists, . . . is the clos[est] likeness and copy . . . of the eternal and blessed Archetype." This refers to the scriptural argument that man, the last of God's creations, is made on the sixth day in the "image and likeness of the Father."

There must be laws protecting not only physical life but *any* offense to the person: "violence, insult, outrage, wounding and mutilating."

We come now to the prohibitions of theft and false witness. Philo's arguments here are very similar: theft and bearing false witness undermine the state *(polis)* and society. In the extended senses of these two sins and crimes, it should also be added that they undermine the economy. Although theologians seem to care little about business and finance, Philo is as practical as a financial attorney. Under stealing are "defaulting debtors, repudiations of deposits, partnerships which are not true to their name, shameless robberies and in general covetous feelings which urge men openly or secretly to appropriate the possessions of others." The last item is so broad that it could cover bad accounting and misleading advertising. Similarly "false witness" includes "deceit, false accusation, cooperation with evil-doers and using honesty as a screen for dishonesty." This also has in principle many modern applications.

Stealing, we are reminded by legislation, may be *petty* or *grand* larceny. The thief is "the common enemy of the State *(polis)*, willing to rob all but able to filch from some." If thieves can do so, they will "rob whole cities, careless of punishment because their high distinction seems to set them above the laws." But the worst are the "oligarchs" who take over the government. They disguise "the real fact of government under the grand-sounding name of . . . leadership." Saint Augustine tells the story of King Alexander, who when he captured a pirate berated him: "Why do you dare steal on my sea?" The saucy pirate replied, "How did you dare to steal the sea?"

Every kind of false witness corrupts truth, "the treasure as sacred as anything that we possess in life, which like the sun pours light upon facts and events and allows none of them to be kept in the shade."

This argument has theological overtones; as we saw above under "taking the Lord's name in vain," one of God's essential attributes and names is Truth. But Philo here attends to the consequences of the application of law by lawyers and judges. The false witness "take[s] part with the offenders and against those who are wronged." Further, there must be testimony when evidential facts are missing; when the jury accepts false witness, the accused are unjustly convicted. Judges can be misled. The worst is that both the witness and the jury have taken oaths: the former knowingly sins and "persuade[s judge and jury] to share their sin . . . and to punish persons who deserve no chastisement."

Interpreting the two last pairs, the sixth and seventh, and the eighth and ninth commandments, Philo seems to speak to what are now called the "secular" applications of the Decalogue. He seems to have a firm grasp on the principles needed to guide decency in personal and public relations. Indeed, Philo is unexcelled in his attention to basic principles of economy and finance, government and law, and in the extent to which he speaks to men of affairs.

The climax of *De Decalogo* is reached with the tenth commandment. It is here that Philo offers a completely Stoic analysis of desire; it is by this section that he should be judged as a moral philosopher. Philo quite forgets the specifics of "Thou shalt not covet thy neighbor's house, wife, servants, land, cattle," for stealing and adultery have already been covered. By generalizing without specifying any object, and by therefore referring to any and all, Philo's tenth commandment becomes virtually "Thou shalt not desire." This is historically very important because Catholic moralists often take the tenth commandment as a condemnation of "concupiscence." Protestants tend to reject such a reading as too ascetic.

Although *De Decalogo* began with pride, the source of all vice — we have had to consider all manner of sin and crime — what has propelled the search for wisdom is the lure of happiness. Philosophers such as Aristotle distinguish *eudaimonia,* being of good spirit, with *hēdonē,* pleasure as gratification of the senses. The Epicureans and Stoics interpreted the fulfillment of the good life as *ataraxia,* a state of contentment or, as we say, "peace of mind." When something appears good, sometimes it "raise[s the soul] to a state of elation, yet [the soul] often finds itself depressed and dejected." We call this state of "grief or pain melancholy." And when we are eager to "grasp the [desired] object, but unable to reach so far," we feel frustrated. Now the psychology of Philo takes on an admonitory tone: "don't let yourself get trapped by the passions." Frequently Philo speaks of diseases of the soul, and he, like a physician, is endeavoring to restore his patient to health.

Because "desire . . . originates with ourselves and is voluntary," there is hope. The admonition of Mosaic law is to warn people against "the lifelong surrender to passion" and to appeal to "those who are capable of reformation." The soul can turn from evil to good. In the chain from Plato to Augustine, there is Philo, a philosopher of conversion.

It is significant that the final commandment, the most important for Philo, is stated in a purely philosophic way. Philo's text seems so thoroughly theistic that we almost overlook the philosophic principles used to justify the theology. Philo's *De Decalogo* is a profound reflection on Order with a capital *O.* We have seen that the Ten Commandments presuppose levels of being and value. Therefore a philosophic analysis must try to state the principles of levels, of higher and lower. The ontological hierarchy, since A. O. Lovejoy known as "the Great Chain of Being," runs downward from the one to heaven, human soul, animal, and the rest of visible nature. Philo needs the scheme to specify good relations of humans upward and bad relations of humans downward. We may say that man is akin to heaven — to God — and should honor and worship what is higher, but man is prone to behave like a beast — and much worse — and to pursue low or bodily goals. Only in this moral orientation do we have a metaphysical basis for judgments of what is virtuous and of what is vicious, what is right and what is wrong. There are many modes of disorder such as excess versus limits and moderation, violence versus harmony, one-sidedness versus wholeness, robbery versus reciprocity between equals, but the chief disorder is insubordination and values turned upside down.

The concept of hierarchy is not greatly esteemed today. Among other reasons, it is distrusted because (as in Pseudo-Dionysius) it was intended to refer to the rule of the priestly orders imitating the ranks of seraphim, cherubim, archangels, angels, thrones, dominions, powers. But Philo is committed neither to earthly bishops nor to angelology. On the other hand — Plato's hand! — hierarchy has come to connote classes, a kind of caste system with a philosopher-king, guardians, warriors, merchants, and workers, or through Nietzsche the contrast between the strong nobleman and the weak, resentful peasants. Philo honors the wise prophet Moses, but for him all men are equally human under God and are to be judged by the same laws. Hierarchy is sometimes employed to cast contempt on matter as "dregs of being," as by Macrobius, or to imply that all is a fixed scheme, down to nothing — all, perfectly planned and ruled. Finally, hierarchy sometimes is made to connote the dominance of male over female, or patriarchy, and the dominance of the commonwealth by an absolute monarch.

None of these forms of hierarchal tyranny can be derived from or justified by what we have in Philo's text. Philo would be revolted by the notion that God is masculine or that one male must be the king and lord as an intermediary between the One and human souls. Needless to say, he does not draw lines between Jew and Gentile as such, and there is no hint of any racial superiority to compromise his conception of universal humanity.

Hierarchy begins with the One, the Creator, the Father of all. Just as the book of Genesis opens with "In the Beginning," translated into Greek *en archē* and into Latin *in principio,* the covenant story opens "I am the Lord thy God." Interpreting in propositions of the first commandment, we may say that "there is one First Cause of the World, one Ruler and King, who guides the chariot and steers the bark of the universe in safety, and has expelled from the purest part of all that exists, namely heaven, those mischievous forms of government, oligarchy and mob-rule, which arise among the vilest of men, produced by disorder and covetousness." Philo adds that "God . . . [is] good, the cause of good only and of nothing ill." The final words of *De Decalogo* are: "it befits the Great King that the general safety of the universe should be ascribed to Him, that he should be the guardian of peace and supply richly and abundantly the good things of peace, all of them to all persons in every place and at every time. For indeed God is the Prince of Peace while his subalterns are the leaders in war." These passages leave no doubt that Philo's monotheism is, as Reform rabbis say, "ethical."

God is one, without beginning and without end, eternal, and invisible. He truly *is,* and is *being itself,* and the first cause. His creative act extends throughout the creation's duration as guiding providence. Philo considers this true God to be living and knowing all things and to have no deceit. What he communicates is truth, and he speaks through his prophet

Moses and everyone who will open his soul. His words are deeds, as in the first step of creation, not quoted, "Let there be light and there was light." What God communicates to all creation is unchanging law to which the cosmos relates unswervingly. Since of all his creations he cares most for mankind, his most sacred treasure, he communicates laws as commandments. These laws include the most general heads, which gather together many particular laws, but they are spoken to each individual. The highest law in the universe can relate to the most ordinary individuals. Each of us has within him an inner voice speaking moral truths. God cares whether mankind obeys, his justice knows all, and all obedience is rewarded and all infraction punished.

Because God himself has communicated his nature, acts, and will, and continues to communicate, there is no need for a "proof" of God's existence. What God says in the Bible is matched by Philo's philosophical understanding of the archetypes of heaven, of man's soul and body, of the appropriate limits needed because of the excesses of human pride and desire, and the order that reigns throughout the cosmos, including the visible and bodily world. *De Decalogo* is saying implicitly: put together all you know and you will find the law of Moses appropriate. For Philo, Moses gets the story right. Philo's picture of the levels of being and value is synthetic, and it does not have to be completely detailed because no analytic approach would fit the theme: the Creator, his order and laws, and the more and less of good, truth, beauty.

Heaven is the invisible world of the models or pure forms of being. Philo appeals to our knowledge of the archetypes. We know numbers, and from the Unit we can derive the plurality — most eminently the perfect, or all-encompassing, because including odd and even, the ten. These invisible patterns hold true for the visible world of point, line, and plane. Much of this is Pythagorean and Platonic, but the ten heads of being, the predicables of Aristotle, are the aspects of existence in which the whole cosmos participates. A wise Creator has made an intelligible cosmos. One of the privileges of our soul's kinship with heaven and its Creator is to enjoy sharing with him, in however limited a way, knowledge of his law.

Man's soul is close to heaven in our knowledge of truth, "our most sacred treasure." We have inward knowledge of the good because the law has been written in our hearts. Philo could have quoted Jeremiah, but we know there is a rational soul and a conscience with "law written in the heart." Just as with the numbers where there is rank order under the Unit or One, so within human nature there is rank order under reason and conscience.

There is higher knowledge (wisdom) and lower knowledge. Some people are chosen to be illuminated specially and are "possessed of God," but all can receive the revelation. Context would suggest that knowledge of general law — of universals, normative standards, principles of order — ranks higher than particular cases, individuals, facts, which we collect under categories. The higher part should rule man's lower part, the passions, which are closely connected with the bodily senses; that way the human person is in good order, in balance, with integrity, whole and healthy. Souls are equal before God, and we are said also to be equally children of one mother. Whether this means we are all equally physical, visible, spatial, temporal, mortal is left to us to infer from knowledge of our nature or from observation. Man's body makes him akin to the animals; Philo mentions dogs and storks.

Cosmos, the ordered world of becoming and change, is our visible world. There was a time when cosmos was not, and there will be a time when it will cease to be. Nature has more than temporal limits, and we ought to learn nature's order to know what limits she has set for us. Philo may have a low opinion of bodily passions — they run amok, and do not know their limits — but even though spiritual sight is above physical sight, he does not denigrate the body because it is physical, or even show contempt for matter. Bodies, male and female, come together, and seed generates new life. Bodies in process of generation are akin to the Creator's creation of the cosmos.

We fumble to find the best metaphor, and there is the picture language of chains, ladders, steps and stages, even trees. Philo uses none of these, perhaps because they are all physical and therefore spatially extended things. The notions of "higher" and "lower" are borrowed from linear experience, but there is never a reference to quantitative size or sheer power or force. Some hierarchical arguments are virtual intimidation of the small by the large. Philo is not a metaphysical bully. His kind of gradation is ontological; the kinds of being we find, and the kinds that concern us most, are qualitative, especially where we have right relations to what is superior and wrong relations to what is inferior.

God is the perfect orderer, and in creating heaven he has created a model of perfect order. Not only is there goodness, truth, beauty, and justice, but the principles of the moral life can be grasped among this range of archetypes.

Among the normative statements, in context of recommending gratitude for favors received, Philo writes of tame animals responding to those who give them food because of likeness to them. This could be an instance of a lower level striving to imitate a higher level, a principle found frequently in Neoplatonic writing. "That is what should happen, for it is *always good* (*kalon*, beautiful) for *the inferior to follow the superior in hope of improvement.*" We might call this the cosmic principle of upward mobility.

The most significant normative principles in *De Decalogo* constitute, when assembled, a kind of hierarchical decalogue. They could have been stated regularly or uniformly as "thou shalt's" and "thou shalt not's," for they are often hortatory, and when not, they condemn evil, vice, insubordination, absurdity, error. Keeping them close to the original language, we may arrange them as follows:

A Hierarchical Decalogue Drawn from Philo's *De Decalogo*

1. "As I am a man, I shall not deem it right to adopt the lofty grandeur of the pompous sage, but make nature my home and not overstep her limits. I will insure my mind to have the feelings of a human being. . . . A man should not forget what he is."
2. "Pride . . . brings divine things into utter contempt, even though they are supposed to receive the highest honours."
3. "Pride is . . . the creator of many other evils, boastfulness, haughtiness, inequality, and these are the sources of wars, both civil and foreign, suffering no place to remain in peace."
4. "Laws [are] not the inventions of a man but quite clearly the oracles of God."
5. It is evil when "everything is debased, the genuine overpowered by the spurious, the true by the specious, which is intrinsically false but creates impressions whose plausibility serves but to delude."
6. "Let no one who has a soul worship a soulless thing."
7. It is absurd for a man to worship an animal, though reasonable to learn from an animal.
8. "The true horror . . . is for image makers to offer prayers and sacrifice to their own creations, . . . better . . . to worship each of their two hands, or if they were disinclined . . . because they shrank from appearing egotistical, to pay homage to the hammers and anvils and pencils and pincers and the other tools by which their materials were shaped."
9. It is to "err [to] magnify . . . the subjects above the ruler."
10. "He who dishonours the servants dishonours also the lord."

Can Philo's hierarchical morality escape the criticism with which hierarchical metaphysics is frequently now accused, that it is deterministic, patriarchal, and exalting the dominion of man above nature, and therefore conducive to exploitation and ruin of our environment?

De Decalogo does ascribe the supreme power to God, but it does not imply that God is omnipotent in the sense of being the sole agent. God grants humans freedom to choose, and always it is human agency that is responsible for evil. Omni-benevolence of God, yes, but not the omniscience that deprives man of an open future. Therefore it is not deterministic and does not generate the problem of evil. Nor is it a theodicy arguing "whatever is, is right."

God is exalted as "the Uncreated, Incorruptible, the Eternal, . . . Kings of Kings." Yet nature is the "common mother of mankind." Evidently, though Philo did not work it out in detail, the masculine principle is balanced in authority by the feminine, and it is "nature" that is our "home [and it is right] not [to] overstep her limits."

God is said to have made man sovereign over earth and sea, and contemporary ecology reminds us of the failures of mankind to tend earth as our garden. Man is to accept a humble role of servant, and nature, his home, has a degree of sanctity that should be respected. All created things are to be respected as "brothers, since all have one Father." He has given us reason also to add "one Mother." Then in not overstepping her limits, man is to limit his consumption to things "necessary for . . . life." The emphasis on maintaining balance would justify interpreting "nature's limits" as "Thou shalt avoid excessive use of nature's bounty," "Thou shalt not produce imbalances," "Thou shalt protect nature's equilibria and encourage the regeneration after depletion," "Thou shalt not pollute."

൙ 3 ൙

Saint Gregory of Palamas:
The Christian Transformation

Interpretations of the Mosaic Decalogue by successive and various Christian commentators provide the subject matter of this study. The essence of such interpretation is perhaps nowhere more clearly seen than in the case of Greek Orthodox Saint Gregory Palamas (ca. 1296-1359). Palamas was born in Constantinople; with his brothers, whom he had converted to the monastic life, he visited Mount Athos, where he learned the tradition of mystical prayer. Though he left Mount Athos under pressure from the Turks, he later made it his base from which he defended his contemplative practices. In 1347 he was consecrated abbot of Thessalonica.

Palamas is best known for teaching the biblical notion of man as a single and united whole, body and soul together, and for his distinction between the essence of God, which remains unknowable, and the uncreated energies of God — identical to God — which can be directly experienced by man in the form of deifying grace.

Useful background for Palamas may be gleaned from earlier examples of Greek Orthodoxy. First, the case of the sixth-century Greek Orthodox thinker Saint John Climacus (ca. 570-649) of the monastery of Sinai. Saint John is named after his celebrated work, *Ladder (Climacus) of Paradise* or *Ladder of Divine Ascent*. At the center of the *Ladder* stands a brief set of ten injunctions. They are addressed to monks who strive for perfection. The *Ladder* treats the monastic virtues and vices and the nature of complete dispassionateness, which is upheld as the ideal of Christian perfection.

Laymen, says John, are casual Christians — not really that serious about the spiritual life.

Some people living carelessly in the world have asked me: "We have wives and are beset with social cares, and how can we lead the solitary life?" I replied to them:

1. Do all the good you can.
2. Do not speak evil of anyone.
3. Do not steal from anyone.
4. Do not lie to anyone.
5. Do not be arrogant towards anyone.
6. Do not hate anyone.
7. Be sure you go to church.
8. Be compassionate to the needy.
9. Do not offend anyone.
10. Do not wreck another man's domestic happiness and be content with what your own wives can give you.

This simple code is strikingly similar to a second example, the Decalogue in the *Shepherd of Hermas*. Hermas (second century) is considered one of the apostolic fathers, and the *Shepherd* was widely regarded as Scripture in the Greek Church of the second and third centuries. Hermas was a Christian slave sold in Rome to a woman who set him free. He married, became a merchant, and prospered, sometimes by illegal means. In a persecution he lost all his property and was denounced by his own daughter. Later he and his family did penance.

The necessity of penance is the great theme of the *Shepherd of Hermas*. Hermas affirms faith in one God, but from the first stresses the virtue of "continence," and mentions "purity by repentance and avoidance of a second marriage," and ends with substitution of "evil desire" with "good and holy desire." Interestingly the Mosaic prohibition of adultery is interpreted in the context of strict monogamy. This has been the common assumption in interpretations of the Decalogue. Yet Saint John's version gives as reason why "coveting the neighbor's wife" is evil: it is "wreck[ing] another man's domestic happiness," which would not apply if a man took an unmarried mistress. But that is not condoned by Saint John's positive command, "be content with what your own wives can give you."

From the virtues assumed by these texts there emerges a general picture of what a Christian layman was supposed to be. Both the *Ladder* and the *Shepherd of Hermas* expect honesty ("Love truth" — "Do not lie . . ."); patience and good will ("Be long-suffering and understanding," "Do not speak evil," "Do not offend," and "Do not be arrogant"); openness and kindness ("Keep singleness [sincerity] and be innocent" and "Do not hate anyone"); and, at least for Saint John, charity ("Be compassionate to the needy").

Both emphasize the moral side of religion. The general principle "Avoid evil and do not do it; do not avoid good, but do it" becomes a principle of Saint Augustine's ethics. In his rules Saint John moves a moral principle to first place: "Do all the good you can."

The religious principle is very simple and in each case practically untheological: "Fear the Lord and keep his Commandments" and "Be sure to go to church." The earlier code emphasizes attitudes — specifically the avoidance of grief and bitterness as well as adopting the positive frame of mind — while the later code specifies seven "do not's," referring as does the Decalogue to forbidden acts.

Now we come to the version of the Decalogue from Eastern Orthodox Saint Gregory Palamas. Best known for his defense of monks who used the "Jesus prayer" and exercises meant to gain immediate knowledge of divine energies and visions of divine light, Saint Gregory, when he became archbishop of Thessalonica in 1347, had to attend to the everyday problems of his flock. The mystical theologian shared his sense of "the immediate experience of God, given to man by God by virtue of the Incarnation."

In Saint Gregory's "New Covenant" there is a marked change from the strict monotheism of Moses' Decalogue. The mystical motivation is the love of Father, Son, and Holy Ghost. Although we cannot know the relationship between the persons of the triune God, in a state recalling the *apatheia* of the Stoics and Philo and of course John Climacus — in "stillness and quiet" — comes the moral motivation to "Keep the Commandments of his Beloved."

Saint Gregory Palamas's *Decalogue* is arguably the document that best reveals how Christians, specifically Greek Orthodox mystical thinkers, refashion the Decalogue through interpretation, making of the Jewish a Christian tradition. The role of the church, its priestly directors of conscience, and the bases of the institutional authority, the essentials of penance and the sacramental renewal, are the vestibule to reward in heaven. The sanction for rejecting the system is eternal damnation and suffering in hell (*"Ghenna"* in the Aramaic of Jesus).

Commentary

I. Compared and contrasted to the Decalogue of Moses, Palamas's *Decalogue* contains no reference to YHWH who brought Israel out of Egypt in the preface or first commandment. We read: "The Lord God is one, known in Father and in Son and in Holy Spirit: the Father unbegotten, the Son begotten without beginning timelessly and passionlessly as Word, who assumed our nature, anointed it, and was called Christ, and the Holy Spirit, also from the Father, not begotten but coming forth by procession." In a theological proposition replacing a declaration of a mighty act in the history of salvation, we have the triune God presented as the one to be worshiped — the "Triad of hypostases," the three persons: Father unbegotten, Son begotten timelessly (the Logos), and Spirit proceeding from the Father. God is the Creator of all, whose creation contains nothing worthy of worship; yet the Word "assumed our nature, anointed it." We ought to heed no angel, particularly no devil, but turn to God as "compassionate and merciful and slow to anger and plenteous in mercy." To do so is to share in the heavenly kingdom; not to do so is to deserve the "fire inextinguishable" of hell.

The motivating force behind obedience is given as the fear and love of God, and not in the next life a reward in heaven or punishment in hell. Saint Gregory passes over the promise of long life in the promised land, plus blessings upon children and children's children to the third and fourth generation. In this context "otherworldly" has ramifications for the present hour.

II. After the summary of the prohibition of idolatry, Saint Gregory turns to the presence of God incarnate, fresh from the Virgin's womb. He paraphrases the Nicene Creeds and draws the concluding commandment: You will make an icon of the Incarnated from love for the incarnation, and through it you will remember and venerate the "incarnation. . . . Likewise you will make and venerate figures of the saints." Here Saint Gregory argues against the iconoclasts who claimed that "images were idols." His defense is: (1) "they are not gods"; (2) they are only venerated, not worshiped; (3) they are venerated only because of their relationship to the saints; and (4) Moses made images of cherubim and the Holy of Holies that "conveyed an image of the whole cosmos," so through icons of Christ we "venerate him who first of all created us according to his own image." We should remember the incarnation, the sacrifice on the cross, the resurrection from the dead, the second coming of Christ, and the last judgment by venerating the cross, making upon us the sign of the cross, and trusting that this "sign of . . . triumph over the devil" will ward off evil powers. We also share in God's grace by venerating the relics of the saints.

III. The third commandment — "Do not take the Lord's name in vain" — is thought to refer to perjury rather than blasphemy. The third also absorbs the ninth commandment, against false witness. When a person must take an oath, it is shameful because it implies that the person does not follow the commandment to be "truthful in all your words." Moreover, you violate Christ's commandment "You will not swear," and you should propitiate Christ "by almsgiving, by prayers, by grief, and by afflicting your body." This is a reference to a distinctive penitential system of atoning for sin. There are degrees of sin; some are called "venial" and others "mortal" — the latter is the more grievous. Mortal sin includes violating the law by swearing falsely, and it puts us in the class "with Herod the prophet-killer." The priestly penalty is severe. "Never take an oath again, and propitiate yourself to God using the aforementioned remedies with tears." Apparently all sins can be forgiven, but some require of the sinner greater penance to earn divine mercy or to be worthy of it. In the Hebrew system it was the penalty that became the application of the prohibition. The Catholic system is penance by the sinner to be worthy of the sacraments, especially since we proceed to the fourth commandment and the consecrated bread and wine.

IV. The new covenant replaces Sabbath, which is not mentioned, with the Lord's Day. The day is not connected, as in Exodus, to the day on which the Creator rested after six days of work. The Lord's Day commemorates Christ "the Lord, who rose from the dead on that day, who showed forth and pledged the common resurrection." Only necessary work is to be done on the Lord's Day, and what is remembered is the resurrection of "our nature." The point of the commandments is to prepare us to be justified in the future life, "the age-to-come." In the temple of God "you will partake of the holy body and blood of Christ, and you will start a most scrupulous life afresh."

V. The literal family of parents and children, discussed under "Honor your father and mother," is ranked second because God is the primary cause of being. (This is a departure from the Mosaic emphasis.) "You will honor and love them after God, if love for them contributes to the love of God; if it does not, then flee from them immediately. Should they be heterodox and an impediment to you and moreover to the true and saving faith, then you will not only flee, but you will hate them." Then follows a kind of anathema upon all who are not orthodox. The justification comes from the words of Jesus, as amplified by Saint Gregory: "Whoever does not hate his father and mother and wife and children and brothers and sisters and above all his own Soul, and does not take up his cross and follow me is not worthy of me." Here Saint Gregory seems, though writing for laypeople, to be urging the young monk to reject his "carnal father and friends and brothers" and to join the religious community through the "household of faith" ruled by spiritual fathers. It is true honor of your father when it is "love [of] the fathers who beget you according to the spirit. They transformed you from being to well being." It is rebirth that makes the person worthy of eternal life.

A Catholic meaning of "Honor your father" is "trust and obey the priest who is your spiritual father." Few, if any, Decalogues make it so plain that the faithful must "declare to him every sin and every thought, and . . . receive from him remedy and remission." Auricular confession is introduced by Saint Gregory because "it is given to [priests] to bind and loose souls, and whatsoever they bind on earth will be bound in heaven and whatsoever they loose on earth will be loosed in heaven. For they have received this grace and power from Christ." Here is the doctrine of the apostolic succession, which is coupled by Roman Catholics with the text used to establish the primacy of Saint Peter among bishops: "Upon this rock I found my church." Whether the authority belongs to bishops and priests generally or more particularly to the successors of Peter, the basis of authority is "grace and power from Christ."

VI. The literal meaning of "you will not commit adultery" is virtually overlooked, probably because the ascetic mind is no more preoccupied with relations between husband and wife than with relations between parents and children. This is perhaps what we should expect of those who have a much higher regard for the soul than the body, who reject "the world" as the bad company of "the flesh and the devil." What is shocking is not so much that people in the world should support prostitution but that a Christian, and especially a priest's daughter — members of "the divine body," the holy community of Christ — should go a-whoring. This is "dishonoring the father" and unlawful. To defile the body of Christ is so sinful that only hellfire is fit punishment.

For Gregory monogamous marriage, even matrimony as a sacrament of the church, is a concession of the church to those too weak to remain virgins; the ideal way is to cling to God only, and to remain "as an angel of God upon earth." The Holy Trinity, although referred to as the Father *begetting* the Son and the Spirit *proceeding* from the Father (or, as the Western Latin theologians added, "and the Son, *'filioque'*"), includes virgin begetting and virgin spiritual begetting of a virgin mother. So the higher marriage is "incorrupt nuptials" as the profession of nun as "bride of Christ."

Saint Gregory slips from the subject of avoiding adultery by not having anything to do with other men's wives, to the general suggestion that to look at the "charm of faces" is lustful. Then, most appropriately as counsel, he warns young monks even more severely of "man . . . brought down dissolutely even to abnormal sodomy by curiously gazing at the charms of the body."

VII. In the law of Christ, the seventh commandment, "You will not kill," is not interpreted as the destruction of the image bestowed by the Father, but as an offense against the Son. To murder is to "forfeit your adoption as a son of the one who brings the dead to life." Thinking of the evil one, Satan, Gregory says to murder is to "become instead, through works, the adopted son of the one who from the beginning brought mankind to death." Later we will examine the Decalogue as ten ways in which the devils command us to kill, steal, bear false witness, covet, etc., and conversely the angels urge us to obey God. The Ten Commandments specify the areas in which mankind is in the middle of a cosmic struggle between the powers of light and the powers of darkness.

At no other place does Saint Gregory use the ideal of Christ to root out all thoughts that are prideful, revengeful, hateful, resentful. The Christian is never to take offense, never to feel insulted, never to be angry, but always to give whatever anyone asks, to forgive everyone, never to speak evil of anyone, never to reproach anyone with a contemptuous word. Saint Gregory portrays the saint as attempting to be absolutely pure of all motives and emotions that fall in the list of vices or sins. If the saint, trying this way of angelic perfection, catches himself in a state of anger, he is to turn his anger against himself and to repent before God and publicly before anyone in the slightest affected. And what is the goal? To "free both yourself and the persons who treat you badly from the murderous fall."

VIII. "You will not steal" is a warning against despising Christ and risking hellfire, but primarily it is an encouragement to do charitable acts. Since

God knows your secrets, "secretly supply the needy." This is the humble way of avoiding any claim to be a philanthropist. The sanction: "a hundredfold blessing and life eternal."

IX. "You will not slander" is Saint Gregory's version of "Thou shalt not bear false witness." The model of slandering is Satan's intimation to Eve that the Lord God deliberately forbade the fruit of the knowledge of good and evil so that mankind should not rise to divine status. Since the serpent is cursed to crawl upon its belly, this commandment, as perhaps all, is a warning: don't bring upon yourself the curse of God.

The opposite of speaking evil of someone is to cover up that person's shame. The reference, again to an early chapter of Genesis, is to Noah, the first vintner, who got drunk and took off his clothes. Commenting on this story, Saint Gregory is saying don't, like Ham, look at your father's nakedness, but like the good sons, Shem and Japheth, walk backward with the cloth to cover him.

X. Saint Gregory's extension of "thou shalt not covet thy neighbor's house" includes his "money or glory." For Gregory, as for Philo, "desire" as such is the root of sin. His interpretation couples sin with death, as in the text: "the soul that sinneth shall die." One's charity, giving to anyone who asks — and as much as possible — would "reconcile him." The general principle is to "conquer evil by good." Is this another aspect of the cosmic struggle in which the forces of light are struggling to raise mankind by saving sons and daughters of Adam and Eve from their fall and restoring mankind to the angelic state?

Although it is said that the archbishop intended to write on the Ten Commandments for laypeople, his text, on examination, turns out to be a Decalogue for monks. But it is no less valuable in suggesting how interpretations for those living in the world must differ from the commandments taken as counsels of perfection for those who have taken vows of poverty, chastity, and obedience.

Richard Rolle:
The Decalogue of an English Hermit

Like Greek Orthodoxy, particularly during the Middle Ages, Latin Christianity entertains a sharp distinction between laypeople and monks and nuns. From Latin Christendom we cite another medieval mystical writer, one of the most noted spiritual guides of England: Richard Rolle (1300-1349). Born at Thornton in North Yorkshire, he studied at Oxford, breaking off his studies when he was eighteen to become a hermit. His last years were spent near the convent of the Cistercian nuns at Hampole. His best-known works in English are lyric poems, his commentary on the Psalms (some of which would later be interpolated by Lollards), and his letters.

Rolle wrote at least two different tracts that are of interest to us. One is for laypeople; the other, more celebrated, was written for a nun. In *The Ten Commandments* Rolle interprets the commandments that are for everyone; these he judges "essential." They include commandments that cover basics like rest from work, avoidance of wicked behavior, and the doing of charitable deeds. Fulfilling the commandments involves keeping a holy day. But then in contrast to the many there are the few. The "contemplatives . . . [ignore] all worldly things so that they may give themselves entirely to God." The "counsel of perfection" demands a life of "prayer and meditation." (In the following texts a few passages have been altered to make the meaning clearer.)

Richard Rolle's Ten Commandments in Paraphrase
(Text Lightly Revised by the Author)
1. The first commandment is: You shall revere the Lord your God, and to him alone you are to be obedient. In this commandment all idola-

try, all witchcraft, and all magic charms are forbidden. They which cannot provide remedy for any ailment of man, woman, or animal; they are the devil's snares by which he does all he can to deceive the human race. In this commandment belief in sorcery is also forbidden, and divination by means of stars or by dreams. To crucifixes reverence is owed: they are a symbol of Christ crucified. To statues the respect is due as to whom they represent, and for that reason alone they are to be honored.

2. The second commandment is: You shall not take God's name in vain. Under this commandment oaths without good reason are forbidden. In three respects a person may sin by swearing. First, he may swear against what he really believes; second, he may swear by Christ's wounds or blood — this is always a great sin even if what he is swearing is a true fact, because it is an expression of irreverence to Jesus Christ. Third, he may betray his own oath and not carry out what he has sworn to do. God's name is taken in vain in many ways: in heart, in speech, and in action. In heart, disloyal Christians take it in vain when they receive the sacrament while their soul is not in a state of grace. In speech it is taken in vain in every act of swearing, of promulgating new doctrines which are of the lips when our hearts are far from him. In action, hypocrites take God's name in vain by making a pretense of doing good externally, but they are lacking in charity, strength, and vigor of spirit to withstand all wicked impulses.

3. The third commandment is: Keep holy your holy day of obligation. This commandment may be understood in three senses. First, in general, utterly abandon all wicked behavior. Second, in particular, abandon all physical acts which hinder devotion to God in prayer and meditation. The third sense applies specifically to contemplative men who separate themselves from all worldly things so that they may give themselves entirely to God. The first sense is essential for all to observe, the third is counsel of perfection.

4. The fourth commandment is: Honor your father and your mother. This has two senses, a physical and a spiritual one. Physically we honor parents by support, so that they can be helped and maintained in their old age. Spiritually we honor them in respect and obedience, not speaking to them discourteously, dishonorably, or disagreeably in a casual way, but attending to them politely, cheerfully, and humbly, in order to gain God's promise, the land of light. And when parents are dead, one is bound to help their souls by giving alms and by prayers.

5. The fifth commandment is that you kill no one, neither by plotting, nor by committing the deed, nor by ordering it or condoning it. And under this commandment, illegal striking of any person is also forbidden. There are spiritual murderers: those who refuse to feed the destitute in their need, those who slander others, and those who mislead the innocent.

6. The sixth commandment is: Do not be lecherous. That means: you are not to have sexual relations with a man or a woman unless you are bound to him or her according to the rites of holy church. Under this commandment additional prohibitions include every kind of deliberate self-pollution.

7. The seventh commandment is: You shall not commit theft. Theft includes all types of removal of property against the wishes of the owner, except in a situation of direct necessity, when all property is held in common. Under this commandment is forbidden the use of deceptive weights, counting, volume or measure, or usury or force or intimidation, including, for example, such acts committed by the underofficers at courts, or the foresters, or the king's ministers, or extortion, as the nobles do.

8. The eighth commandment is that you shall not bear false witness against your neighbors, such as in the assize courts or in matrimonial cases. This commandment applies to all kinds of lies, including perjury. Yet not all lies are mortal sins, only those which harm someone physically or spiritually.

9. The ninth commandment is: You are not to covet unjustly the house, or any movable or fixed property of your neighbor, nor are you to retain possession of other people's property if you can restore it to them.

10. The tenth commandment is: You shall not covet your neighbor's wife, nor his servant, nor his maidservant, nor his property. Anyone who keeps these commandments through love, loves God. He is bound to love his neighbor as himself: wishing for him to have the same good things which he values for himself, for him not to have any harm at all, and to love his neighbor's soul more than his body or any worldly goods.

Commentary

1. Mysticism is often a revolt against dogmatic assertion of authority. The biblical injunction "taste and see" can be addressed not only to mystics as an encouragement to experience the goodness of God, but negatively to all of us as a reminder to unmask superstition and dethrone false gods.

To discover true religion is difficult, but if false religions can be refuted, we can eliminate most of them — or nearly all. If magical charms, witchcraft, sorcery, divination, etc., "cannot provide any remedy," these false gods can be rejected.

Rolle's interpretation of "worship the one invisible God, the Creator" recommends the rejection of alternative gods. Coupled with this empirical argument is an analytic, even a semantic, argument. A symbol as such, although a reference to some event or agency, is not itself an effective cause. You may shout "Sieg heil" till Nazi hope and wind gives out, yet defeat may come and not victory. A crucifix or a statue is to be honored only because of what it represents. Perhaps Rolle's mind was shaped by thinking of the bread and wine representing the body and blood of Christ: "this do in remembrance of me."

2. The exposition of the second commandment against "taking the Lord's name in vain" could also be on empirical and analytic grounds. Using God's name does not give one any power in itself.

A wise way to state a general rule is to make allowance for exceptions in stating it in the first place. The first instance of this is "oaths *without good reason* are forbidden." A good reason would include the legal practice of preventing perjury by putting the witness under oath — at least if the reflective witness takes penalties for perjury into account. Other instances will come shortly. Apart from the irreverence of blasphemy, and the irresponsible participation of an unprepared person in the sacrament, five reasons are given for the prohibition. Saying that what is false is true is contradictory logically; when knowingly done, it is a lie. To go contrary to one's conscience is insincere. Not "carrying out what he has sworn to do" is breaking a promise. Proposing new doctrines without basis is "frivolous," and contravenes any responsible choice of knowledge above opinion. And pretense to good works one has not done is the vanity called "hypocrisy," counted by some the worst of vices. So there are at least two sins: blasphemy and sacrilege; and five vices: lying, insincerity, promise breaking, intellectual frivolity, and hypocrisy.

Is Rolle not inducing his reader to analyze the character of the act by breaking it down into all the reprehensible aspects of it? If this is "didactic," so be it, but it is encouraging critical thought about the language one uses. The phrase "may God despise him," said of the blasphemer, may be a way of saying "just tell the truth." If that is trite and pedestrian, so be it; Rolle has found a very interesting way of saying it. Rolle does introduce the consideration of the familiar "thought, word, deed" sequence which presupposes intellect and intent behind agency, and may be further amplified by considering consequences.

3. "Remember to keep holy your holy day of obligation" is Rolle's version of "Remember the Sabbath to keep it holy." This is a gain in generality. It does not say that the holy day has been changed from the seventh day to the first by Christ's resurrection. The Moslem is left quite free to keep his Friday holy. This interpretation is generous, ecumenical; it doesn't rule out all work but only "wicked behavior" and "physical acts, which hinders devotion to God." How broad an understanding of "rest" had Rolle? If it would include relaxation, then play might be encouraged. This reading of the third commandment may well follow "Sabbath was made for men" in not requiring attendance at church, though that may be implied by "keeping holy your holy day." Holy days may be many or few, and Rolle leaves it up to us whether acts are fitting or unfitting the day of rest.

4. "Honor your father and your mother" gives priority to kindness to the elderly rather than to just paying their bills. The promise of so doing is not long life in the promised land, nor only reward after death in heaven but in "the land of light." How alms and prayers for the dead help them is not explained.

5. "Kill no one" is broadened to include plotting against anyone, striking someone, or just condoning violence. And it is further broadened to three types of "spiritual murder": lack of benevolence, malicious talk, and "mislead[ing] the innocent."

6. "Do not be lecherous" is, as in many medieval Catholic Decalogues, the interpretive version of "thou shalt not commit adultery." The limits of sexual relations are to be set by what "holy church" considers matrimony. Monogamy is understood according to the standards of "natural behavior." If this is no improvement on specifying forbidden relations, as in Scripture,

and if invoking the norms of "natural" is intellectually preferable, it at least makes the complex problem a matter of discussion.

7. "You shall not commit theft" is Rolle's most carefully qualified and extended commandment. As in allowing oaths when swearing in vain is prohibited, or permitting necessary labor and good works when rest is commanded, here the prohibiting of theft does not apply to the celebrated case of the parent who takes bread for his or her starving children. This is the third case where Rolle anticipates the exception while stating the rule. Is taking interest on loans theft by usury? Less debatable, and quite in keeping with Jewish law, is the prohibition of deceptive weights and measures. Very interesting under "stealing" are government acts that Rolle judges unjust. The complex problems of equitable taxation lie beyond the range of condemning "force or intimidation . . . or extortion." At least we may say Rolle's seventh commandment includes a protest against unjust government.

8. "You shall not bear false witness" applies to courts under both civil and canon law, and to lies as well as to perjury. Yet there are lies that harm no one and are not "mortal sin." The eighth commandment is the fourth time an exception to a universal principle is made, apparently condoning what are called "white lies" or polite compliments not strictly accurate.

9. "You are not to covet *unjustly*" apparently points to the wanting of a neighbor's property sufficiently to take it in violation of a law, and the return of property *when possible*. An act of penance is worthless without the restoration. One wonders whether this is meant generally of the cases of theft under the seventh commandment and others.

10. "You shall not covet your neighbor's wife, nor his servant," nor his "property." Why not? The motive is love of neighbor and of God. To keep commandments is to "love God." The principle, stated as a conclusion, is an intense and positively stated Golden Rule: to wish for the neighbor "to have the same good things which he values for himself, for him not to have any harm at all [which rules out hatred, envy, ill will] and to love his neighbor's soul more than his body or any worldly goods." This is a comprehensive statement of what it is to have good will.

Rolle's conclusion, defining the Decalogue as the way to be a person of good will, is a remarkable statement. It includes only minor consideration of God's promise of the "land of light" (fourth commandment) or the displeasure of God (second commandment). Otherwise there are no earthly or heavenly rewards or consequent curses upon oneself on earth or in hell. The appeal is to virtue for its own sake. There is no basis for judging right and wrong by the consequences for oneself or society.

Rolle's picture contrasts sharply with Saint Gregory's, who includes the creed in the Decalogue — and not just for theological orthodoxy, but for the cosmic struggle between the angels and devils, with the apocalyptic trust in the restoration of Adam to his angelic state before the fall. Rolle is relatively humanistic and contemplates no angry God and eternal punishment of the wicked. The afterlife is shadowy: we may by alms and prayers aid the souls of the dead. We should do penance, but Rolle gives no specifics of purging the soul of the seven deadly sins and no calculation of penalty of length of days in purgatory.

Only in the penultimate paragraph of the letter to a sister does Richard use the threat of hell and the promise of bliss of the vision of God. In spite of all the virtues intrinsic to the religious life, the sister had protested that she can't give up the world. "But it's possible you will say, 'I just can't despise the world. I can't find it in my heart to torment my body; and I've simply got to love my friends whom I know in this life, and take rest when the opportunity comes.' If you should be tempted by such thoughts, I beg you to consider where, from the beginning of this planet, the lovers of the world are now, and where the lovers of God are."

The prudential argument follows: if you live for sensual pleasure, some day you will know you were a fool and "disgustingly self-indulgent." Either a few quick and brief pleasures now and eternal misery hereafter, or a few sacrifices during this life and unending bliss and infinite "delights of the vision of God" in heaven.

Only one out of ten paragraphs is prudential. Nine paragraphs of *The Commandment* concern love for God, the growth of spiritual strength, and the virtues that prepare the soul for the vision of God. Apparently "it comes" after long delay, in this life, so that the "sweetness of heaven" is not put off until after death.

Rolle keeps *The Ten Commandments* distinct from *The Commandment*. He never belittles the active life, nor what the philosophers called the "political virtues." But *if* someone heeds the counsels of perfection, then he or she can begin where the appeal to the ordinary good life ends: the love of God. Apparently the contrast is that the layperson shows love of God in and through the love of neighbor. The religious concentrates on the love of

God. The avoidance of all the sins detailed in *The Ten Commandments* is presupposed. The religious have other temptations: when they are avoided, the way of contemplation leads to a sequence of virtues.

Richard Rolle: God's Commandment

God's Commandment is that we should love our Lord with all our heart, with all our soul and with all our thought. With all our heart: that means with all our understanding, without making any mistakes. With all our soul: that means with all our free will, without any refusal. With all our thought: that means we must think of him without any forgetting. Loyal and true love operates in this way; in other words as an act of human will. The reason is that love is a voluntary stirring of our thought towards God to such an extent that it is unable to take in anything that is against the love of Jesus Christ, and at the same time is enabled to persevere in sweetness of devotion.

What has the life of a monk or a nun to do with the Ten Commandments of Moses? There are the obvious differences between the this-worldly and the otherworldly, between thinking of human relations and institutions and thinking only of the soul's relation to God, between success and reward from work, good marriage with children, and defining one's own character and career. Why take vows of poverty, chastity, and obedience?

In Orthodox Christianity, and in Venice, under a patriarch, there are churches dedicated to Saint Moses, Saint Job, Saint Zechariah, Saint Jeremiah, and this high rank of sanctity is acknowledged for the apostles and the celebrated founders of the great monastic orders, Saints Benedict, Bernard of Clairvaux, Francis of Assisi, Dominic, and many others.

If the coupling of *The Ten Commandments* with *The Commandment* means anything, it is that the search by a contemplative in the monastery is a further stage of development beyond the achievement of a good life in the world. Clearly this lover of Christ has accepted and lived according to the commandments of Moses. "Now this is the ultimate state of perfection in this life; to it all grave sin is opposed and inimical." It is impossible to take this further because mortal sin would destroy love. Yet if one conforms to the Ten Commandments, there is still "venial sin [which] does not destroy love, but merely inhibits its application." Therefore this coupling of *The Ten Commandments* with *The Commandment* means that the "man [or woman] of YHWH" becomes the "lover of Jesus Christ" when the love is uninhibited.

There are several very serious objections to thinking that Christian sainthood is the fulfillment of the law. Hasn't the Christian chosen to worship a god other than the God of Moses? Moses said nothing about a Son of God, differing in person but one in substance with the Father and the Spirit. That is the theological divide between strict Yahwism and Christianity. Rolle does not see this break because there is from the beginning a divine plan whose encompassing scope has finally become decipherable. The Creator and Redeemer are one God.

Two difficulties concern the two tables of the law. If the second table as a whole is interpreted by Jesus in the phrase "and thy neighbor as thyself," why should the monastic life be exclusively based on "Thou shalt love the Lord thy God with all thy heart, mind, and strength"? Philo would object to the one-sidedness of those turned Godward if they turned their back on man. Isn't monasticism at best one-sided, at worst a rejection and a perversion? Rolle would say the good layman shows his love of God through love of neighbor. Hence, why not the good monk showing love of neighbor through love of God? The perfect monk (or nun) is "constant in virtue in his principles, and full of charitable feelings towards God and his neighbor." The missing link is between struggles inside and outside the monastery. Through prayers the monk and nun aid the struggling souls outside, just as our prayers assist departed souls. God's grace, in the added Catholic premise, is that of a community in which the member shares. (Without the Catholic premise of the pooling of grace, we have the individual Protestant, for example, John Milton, who belittles "cloistered virtues.") If evils spread by bad companionship, why should virtues be sealed off into individual uncommunicating units? Doesn't a prayer somehow unite persons? "Influence" may have subtle conduits.

If the religious person, to go on to a second paradoxical difficulty, turns his/her back on the world, convinced that he/she has chosen "the better part," how can he/she not take pride in the act? If the sin of pride is evidenced in a feeling of being "holier than thou," as in the case of Mary speaking to Martha, the way of the religious and the contemplative, claiming higher virtues, shows that it is tainted by the greatest vice.

Rolle warns those who aim at perfection not to "esteem their own condition above all others." But how can a Mary not pity a Martha? Over the door of the monastery seems to be written "Beware of the spiritual trap." We saw that Saint Gregory Palamas's appeal to forsake fleshly pleasures is joined to the exaltation of the angelic state. In both *The Ten Com-mandments* and *The Commandment,* Rolle skillfully avoids this trap. The so-lution to the paradox is for the religious to think only of God and to "talk very little," and by silence to avoid "flippant talk and nasty remarks." In this concentration on removing even venial sins which inhibit love, the goal is to remain always kind and to consider "every person better than himself." Then apparently God's grace can fill the soul emptied of "idle and malevolent nature."

Rolle's rules for achieving this state might have been written as a decalogue. If numbers are supplied, the commandments stated continuously are:

1. Be in awe of the decrees of God, so that you do not anger him in any way.
2. Make your soul constant in his love and pour out of yourself all sins.
3. Throw away lethargy.
4. Exercise yourself vigorously in goodness.
5. Be courteous and humble to everyone.
6. Don't allow anything to rouse you to fury or malice.
7. Decorate your soul prettily; construct inside it a stronghold of love for the Son of God and make your will eager to receive him as you would the arrival of something or someone you loved most of any-thing.
8. Wash your thoughts clean with tears of love and burning longing so that he doesn't find anything dirty about you, because he is happy when he sees you beautiful and lovely. Your beauty of soul, which is what he desires, is this:
9. You are to be chaste and humble, polite and submissive, never grum-bling about doing his will, always finding all wickedness repulsive.
10. In everything that you do, concentrate all the time on arriving at the vision of his beauty, and place all your resolve on this, so that you will attain this on your death. Indeed, this ought to be the purpose of all our endeavor: while we are living here, we should constantly be yearning for that vision with our whole heart, always finding it a long delay until it comes.

Did Rolle deliberately make a list of ten commandments, or had the decalogic archetype so guided his thought that they turned out to be ten? Or has the tenfold pattern been imposed upon the injunctions? The virtues here enjoined are stated, except for the third, "be zealous," and the fourth, "exercise yourself vigorously in goodness," in relation to someone or some ideal. The only "don't" in this decalogue is probably intended to rule out anger and *hatred of anyone,* and if the third means *zealous in carrying out projects* and the fourth, *to exercise goodness toward* others, then the whole decalogue is a blending of relations to God and relations to other people. Therefore Rolle's decalogue has balance between the Godward and the manward orientation. It is not as self-centered as it may have appeared at first.

The validity of this contemplative way of life is authenticated by the character resulting from this way of living. The bulk of the essay is about the virtues which come from practice and discipline. These may be summarized under ten heads, though the important point is that these are the results, the proof of the pudding. These may be called ten saintly virtues, and in the sequence of development they seem to be:

1. *Quietness* of the humble person who talks very little.
2. *Joy* of one who gives pleasures to those he loves.
3. *Patience* of a person who accepts suffering.
4. *Perfect freedom* of one who does not want to do anything but what one should.
5. *Moderation* in meditation and fasting of one who does neither too much nor too little.
6. *Unanxious* quality of one not vexed and not antipathetic to people or "embroiled in a frenzy of activism."
7. *Satisfaction* of one who feels rich with faith, hope, love, though without outer possessions.
8. *Activity* of good works, including "making useful things."
9. *Sincerity* and lack of hypocrisy.
10. *"Purity of soul."*

King Alfred:
The Decalogue and Anglo-American Law

Alfred the Great (849-99), king of the West Saxons (his kingdom even-tually included London), could have been influenced by Charlemagne of the Franks; historians of law have not told the full story. Yet the individ-ual case of Alfred's law is of particular value because American law is con-tinuous with that of England.

The command of Jesus to "render unto Caesar the things that are Caesar's; render unto God the things that are God's" is interpreted in two contradictory ways. The first is seen in the radical and revolutionary doc-trine that political power and religious grace are so totally antithetical that, in another word of Jesus, "a man cannot serve two masters, either he love the one and hate the other, or hate the one and love the other." A religious prophet, and there are many of this dualistic conviction, may oppose Caesar; he may feel all cooperation is a compromise in which Caesar wins and Christ loses. He may even scorn Christianity as a religion of a whole people, under Christian rulers, a nation with a church together obeying the commandments.

The other reading of the ambiguous Caesar/God dual loyalty is that there are two sides to every complete picture. Each has its sphere; when de-limited, each can keep from treading upon the other. Cooperation is neces-sary for a Christian nation. The hostility between the Roman Empire and Christians ended with tolerance from Constantine, and then he gave to the church the support of the state. The pattern of Roman conversion was fol-lowed in all the nations of Europe — among Latin nations, Germanic, Scan-dinavian, Slavic, etc. Does this mean that the Mosaic Decalogue became part of the law of these peoples when they were converted to Christianity? And how did changes introduced by the gospel affect the legal code?

Political historians and historians of law do not offer us a general and comparative study, but one notable case is the code of King Alfred the Great. This is particularly of interest since it shows the Decalogue as basic to the civil religion of England, and of the many colonial offspring, which build upon the traditions of common law. Thanks to Alfred the law is also the king's law.

The problem faced by a medieval king was the tension between three principles: the Roman imperial conception of law as the voice of a sovereign authority, the Hebraic revealed will of a divine Lawgiver, and Germanic custom. Descended according to West Saxon genealogy from Woden, Alfred had the problem of continuity with Germanic tribal precedent, but he used Roman precedent to set down the "dooms" in written form. Alfred accepts the role of transmitter of customs: "I dared not set down much of my own in writing, for it was not known to me which would please those who should come after us." As a Christian, he acknowledges God, whom philosophy or "Wisdom" says is "King or lord and well-spring and beginning and law and wisdom and righteous judge." God's righteous will is found through the lawgiver Moses. The task was to bind together the threads from various tribes, Kentish, Mercian, and West Saxon, and to harmonize them. "I gathered together here such as seemed to me the most worthy, and the others I rejected." Alfred, King of the West-Saxons, "showed these to all my *witan* (wise men), and they then said that it pleased them all to hold them."

In the name of the king, the authority of custom is given a higher status as an extension of the law of God. It is approved by wise men who advise the king. That the "Mosaic Laws are not abrogated by Christ under the new dispensation" is a valuable precedent for the argument that good laws should be augmented. When Alfred the king introduced harsh injunctions from Mosaic law, based on the principle of *lex talionis,* "an eye for an eye, a tooth for a tooth," Alfred the Christian modified them by mild and encouraging precepts based on mercy.

The philosophic interpretation of Alfred's act, apart from the appeal to historic prototype, is that Scripture contains a principle of justice. "Whatsoever ye will that men do not unto you, do not to them." This is the underlying principle of all lawgiving. Alfred makes connections between the stages, showing how they can be logically deduced. Thus what was taught by the apostles is renewed in England. As Moses followed the divine commands of Exodus 20 with legislation in Exodus 21, 22, and 23, so Alfred adapts these dooms to conditions of his people. Notably "If thou buyeth a Christian slave [for Moses, 'Hebrew'] for six years he shall serve thee, on the seventh he shall go free."

Alfred, in his first restatement of the Decalogue, omits the second commandment, against making and worshiping idols, but then adds another version against making gods of silver and gold. As in restatements in catechisms, the expansions in Exodus and Deuteronomy are shortened. Where the Vulgate reads *Dominus,* translated "Dryhten," Alfred adds "Crist," as Christ in the New Testament is "the Lord." The promise of the land to those who honor father and mother becomes earth generally. When Alfred adapts, he is following the precedent of the law of synods which were not altogether ecclesiastical.

In how many lands does the Decalogue have the central position it enjoys in the tradition of Britain, the dominions, and former colonies? Histories of law should tell us, for there is no other example of established moral norms with the heritage of the last thousand years, on the basis of the previous two thousand years.

Since a general answer to these questions of the law of nations dependent on the Decalogue is locked in the archives of a score of nations and hundreds of cities, we must settle for a single example. The republic with the longest continuous recorded and available history, Venice, shows in the sixteenth and seventeenth century that it was a most serious threat to the state for anyone to deny the authority of Moses and to challenge any accepted commandment of the Decalogue.

On a column of the Ducal Palace of Venice, close by the entrance to the great courtyard, is Moses on Mount Sinai receiving the tablets. In 1610 the Holy Office of the Inquisition tried Francesco Faggiani for offenses, among which were claiming "that the laws and ceremonies that are observed in the church were instituted by the King for reason of state. That Moses did not fast the forty days, but that his servant carried him something to eat. That Moses had a cave made in the mountain, and put some dust in it, then said to the people that he had laws given him by God but they were of his own invention." In spite of these thoughts, similar to those of young Thomas Hobbes (born 1588), Father Francesco took holy orders, and from 1621 to 1624 was an ordained priest at Misericordia. He then was tried again for breaking particular commandments, such as taking the Lord's name in vain and not keeping holy days: "blessing playing cards in a gambling den, heretical cursing, and non-observance of fasts." Another was a commandment of the church he violated: he "said mass without having confessed."

Obviously, then, the authority of Moses and his laws was considered basic to the public order of Venice, and denial of such a basis was a heresy, and because of serious consequences, such heresy was not to be tolerated.

Ramón Lull:
A Decalogue of Medieval Reasons

Within Christianity, Catholic Christians have made a unique contribution to the ongoing interpretation of the Ten Commandments: the development of both a theology of the Decalogue and a philosophy of the Decalogue. In Judaism there is a comparable
differentiation in the work of Moses Maimonides and Philo Judaeus.
Both of them, directly and indirectly, influenced Saint Thomas Aquinas
(1224-74). Maimonides (1135-1204) systematized the 613 laws of the
Mosaic code in a way that was celebrated by succeeding rabbis: "From
Moses to Moses, there is none comparable to Moses." He is better
known for his *Guide for the Perplexed,* written in Arabic, which shows
what medieval Islam had in common with Judaism and Christianity, to
wit: that much, if not all, of what a faithful Moslem, Jew, or Christian believed could be arrived at by reason. "Reason" was of course the reason
of Greek philosophy, of Plato, Aristotle, the Stoics, Plotinus, and other
Neoplatonists. The central burning conviction was that what Moses said
of God, the world, and man made sense, not least of which is the
Decalogue. We have already singled out Philo's *De Decalogo* to show in
detail that the Ten Commandments are fundamental to the good life of
the individual in a good society.

It is an error to think of Thomas as the only Catholic theologian-
philosopher of the Middle Ages. True, he was given a special place by the
papal encyclical *Aeterni patris* of 1870 and has been a paramount authority,
but he could not have done his work without many brilliant predecessors,
especially Saint Augustine. Among his contemporaries was the Franciscan,
Saint Bonaventura. Moreover, other, later brilliant Franciscans — Duns
Scotus and William of Ockham — continue to fascinate philosophers.

There is unfortunately no comparative study of their understanding of the Decalogue.

Ramón Lull (1232-1315), a member of the Third Order of Saint Francis, which was open to lay and married people, wrote with confidence that reason could arrive at all the dogmas of faith. There is in his system no theology of the Decalogue distinctive from a philosophy of the Decalogue. By reading him first we are better able to see the achievement of Saint Thomas Aquinas.

Lull was a knight of the island of Majorca, a poet who founded the Catalan tradition of literature, a man of vision who, when converted, devoted himself both to elaborating a metaphysical system of great originality and to stating a universal religion to which he set out to convert Moslems. He is remembered in La Palma as a martyr, for he died returning from North Africa after having been stoned. But he was also a rationalist, a thinker who invented simple machines for making calculations of all sorts, and an inspiration of Leibniz's universal calculus, which is the tradition out of which comes the computer.

Lull's version of the Decalogue is unique in its reordering of the commandments. This is never arbitrary, and his reasons will be explained in the paraphrase of his text.

1. *Non Adorabis Deos Alienos*
   Thou shalt not worship other Gods.
2. *Sabbathum coles*
   Thou shalt keep the Sabbath holy.
3. *Non accipias Nomen Dei in Vanum*
   Thou shalt not take the Name of God in vain.
4. *Non facias falsum Testimonium*
   Thou shalt not bear false Witness.
5. *Honora Patrem & Matrem*
   Honor Father and Mother.
6. *Non facias Furtum*
   Thou shalt not Steal.
7. *Non occides*
   Thou shalt not Kill.
8. *Non moechaberis*
   Thou shalt not commit Adultery.
9. *Non invideas Uxorem tui Proximi*
   Thou shalt not covet thy Neighbor's Wife.

10. *Non habeas Invidiam de Rebis tui Proximi*
Thou shalt not covet thy Neighbor's Things.[1]

I

Lull's version of the Ten Commandments is in ten chapters of his *De proverbiis moralibus;* each chapter has twenty epigrams, each of which begins as the first commandment does: "*Deus* Praecepit Hominibus" (God taught men).

For Lull the first commandment means not to believe in idols — not to idolize things. "To believe in an idol" means to love "anything . . . more than God."

Idolatry is to deny "What is in God, and to affirm in God what is not in Him." This precept posits God as the most intelligible being, supremely excellent in every respect. Therefore man is a servant to the Lord God more than to "any other Lord."

This first commandment is "the precept of all other precepts" and states the obligation that is the obligation of all other obligations. Theological reason then leads to an imperative: "before thou obeyest any other, obey God."

Then follow ten epigrams about the first commandment, which plays the role of love of the good in Platonistic systems. It is infallible, supreme, expressing in giving the command greater love of God than man shows in obeying; therefore it is "easy." The divine precept is absolute: all other precepts are relative to circumstances ("in omni praecepto considera conditionem, excepto divino"). It is impossible to obey God unless one loves him, and he is the precept of love.

Because of this inner motivation, in contrast to external compulsion, "The precept, which God gives, makes men free, whereas every other command (from a lesser Lord) enslaves them." The divine precept does not rob man of autonomy, because every precept of God is with justice. Moreover, God makes a command not for his own sake, but for man's.

1. *De Proverbiis Moralibus, Tertia Pars Caput VIII–Caput XVIII, Tome II,* in *Opera Omnia* 42 (Mainz, 1721; reprint, Frankfurt am Main: Minerva, 1965), vol. 2, pp. 93-96. Quotations from Lull in this chapter come from this work.

II

Lull moves the commandment of the Sabbath to second place, apparently to emphasize the closeness of God and man. It is a positive command — "Sabbathum coles," "Keep the sabbath holy" — and the negative prohibition of perjury will follow. In Lull's reasoning it is not that the Creator rested on the seventh day, but that God himself is festival. "God commands that man should keep festival, because He Himself is Festival" ("Deus Fecit Praeceptum, Quod homo faciat Festum, quia ipse est Festum"). What is it for God to be a festival, "Festival of rest," "Festival of joy, which is glory," "Festival of remembering, of understanding, and of loving God"? Because "Deus est festum quietis" and "Festum laetitiae." Therefore God wills that man should keep festival, because by these spiritual activities ("Memorare, intelligere, et amare Deum") man shares in God's rest and glory. The means is one day in seven to include nothing other than "knowing and loving God and his honor."

A spiritual Sabbath festival is not kept by physical eating and drinking but by remembering and recognizing one's sins. Nor is a spiritual Sabbath celebrated by wearing silk and purple, "that one makes a greater festival, who clothes his Will in the Love of God" ("Ille fecit majos Festum, qui suam Voluntatem vestit Amore Dei . . ."). The true festival is not made by the finest food or richest dress, but by prayer, humility, "Worshipping God and feeding the poor," "True knowledge rather than a beautiful voice."

For Lull, if one does not keep the festival of God, one celebrates the devil; and "he who does not keep festival for God in this life, for that one God does not prepare a festival in the other life." Actual punishment in the next life for disobedience or punishment in this life is not emphasized, nor is attending church services: "keep festival of the cross with thine eyes, and [a festival] of the words of God with thine ears."

Then are coupled two negative commandments, the prohibitions against taking the name of the Lord in vain and bearing false witness. This is going from the second to the eighth; apparently Lull ignores the division of duties to God, the first tablet, and the duties to fellow man, the second tablet. This rethinking also departs from the Augustinian division of the first three commandments referring to God the Father, the Son, the Holy Spirit, and thereafter the other seven referring to relations among men. Lull then rejects the division between theological and moral commandments. Not to take the Lord's name in vain is as moral as not bearing false witness is theological. But we shall later observe a shift from reference to God in every proverb (as in the first) to concentration on virtues of man (as in the last five).

III

The prohibition "Thou shalt not take the name of God in vain" means not to use the final goal ("Finis") as a means ("Instrumentum"). To speak "in the name of God" and to honor him require respect for "what thou lovest most" and for what is "the purpose of all things" ("Deus est Finis omnium rerum"). To perjure is to "sell the Name of God," and that is to use an end as a means. "Thou are not to sell what thou lovest." The imperative follows from the commandment as Lull interprets its meaning.

The end of speaking is to speak the truth, and to lie goes against this end. To speak in the name of God is to speak in the name of the truth, and to speak truth rather than falsehood is to act virtuously rather than to indulge the vice of lying. Therefore, to lie in the name of God is a "great evil."

It is better to honor the name of God than to honor the king and all things, and more important to speak reverently of God than to have all the money in the world. "He who speaks the name of God with Truth, participates in God" ("Qui nominat Nomen Dei cum Veritate, participat cum DEO"). "He who swears falsely, blasphemes God." "Name God for his love, and not for any other thing." And: "Every devil fears when he hears men speak of God's name."

IV

The eighth commandment is stated next, after Lull's third, for the logical reason that it follows from it. The purpose of speaking is to tell the truth; therefore, "Thou shalt not bear false witness."

Lull uses the traditional definition of truth: to say of *what is* that it is, and of falsehood, to say of *what is not* that it is. The principle is "that one bears false Testimony of God, who . . . affirms that, what in that one is not, and who denies of that one, what is in him."

The first reason why the commandment of God is "Thou shalt not bear false witness" is that to bear false witness is to deny its end, truth, which is to deny truth of God. And to deny the good reputation of a saint cannot be repaired by a lie.

"False testimony is testimony of a devil," and no devil can give true testimony. Whoever gives false testimony is an ally of the devil. To give false testimony is to give misinformation ("falsam cogitationem"). This is a wicked deed, an act far from charity, and one depriving speaking of its proper end.

"False testimony causes many men to go wrong and to lose faith." From false testimony, which one cannot conceal, comes great evil. False testimony does greater wrong to public leaders than to individuals ("Falsum Testimonium communis personae est magis malum, quam alterius particularis"). False testimony makes many enemies.

In the day of judgment every false testimony will be revealed.

It must be observed that a narrow interpretation of taking the name of God in vain might be to speak falsehood when under oath in court of law. And then the second commandment would imply the eighth, also narrowly interpreted as giving false testimony in court. But the metaphysician seeks the broadest possible imperative, which might be stated as "speak the truth!" or "don't lie!" Since God is the truth, to "Have no other God" and to "keep festival" imply worshiping God by telling the truth. But much more is implied by keeping commandments of love and justice, and celebrating God's glory with joy.

V

Lull's fifth commandment, true to the principle of keeping God as the center, interprets "Honor thy Father and Mother" as based on "Honor God, who is thy Father through creating and sustaining thee." This is accompanied by the commandment to honor one's mother the church, who guides one in the way of salvation ("Honora Sanctam Ecclesiam, quae est tua Mater per viam salutis").

After the allegorical meaning of Father God and mother church comes the literal "honor thy Father and thy Mother who begat and bore thee" and "who fed thee." The second argument is then one of natural indebtedness or gratitude. Parents are original sources of being, and so they are called "principles." He who does not honor his father and his mother dishonors his principles.

Then comes a third argument, not to shame parents or oneself. "From

a dishonored Father and dishonored Mother [comes] a dishonored son."
"He dishonors himself who dishonors his Father and his Mother." And remarkably, "He who dishonors himself honors no one."

Next, a return to the theme of honoring God, which reinforces the
honor due oneself, in descending degrees. It is God who links the degrees
of honor. "If God loves the honor of thy human Father, how much more
does he love honor for himself." And: "He who loves honor in small things
how much more ought he to love honor in great?" And: "The greater honor
belongs to God, than to all things." And last: "He who does not honor God
more than all things in no thing does he honor that one."

A man of distinctions, Lull argues that God is not to be honored with
meanness, nor with smallness (stinginess, pettiness, miserliness, insignifi-
cance). "If thou honorest thy Father and thy Mother equally [with God],
thou dishonorest God, who gives thee thy principles for being."

Then Lull returns to the punishment of the third argument, an attack
on self-respect: "He who dishonors any one else, is not able to honor himself" ("Qui alium inhonorat, non potest se ipsum honorare"). Having uni-
versalized the commandment to the degree of reading the fifth commandment as "honor all persons to the degree proper to their station," he
develops the distinction between what puts one higher and what puts one
lower: "Virtue honors, and vice dishonors." This is the concept present in
"a hierarchy of virtue." This is then applied to friends: "Honor thyself and
thy friend with virtues." The commandment "Honor thy father and
mother" has its last application to civil obedience: "He who dishonors his
earthly Lord, dishonors himself." And finally, the condition of the person
who cannot be dishonored: "He who honors himself with Patience and Humility, cannot be dishonored."

We are now in the realm of social relations. Lull reorders the central
"Thou shalt not kill, thou shalt not commit adultery, thou shalt not steal."
Why does Lull put first "non facias furtum," next "non occides," and last
"non moechaberis"? The reasons seem to be that theft is the most common,
and that the prohibition "Thou shalt not steal" is logically based on very
general principles which imply also "Thou shalt not kill" and "Thou shalt
not commit adultery." Clearly Lull has extended the meaning of "Thou
shalt not steal" to the fullest extent, and perhaps further than any other interpretation.

VI

The central principle that would prohibit theft is "Love thy neighbor" — all good is a gift of God. So the beginning is "God wishes, that thou shalt not steal, so that thou puttest hope in him, and hast charity toward thy neighbor. He who claims that he has done a good that GOD has done, steals that good from GOD" ("Qui sibi ipsi attribuit bonum, quod *DEUS* facit, furatur DEO illud bonum").

The contrast is between giving, which is divine, and stealing, which is devilish: "Give thyself *to God,* and steal thyself from the Devil" ("Da te *DEO,* & furare te Diabalo").

Following the previous commandment to honor all persons, the first theft prohibited is to take from anyone his good repute ("Non fureris alcui suam bonam famam"). This is developed in a parallel prohibition: "Non fureris alcui suum honorem"; "He commits grander larceny who takes away a good name than he who steals a treasury."

Charity is expressed by almsgiving. The justification is that the poor have a claim on any unused money and food. Not to give is stealing from the poor, because of their claim, and stealing from God, because he commands this kind of good ("Otiosos denarios non fureris pauperibus"). "Panem, quem non putes comedere, non fureris pauperibus." "Bonum, quod potes facere, noli furari DEO." "What is stolen from his neighbor is stolen from GOD" ("DEO furatur, qui suo proximo furatur").

In addition to stealing from others, stealing from oneself is also prohibited. "Thou shalt not steal from thyself that which is thine." This has a threefold application: "don't steal from the Memory anything good to recollect"; "Don't steal from thy Intellect any true knowledge"; "Don't steal from thy Will anything good and right to love." What memory deserves is "Bonum recolere" — to remember what is good; what intellect deserves is "verum intellgere" — to understand the truth; and what will deserves is "bonum & justum amare" — to love the good and the just. This is an application of honoring oneself, reflecting Saint Augustine's conception of the threefold self.

Then for the senses and imagination, which Augustine regarded as the fantasy or picturing of tempting evils as good, the commandment is applied in three imperatives: "Steal, Steal, Steal!" "Steal from thine eyes pretty things, and from thine ears vain words." "Steal from thy hands evil deeds, from thy feet false ways, from thy tongue sweet foods." "Steal from thine imagination vanities."

The exposition is then rounded out by returning to the omni-
benevolence of God, which is applied to the person and to his relation to
his Lord. "Don't steal because God always has what he shall give thee." Evidently God's plenitude of being includes maximal generosity.

VII

"Thou shalt not kill" ("Non occides") requires a statement of the exceptions, that is, when killing is legal and not condemned as murder. Lull includes justifications of legal killing, which is what we should expect of a
knight who serves his king. But Lull speculates generally on what should
be killed, much as in the previous commandment he stated what should be
stolen.

The theological ground of the prohibition of taking human life is that
it is God "who gives a man life." Lull does not say it is offensive to the Creator to destroy the image of God. God as judge is evidently also the giver of
death, for "Thou shalt not kill" includes killing oneself. "Thou shalt not
kill thyself, because thou art not judge of thyself."

The seriousness of the crime of killing, in contrast to the stealing of
goods which can be paid back, is contained in the fact that "he who kills a
man is not able to give him back his life." On moral grounds alone, apart
from theology, the argument against murder is, "From evil comes evil, and
from murder comes murder" ("De malo malum, & de homicida homici-
dium").

The most general exception is stated last: "Kill, who wishes to kill
thee unjustly." This is justifiable self-defense; it is assumed in making the
case for just war, when a society and its property are defended against an
armed enemy. This may well be included in the exceptions: "only the
prince has the right to kill a man in doing justice." "To kill one man that he
shall not kill many, is not evil."

There is the basic goodness of life that is stated as an imperative:
"Live! So you don't die" ("Vive, ut non moriaris"). The goodness of life in-
cludes both the soul and the body: "Thou shalt not kill thy soul with sin!"
"Thou shalt not kill thy body for the sake of money" ("Non occidas tuum
Corpus pro denariis"). Apparently the goodness of charity is to give more
than alms: "Thou shalt not kill the poor with money."

Is it also murder to kill animals? There is no general prohibition of
slaughter by butchers, but there is a positive protection of animals that are

needed alive: "Do not kill an ass, for he helps thee live." "Do not kill a dog who guards thee." But "kill a serpent, because it has venom." Apparently self-defense extends from defense against enemies to defense against vermin.

The conclusion is the metaphorical extension of "Thou shalt not kill" from "thy neighbor" and "thy neighbor's good name" to "thy goodness with ill-will" ("Non occidas tuam Bonitatem cum malitia"). The justification of these prohibitions is: "It is not right to kill virtues."

As for vices, the commandment means "Kill!" Examples given are the chief sin of the soul and sin of the body: "Kill pride with humility" and "Kill great pleasure of the senses" ("Occide tuae sensitivae suas magnas delectationes").

Last Five Commandments as a Group

In the last five commandments in Lull's interpretation, although each begins with what "God wills" or "God teaches," increasingly God plays a smaller role in the reasoning: from six maxims in "Thou shalt not steal" to two in "Thou shalt not commit adultery" and two in "Thou shalt not covet thy neighbor's things." The commandments are commandments of God, but the justification is increasingly moral, arguing against vice and the evil consequences of vice. The first five in Lull's listing might be called "theological commandments" because in restating them the chief ground is the nature of God. The second five might be called "moral commandments" because the chief ground is the nature of human virtues and vices and the bad consequences of vice. The penalty of breaking a theological commandment is to side with the devil against God and to be condemned to perdition. But the chief sanction of the last five commandments is that breaking them brings misery in this life. The last five are sometimes called "secular commandments."

Lull's eighth commandment, "Thou shalt not commit adultery," is argued first from divine authority: "God wishes, that thou shalt not live lasciviously, so that thou mightest love matrimony" ("Non facias luxuriam, ut ames matrimonium").

"The man who is luxurious [deviating from strict matrimony in adultery, etc.] does not use reason" ("non utitur ratione, qui est luxuriosus"). Why matrimony? "So thou mightest be holy." In addition to the sacramental bond of holy matrimony, there is the legal reason, with the good consequence for the family of a "legitimate heir" ("Non facias luxuriam, ut habeas filium legitimum"). Then there is the reason that marriage lengthens life ("Non facias luxuriam, ut diu vivas").

Both the life of virtue and the life of vice are habit-forming. The argument for chastity, which depends on the will, is that no pleasure in a luxurious life compares with it ("Nulla delectatio tantum valet in luxuria, quantum castitas in Voluntate"). The more a chaste man hates luxury, the more he will hate it. The more a luxurious man thinks of loving luxury, the more he loves it. Lull speaks in the second-person singular (thou) to each. The chaste man will not "carry the signs of luxury," but a luxurious man, going on from luxury to luxury, will have no rest, and growing old in his luxury, dies with it.

IX

"Thou shalt not covet thy neighbor's wife" is meant most generally: "every man [homo] is thy neighbor." Homo then clearly means a human, whether female or male, and applies to the adulterous wife as well as the adulterous husband. So God wills that "Thou shalt not covet thy neighbor's husband."

Coveting is defined as desire for what God gives, and so it is theological usurpation of authority ("Non habeas invidiam de hoc, quod DEUS dat").

From desire for what is thy neighbor's springs envy and discord in the community. "Envy divides the friendship of men" ("Invidia dividit amicitias hominum"). Often the man who desires another's wife sows suspicion in his neighbor ("Saepe bonit suspicionem in suo vicino, qui concupiscit illius uxorem"). "If thou lustest after the wife of thy neighbor, thou puttest all thy neighbors in suspicion." And: "Because of a bad neighbor thou hast a bad evening and a bad morning." And: "Every day envy of the neighbor grows." Finally: "No war is worse than a neighbor's war."

Steps can be taken to prevent such a feud. "When thou seest thy neighbor's wife, if she is pretty, shut thine eyes." "Don't praise his wife to a neighbor." Likewise: "Don't praise thy neighbor to thy wife." What's more: "Don't speak with thy neighbor about thy wife." Indeed: "Beware of thy neighbor more than of any other man." In conclusion: "Give or sell thy houses and flee from the bad neighbor."

X

"Coveting thy neighbor's goods" continues the same lines of argument. To envy what your neighbor has is to reject God because he gives these things.

The shift is from coveting to envying as the vicious motivation.

Concupiscence or envious desire is self-defeating and unproductive. He who causes his good things to be desired, makes enemies. "The envious man does not sleep." The steps to avoid arousing envy are simple: "Thou shalt not praise thy wealth to thy neighbor" ("Non laudes tuo vicino tuas divitias"). "If you praise your riches to your neighbor, you get envy."

It is very instructive that although some doctors of the church classify pride as the chief of sins, Lull does not mention *superbia*. Lull makes honor a great virtue, and includes honoring oneself as essential to honoring God, virtue, one's parents, one's ruler, all men. The greatest opprobrium belongs to *invidia*.

Invidia, which might well connote hatred as well as envy, because it's an opposite to charity, brings Lull to prescribe love as the cure of envy: "Kill envy with charity." "The envious man has neither Justice nor Hope," which means the envious man lacks the chief pagan virtue as well as one of the three theological virtues. The envious man violates the principle of virtue (in Aristotle's analysis, moderation), since he goes to the extreme of envying the king.

"All envy brings sadness" ("omnis invidia dat tristitiam"). "The poor envious man has no rest" ("Pauper invidus non habet quietem"). "Envy is the messenger of betrayal" ("Invidia est nuncius proditionis"). "Envy raises up, and does not spare" ("Invidia tollit, & non parcit").

It is not that all desire is evil. Even a desire to be as rich as someone else is permissible. "Thou mayest desire similar riches, but not those which thou lustest for" ("Potes desiderare similes divitias, sed non illas, quas concubiscis").

Just as Lull advised getting away from a bad neighbor by selling houses, even giving them away, so he concludes it is better to have nothing to do with an envious man. "Don't give an envious man anything of thine own" ("Invido nihil commenda de tuo"). "Don't confer with an envious man" ("Non habeas consilium cum invido homine").

Clearly Lull's mind was one of excitement and fearless originality. Although the age in which he lived is known as the "age of faith," it is truer to say that Lull represents an "age of faith and reason." There are no mysteries of faith that cannot, according to this saint, be made intelligible, and he presents the Decalogue as an understanding of God's will and man's felicity.

ᵔ 7 ᵔ

Thomas Aquinas:
Firmness and Flexibility in the Decalogue

Saint Thomas Aquinas is unique among Christian interpreters of the Ten Commandments because he wrote treatises on the Decalogue both as a theologian and as a philosopher. Apparently there is no total and absolute distinction between the subject matter of the moral law based on revealed Scripture and that based on reasoned dialogue, for the theologian addresses the intelligence of his reader and the philosopher asks him to think critically about biblical texts and uses Scripture and doctors of the church, notably Saint Augustine, to state the position to be defended.

As theologian, Thomas presents the Decalogue in the context of the creed and the Lord's Prayer. These are learned in catechetical instruction, where the purpose is to answer the question, what should a person do to be saved? In this context the person must believe the creed and pray, and then must "know what is to be done and what is not to be done." The human faculty of intelligence needs to be enlightened by God. We begin by noting that Saint Thomas addresses himself to the intelligence of his reader. He never demands that the believer blindly accept what the church teaches; but rather, since intelligence is enlightened by God, he wants his reader to grasp the truth of what Moses and Christ taught.

Unfortunately, begins Thomas, man is not as originally created. He is now blinded by passions. The human condition is as described by Saint Paul in Romans: "I know in my members another law, which fights against the law of my mind." This knowledge allows a further observation: "[This law makes] me slave to the law of sin, which is in my members."

Both Moses and Christ are presented as liberators. The motive for obeying the commandments is fear, and Moses' wisdom begins with fear of the Lord. But there is another motive: love. This is the commandment of

Christ. He is making the contrast between two ways: fear makes us slaves but love makes us free; the first way leads us to worldly goods, the second to heavenly. Moses' commandments are a heavy burden, but Christ's commandments are light and easy to bear.

The laws of love cover all human acts; the result of living according to love is compared to a work of art which conforms to rules appropriate to that art. The analogy is between a virtuous life and something beautiful and perfect.

Why live according to the twofold love, love of God and love of neighbor? Because the results are a spiritual life, observance of the divine laws, a defense against all adversity, and happiness. Love *(caritas)* leads to forgiveness of sins, illumination of the heart, perfect joy, and perfect peace. Thomas assures the reader that this way to such results is possible, and he does not neglect to explain how. The beginning for us is to love ourselves; if we do this in the proper way, we love the source of our being and others, particularly those to whom it is natural to be grateful. Intelligence develops from nature and bridges to grace; nature is perfected by grace. Much of this is specified under the individual commandments of the Decalogue.

Aquinas's method involves first quoting the text of each commandment and relating it to other scriptural texts. The purpose is first to establish what the Scripture means. In the first commandment, "Thou shalt not have other gods before me," the text does not say what these "other gods" might be — perhaps the stars, or elements of nature, heroes, etc. So one must form an interpretation of the phrase "before me." Then comes the question *why*. In sequence Thomas presents five motives for worshiping one God only: the dignity of the Creator, his generosity in sharing being, then the necessity of renouncing the devil and avoiding slavery to him, and finally the goal of winning the greatest prize, eternal life.

For the second commandment, forbidding "taking the name of God in vain," it is necessary to distinguish when it is right and necessary to use the name of God. For example, there is the good motive of using God's name when confessing. Several other theological techniques are employed for "Thou shalt keep the Sabbath holy." One is to show *how* this is done in thought (in one's heart) as well as in word of praise and in deed. In great detail Thomas tells us how to keep the Sabbath — and, he adds, other festivals. The Eucharist, for example, is by sacrifice offered to God, and he specifies that this should be done spontaneously, with glad and willing heart. What is to be done also on festivals is giving of alms to the poor, study of the word of God, and devotional exercises.

The commandment of the Sabbath specifies "rest" from six days of labor; we must learn the principle Jesus recommended to restless Martha and turn ourselves from the distraction of "many things." There is also the metaphorical "rest" from turbulence of sin and "rest" from passions of the flesh. But the highest meaning, the "anagogical" sense, is that "rest" signifies the change from remembering the Creator's rest to celebrating our new creation in Christ. "Rest," then, is the anticipation of life in heaven.

The commandment "Honor thy father and thy mother" begins from a basic moral principle: do good and avoid evil. This is not explicit in the biblical text, but theology makes explicit what everyone knows and what the text presupposes. With this as basis, it is only logical that (paraphrasing Aristotle) having received from our parents our existence, nutriment, and education, the good we owe them is gratitude.

Other expositions, Lull's for example, as we have seen, interpret "Honor thy father" with a mystical reference to our "heavenly Father," but Thomas is as literal as Philo in stressing our dependence on parents in the family. This we share with animals. Thomas, like Philo, appeals to ancient naturalists who tell of younger birds taking care of their aged parents. This is to indicate how *we* are to honor parents.

This is a commandment with a promise; and beyond expounding *what* it means, there is the *why.* Not only is "long life" held out as a natural reward, but also a good life, one full of virtues, and not only that, but a "life of grace and glory."

Aquinas makes this an expanded exposition on giving and gratitude. There is empirical observation of the commonsense advice to parents: don't give sons too much power.

Gratitude is not only owed to our natural fathers (Thomas is under the ancient misconception of children as extensions of active seed with little role played by the mother's egg), but to other fathers as well, of whom Thomas includes apostles and saints, famous men, priests, rulers, *and* benefactors. All these should be venerated, in the keeping of the fourth commandment.

As mentioned above, when we seek the meaning of "Thou shalt not kill," we need to consider various interpretations. We must sort out what is true and what is false in our predecessors. Perhaps this is the most ambiguous of commandments, or one in which the reader has already met various conflicting meanings.

"Killing" has many meanings, and beyond causing death to another human being by blow or with sword, there is going after another, provoking him, or accusing him, or calumniating him.

It is apparently self-evident *why* killing is wrong, and Thomas goes from *what* killing is to *how* to prevent the act. Begin with the motive, anger; by controlling anger, a person removes the root of murder.

Quite in contrast to "Thou shalt not kill," where Aquinas assumes human nature abhors the act, is "Thou shalt not commit adultery." Here, as in the *Summa*, adultery is so pleasant that he must ask *"why not?"* The exhaustive analysis of the many wrongs done to everyone involved bears comparison to Philo's case against what he considered the chief sin, worse than murder because so many persons — indeed, Philo and Aquinas agree, everyone involved — come out wronged and damaged.

As for "stealing," there are many ways to break the commandment "Thou shalt not steal" — likewise for "Thou shalt not give false testimony." Both call for explanations of *why* we should guard against them, and Thomas adds a list of motivations of bearing false testimony that may have had the role of helping the reader examine his conscience.

What coveting is, is fairly obvious, but here Thomas dwells on *why* it is forbidden. The ninth commandment leads naturally to the tenth. Also this begins "Thou shalt not covet," and here the sin of concupiscence is analyzed. A different technique is introduced: scaling the sin by degrees. Thus the reader is given a way to conquer excessive desire for others and their goods, just as the reader had been helped with anger.

Having looked briefly at each commandment, we now pass to Thomas's philosophy of the Ten Commandments.

The Philosopher of the Decalogue

In the philosophical context of the *Summa theologiae*, the existence and nature of God are demonstrated according to reason. Thomas draws upon the natural philosophy of Aristotle, with its concept of causality, to prove that there must be a first efficient cause and a final cause of the world, and what God's essence is. Man is demonstrated to be a free and responsible agent who knows that his end is happiness, an agent who knows which habits conduce to happiness and which produce misery. Aquinas draws upon the *Ethics* of Aristotle to state the virtues a man should develop and the vices he should avoid. Justice is the chief virtue.

What are the moral precepts of the old law? Answers come from philosophy and experience as well as Scripture. In the letter to the Romans, Paul states that what the Jew received through Moses, the law of the covenant of God with Israel, is identical to the moral wisdom of the pagan philosophers: "The Gentiles, who have not the Law, do by nature those things that are of the law" (Rom. 2:14). Thomas's method of defending the proposition is to consider in twelve articles various difficult questions. There are no fewer than forty-two difficulties to address. First he states the difficulties that seem to refute the identity of revealed moral law with natural law, then he quotes a statement of truth, from Paul or some theologian, and then usually an answer to each difficulty.

Question 100, the first part of the second part, is part of the section entitled "Law." It is only 1 of 119 sections and considers only the "moral precepts of the Old Law," distinguishing these from the ceremonial and the legal, which follow.

The great value of the scholastic method used in the *Summa theologiae* is that it clarifies the question. The most important of the twelve articles are:

1. Whether all the moral precepts of the old law belong to the law of nature.
2. Whether the moral precepts of the law are about all the actions of the virtues.
3. Whether all the moral precepts of the old law are reducible to the ten precepts of the Decalogue.

Thomas's problem was to square the Decalogue with the ethical doctrine of Aristotle. Is the person who keeps the Ten Commandments the same sort of good person who has practiced the virtues of temperance, fortitude, prudence, and justice? Maimonides formulated the question of whether the good Jew, illustrated by the prophets and wise men of Israel, had the cardinal virtues taught by Aristotle. Not only does the evidence support the affirmative: the good Jew surpasses the good pagan by having also developed righteousness, judgment, and loving-kindness; but had Thomas framed his question that way, his parallel answer would be "Yes, and the good Christian surpasses the good pagan in humility and in the three cardinal virtues added to the four pagan: faith, hope, and charity."

Why did Thomas ask whether all the moral precepts of the old law belong to the law of nature? Moral rules are learned; "moral institutions are various for various people"; good morals are based on faith. Thomas was facing the problem that all the "Thou shalt not's" may be only taboos, that folkways are as various as cultures, and subject to change. Since all moral rules seem to be relative, and none absolute, all we can have are opinions. Relativism breeds moral skepticism and subjectivism. Anything and everything should be permitted — and there are no rational limits to tolerance.

We learn from Thomas that when an objection has some truth, we should say, "Yes, there are many rules that are particular, arbitrary, and subject to change." Thomas so regards ceremonial rules. There is no necessity that the day of rest be the seventh day, as it is among Jews. For Christians the Sabbath became Sunday, the Lord's Day, the first day of the week. But over and above various human institutions, it still makes sense to recognize "Divine law [that is] more perfect." That is: some time ought to be devoted to thinking of things other than our daily work. If this is the principle, then Moslems can satisfy it by keeping Friday holy. Thomas stated simply that we owe some time to things of God.

Thomas was certain that human reason can grasp principles which are universal, necessary, and unchangeable. Each man has reason, even if he does not always activate his potential and apply himself to finding "first common principles." How was he certain, and can we also be certain about principles? Part of a scholastic doctor's training was logic, or the science of relation between propositions. There are formal truths so obvious that they are almost never stated, such as "if a proposition is true, then it is true," or "if a proposition is true, then it is not false," and formal patterns of valid steps from the truth of one proposition to the truth of another. Thomas had studied the Aristotelian syllogism: if all A's are B's and all B's are C's, then all A's are C's. It is impossible to reason without *modus ponendo ponens,* as the scholastics named the very simple validating form: *if P is true, then Q is true; and P is true, therefore Q is true.*

In this short question Thomas applies his logic to the commandments. We shall consider the problem of the relation logically between "Thou shalt not do *x*" and "Thou shalt do *not-x*."

Now, if reason can grasp and use principles in the area of the truth, why not also in the area of the good?

One example of analysis that uncovers what everyone knows concerns the application of rules to acts. We constantly judge persons, others and ourselves, according to whatever rules there are in human relations. The principle here, Thomas argues, is that whoever transgresses a precept of the law deserves to be punished. But suppose the person has had no opportunity to know the rule he is said to have violated. Suppose the act is accidental, and the man has not acted from choice or deliberately. If he has not acted "of violation and of intention," then he is not to be condemned. A person is blameworthy or culpable only if he has knowledge of the rule and has had opportunity to follow or violate it. Thomas adds a third condition: that he *should act from a firm and immovable principle,* which firmness belongs properly to a habit and implies that the action proceeds from a rooted habit.

Between the questions about the Ten Commandments and Thomas's answers come expositions of Thomas's own position. It is best to consider these separately; otherwise the sheer multitude of points and counterpoints may give the impression of trivial logic chopping; or worse, the scholastic doctor may look like a clever lawyer scoring against any and all who would challenge him. Nothing could be further from the seriousness of Thomas's search for wisdom.

In the sequence in which they are developed, Thomas has taken positions which remain of great value to the contemporary thinker.

Ten Starting Points for Interpretation
1. How natural law is known
2. Advantages of natural law
3. Logic works back to first principles and on to the implied precepts
4. Adequacy of the Decalogue
5. Precepts added to the commandments
6. Proper order of the commandments
7. Application requires psychology and sociology
8. Dispensations for exceptions to the rules
9. The mode of virtue, how a rule is obeyed
10. Obeying the rules does not justify us before God nor earn his salvation.

How Natural Law Is Known

Anyone who accepts a principle and any set of standards must face the objection that such beliefs are commonly believed to be only private opinions or the folkways peculiar to some subset of rational creatures. Thomas begins in article 1 with objections that no moral rules can be universal, necessary, and unchangeable. The relativist position is that commandments are cultural *taboos* — particular, arbitrary, subject to change. Thomas grants that taste and convictions vary with class and role in society, yet insists that there is "Divine Law [that is] more perfect." Morals are commonly believed to be emotive, not knowledge at all, but at best an expression of faith. Thomas unfolds law from his rich concept of nature, natural reason, the law of nature, and so on. Certain commandments are known by natural reason: honor thy father and mother; thou shalt not kill; thou shalt not steal. Others belong to the law of nature, and some are known by means of divine instruction (the law against graven images, the law against taking the name of God in vain).

A common first principle is: "Do evil to no man." It is practical reason by which we know this. Because we know this as an important aspect of human nature, it does not need to be taught. It is presupposed in knowing that some acts in relation to other persons are good and some are evil, and it is therefore on a higher level of discourse than specifying which particular things are good and which are evil. Because it is true without demonstration, it is a self-evident truth. Because it is a more perfect law than any human law, its status is designated as "natural law" — and, Thomas adds, man here knows something "immediately from God."

Advantages of Natural Law

There are many advantages to the natural law interpretation of the Decalogue — at least four, each of which answers a difficulty often expressed in a theory that puts reason in central position in moral life. The first difficulty, made famous by David Hume, is that reason is not a motive force, as are the passions. Reason, he argued, is only a tool for aiding us in getting what we want. The second difficulty is that we often discover no reason in judgments of taste, reduce moral to aesthetic judgments, and say there is no arguing about them. The third difficulty is that we commonly think ascribing the natural law to "God" is only a mode of speaking, and that Moses got Israel to agree to the covenant by ascribing his moral rules to "God." The fourth difficulty is that we have reduced the demand for "fairness" to a kind of rhetorical insistence that institutions bow to our demands; hence "fair" is a tool used in gaining or defending power. Devise ways to apply pressure, and your opponent must give in and grant your claim. If that is all there is to "moral" discourse, then "natural law" is a loaded concept.

If the two tables of law are duties to God and duties to one's neighbor, where are duties to oneself? Thomas recognized that there is no explicit statement "Thou shalt preserve thyself, satisfy natural needs, educate and advance thyself by diligence, defend thyself against attack." But the duty of self-preservation is part of the natural law, along with protecting the freedom needed by a responsible agent to do what the agent knows is right (Art. 5, 1, 834-36). If a person exercises these rights, he will not be angry, and he will not be envious of others' success, for he too has done what he could with his opportunities. Thus acting as a free agent avoids disorders on what Aquinas quaintly calls the "irascible part" and the "concupiscible part."

Some Christian moralists observe that self-love can be a strong rival of love of God and love of neighbor, and observe that man by natural law has no lack of self-love. Thomas is more optimistic about the basic driving motive of human action, as many observe the second great commandment, "Thou shalt love thy neighbor as thyself." "Reason" therefore is not mere calculation, a sort of means, but a directing agency. Natural reason is the source of moral precepts, even ones not included in the law of Moses.

A second great advantage of a natural law interpretation of the Decalogue is that it appeals to man in his dignity as the highest of earthly creatures. The natural law interpretation is addressed to the whole person, and not to some restricted or specialized relation, as are some other interpretations which consider man qua sinner in the judgment of God or man as moral man who needs to reform immoral society.

A third advantage is meeting the argument raised by the story of Moses — of a very special person in a unique circumstance. A skeptical person can say, "God never spoke to me from a burning bush; I have no personal acquaintance with the Holy One, who on Mount Sinai wrote with his finger upon tablets of stone. What does it mean to say that God himself gave the precepts of the Decalogue? A very significant story about the making of a covenant between YHWH and Israel, but completely remote from our own experience, perhaps only a myth." The natural law approach, following Scripture that law is "written in the heart," can say to the skeptic that each of us can know what it means for God to give the law. Each of us, finding precepts of natural knowledge, has knowledge immediately from God. This is appropriate to man, whose mind is the "image of God."

A fourth advantage of the natural law interpretation, prominent in Thomas, is his account of judging our acts according to the rules. On the one hand, obedience to a rule involves principles. On the other, some judgments are unjust, as when we have acted in ignorance or done something "accidentally." The advantage of the Decalogue is that it takes intention or motive into account, and judges our acts when we act deliberately or from choice. Divine law considers intent as equally blameworthy with act.

Under natural law, reason can operate in the moral realm with objectivity.

First Principles and Implied Precepts

The use of logic in thinking of the Decalogue as part of the natural law has several valuable results. The simplest is to go beyond the obvious grammatical observation that only two commandments are positive "Thou shalt's" while eight are negative "Thou shalt not's." If one chooses to have ten "Thou shalt's," it is simple logic to convert negative to positive. Thomas gives one example with regard to stealing. Its strict meaning is preserved in commanding "Thou shalt keep another's property intact and thou shalt return property to its owner."

But Aquinas is sharp in logic. He knows that the affirmative goes beyond the negative. If the positive demands that we protect the property of the owner, it involves much more than *not* stealing.

Calvin in his *Institutes* followed Aquinas in turning negative into positive. The commandment "Thou shalt not kill" is included in "do all thou canst to help the neighbor's life."

Thomas, however, points out that the negation of all cases has a greater extension than the affirmation of a single case or only some. The "Shalt not's" prevail eight to two over the affirmative commandments to honor parents and observe the Sabbath. The two affirmative commandments are then brought logically under the more inclusive class of acts required out of gratitude.

Because it appeals to reason and uses logic, sometimes natural law theory is thought to be a deductive system. Thomas does not go so far as to systematize precepts under axioms, with postulates and QEDs. He does grade according to the hierarchy from general down to particular and, interestingly, according to the certainty of the proposition and to the type of evidence. The Decalogue is somewhere in a mean between self-evident truths of great generality and more particular applications of the commandments.

We began with his defense of the most general "Do evil to no man" and now must consider "moral precepts added to the Decalogue" (Art. 11). The added precepts are, as in geometry, called "corollaries." But does this amount to saying that the Ten Commandments revealed to Moses are deficient?

Adequacy of the Decalogue

Although the statement about the existence of more general imperatives than those stated in the Decalogue and the adding of "moral precepts" seem to imply the imperfection, deficiency, or inadequacy of the Ten Commandments, Thomas argues this is not so. The more general are parts of the natural law, given to every man, and although not explicitly stated in the Decalogue, they are logically presupposed by it. It is presupposed that we have the ability, for example, to distinguish good and evil, right and wrong, and to recognize that what is good and right is commanded, what is evil and wrong is prohibited.

If we ask about duties to ourselves, Thomas justifies only two tablets because we are constantly motivated to care for our own interests; it is God and our neighbor who are forgotten and neglected. Similarly, why is not "Honor thy father and thy mother" coupled with "Care for thy children"? Thomas says no ordinance is here needed because children are extensions of ourselves. The impulse to covet what is our neighbor's is motivated by appetite, since pleasure and use are good in themselves. It needs to be prohibited. But Thomas recognizes no natural impulse that leads to either murder or to lying. And further, since it is excessive or misdirected desire, for "concupiscence," which has a second effect, hatred, the prohibition of lust and covetousness suffices.

"The law of the Lord is perfect."

Precepts Added to the Commandments

Toward the end of the question on the moral law (Art. 11), Thomas runs through eight commandments showing amplifications found in Scripture or in church tradition. He says the Ten Commandments are principles and the other precepts are like corollaries. The commandment against idols is interpreted in Deuteronomy 28 to include human sacrifice, use of wizards, and so on.

Thomas does not put these "added precepts" on the level of "the love of God and our neighbor" or of "the common good." Although he cites Scripture verses to justify most of these rules, this alone does not give them the rank of commandments.

Thomas was so firm in his absolute first principles and ends of action that we may be taken by surprise by his flexibility in their instrumentation. Perhaps because he had put the commandments in a rational context of natural law, he had fixed standards by which he could judge freely which of many alternative means can satisfy such very general norms. This raises his thought above the limitations of the "medieval" and gives it a most remarkable timelessness.

Proper Order of the Commandments

As with distinguishing the different commandments, so with grasping how they are arranged, perception varies from person to person. Some judge in which respects commandments are like or unlike, similar or different, and how one is related to another.

We might arrange commandments in the order of our knowing, for we learn love of neighbor before we learn love of God. We might follow the order in which vices should be curbed. We might think first of our thought, rather than prohibit first the sinful act and then come to the motivation. Perhaps because Thomas, a great expert on ordering relations, can consider several relevant organizing principles — order of learning, order of gravity, and order of execution — he recognizes that the order in which we receive the Ten Commandments has the rational merit of beginning with the end of action, the final purpose. God is the first principle of order; as Saint Paul says, "The things that are of God are well ordered" (Rom. 13:1).

What Thomas presents as the "order of reason" does satisfy the principle of the order of execution, for our thought of God motivates the sequence of acts. It satisfies the order of learning by continuing in the recognition of parents to whom we are indebted. And the order of prohibited sins — murder, adultery, and theft — is an order of gravity.

But what is the rationale behind the last commandments, against bearing false witness and coveting what is the neighbor's? Are these last because it is even more difficult to control words and desires than acts?

Thomas's silences are an invitation to us to continue thinking.

The choice of the order of an army, one of Aristotle's metaphorical models, may be explained by the stress on loyal obedience to the commander. But the repayment of a debt shifts the metaphor to the marketplace. The order of learning belongs to the school, while the decree of criminality reminds us of judgments in courts of law. Thomas turned to the world for his models of order rather than using the spiritual model of hierarchy, the ascent, by return, to heaven. But as we shall shortly see, Thomas pays most attention to the order of the family and of the community, to which orders the commandments are particularly adapted.

Application Requires Psychology and Sociology

Although Thomas is following the "order of reason" in this account, and refers to added precepts as "corollaries," we are not presented with a deductive system. Thomas's moral reason is practical reason, and it is applied in the empirical search for what is natural in human institutions. In no passage is his psychology more apparent than in his characterization of the family. Thomas's cheerful note is that parents do not need to be commanded to show affection to their children. It is just as natural for people to love their children as it is for them to love themselves, and he quotes a gloss on the Decalogue in Deuteronomy: "Parents love their children as being a part of themselves," and supports this also from Aristotle's *Nicomachean Ethics* (8.12). Obviously "natural" connotes, as we sometimes say, "normal."

But the "natural," although in search of the good, can be spoiled by excess and needs to be restrained. He answers the apparent irregularity that only some commandments prohibit thought as well as act, and some explicitly only act, by noting that adultery and wealth pertain to the appetite and must be addressed not only as deeds but as desires, whereas murder and falsehood may be addressed as deeds only.

Thomas's sociology is clearly that of "a community or commonwealth of men under God." The relations, through thought, word, and deed, are of loyal and grateful service, and of "doing harm to none." Marriages, families, neighborhoods: civil arrangements depend on the Ten Commandments.

Dispensations for Exceptions to the Rules

The whole tone of discussing added commandments, classing them as less than evident; the recognition of alternative principles of ordering them; and the empirical approach to the commandments relating to family and community prepare the way to recognize that some rules have exceptions. There are conflicts between rules, most notably between "Thou shalt not kill" and capital punishment (Thomas has already recognized that the state defends itself in war). Why is execution of a criminal not murder? He paraphrases Augustine's distinction between murder and the killing done by civil society in self-defense.

God, according to Scripture, makes exceptions to his own commandments. The most troublesome case is the command to Abraham to take Isaac his son, his only son, and sacrifice him on Mount Moriah. Did Abraham violate the commandment "Thou shalt not kill" in his compliance? If the intent to murder is as sinful as the act, then "justice itself" commanded the death of an innocent. If God was only testing Abraham's faith, then Abraham, loyal to God, should have protested injustice. If God never intended the father to kill his son, which would have cut off the very possibility of God's promise of many descendants, it would have been deceiving his faithful servant as well as frustrating God's own plan for the people sprung from Abraham. Thomas might have rejected Scripture or consigned this to a primitive barbaric misunderstanding of God, and saved his rational ethics. But he could not cease to be Thomas the theologian, considering a case of exception to the rules. Less horrendous than the Abraham story, which drove Kierkegaard into the agonized existential analysis of *Fear and Trembling,* Thomas also finds that God commanded theft and adultery. The instance of theft is the command to Moses, leading the fugitive slaves out of bondage, to carry off the spoils of the Egyptians. (This might have been justified as recompense for unrequited, uncompensated toil.) Then there is the command to the prophet Hosea that he marry, taking back an adulterous wife. (This might have been justified as an analogue to God's taking back an adulterous people.) What is Thomas's account of God himself commanding theft, murder, and adultery? God, the Lord of life and death, is the author of the institution of marriage.

Few theologians state these scriptural exceptions to the commandments, and there is the further problem whether this theology, based on Scripture, can be consistent with the theology, based on philosophy, that God "cannot deny Himself. But he would deny Himself if he were to do

away with the very order of His own justice, since He is justice itself"
(Art. 8).[1]

How a Rule Is Obeyed

"Mode of virtue," how a rule is obeyed or how one is judged to have violated a law, covers the questions "Is justice done justly?" "Is the rule
obeyed out of fear of punishment for not obeying?" "Is the rule followed
because one must do what is commanded?"

The first question, when is a person judged justly? was answered by
Aristotle. Thomas paraphrases the *Ethics* by distinguishing between delib-
eration, choice, and ignorant accident. The second question bears on the
contrast made by the theologian Thomas between the law of Moses and the
law of Christ. The first is obeyed out of fear of punishment for disobeying,
the second out of love. Of course, the philosopher knows that both "Love
the Lord thy God" (Deut. 6:5) and "Love thy neighbor" (Lev. 19:18) are
part of the Torah of Moses and were combined by Jesus into the twofold
commandment. The contrast then is upon the emphasis of Christ, and
could not be a rejection of the old law, for the new fulfills the old. Good
works are not sufficient in themselves: they must be done out of loving-
kindness. Thomas argues that we are enjoined to keep all the commandments, one of which requires love of our neighbor.

It is sometimes objected, as by Immanuel Kant, that to say "Love one
another" is absurd. Love is an affection which cannot be commanded. Only
actions can be commanded, not affections. Kant's objection was made five
centuries after the time of Thomas, who would have answered: "One can
dispose himself to receive charity from God." The human mind is open to
divine inspiration. The human heart, related to a loving God, is open to
"infusion of faith," and responds, if it is ready, to the divine eros.

If an act is done out of calculating the punishment or the reward, and
the choice made out of prudence alone, it may be done "with sadness or necessity." The mode of virtue is very important because if the act is done
"willingly and with pleasure," it is done gladly, "then," following a gloss,
"you will do it well."

---

1. *Basic Writings of Saint Thomas Aquinas*, vol. 2, *Man and the Conduct of Life*, ed.
Anton C. Pegis (New York: Random House, 1945), p. 843.

Simple Obedience Is Not Enough

The question of man's final end and ultimate destiny was put urgently by a rich young man to Jesus: "What shall I do to inherit eternal life?" Is it sufficient to have kept all the commandments? The answer must be no. Even if one has done all to satisfy the norm of justice, "rendering to each one his due" or acting "for the common good," this does not cover all the virtues. The relation of man — "reason or mind, in which is God's image" — to God requires "interior passions" as well as "outer action" to complete the whole "order of virtue." Justification before God is true justice. This is not merely habit and act but the state of the person "caused by God Himself through His grace."

We have now reached a conclusive statement of Catholic Christianity on the Ten Commandments, and as summed up by the greatest of Catholic theologians and philosophers, a significant point of the continuity of what are sometimes divided absolutely, Catholic and Protestant interpretations. Soon we will hear Luther denouncing the belief that works alone will earn heaven, and we will hear his insistence upon faith and love, and consider the conclusion that good works flow from this inner response to God's grace.

On this central point of the Protestant Reformation, Luther was applying exactly what Thomas had taught. Had Luther known the teaching of Saint Thomas Aquinas rather than the degenerate scholastics of the Renaissance, he could have improved his argument with Roman Catholic authorities, and they would have seen that the passionate monk was justly rebuking practices of trying to buy salvation, which Thomas also would have condemned.

~ II ~

REFORMATION

Girolamo Savonarola:
The Decalogue of a Fanatic

Not all medieval Catholic versions of the Ten Commandments are written in the various styles of spirituality, from ascetic and withdrawn to activist and involved. Not all medieval and Catholic versions are either on the high level of Dante or on the elementary pedagogical level of rhymed versions which are part of catechetical instruction. Nor are all full of either simple maxims or nuggets of common sense.

Some versions, particularly in sermons, are from preachers distressed by a world of wickedness and in fear of divine wrath, preachers who held up the tortures of hell to shock their hearers into abandoning their wicked ways. Some great preachers had a keen eye for the vices not only of laypeople, but of monks and of the highest ecclesiastics, and still managed to breathe some logic and much common sense into their sermons. The sermons of Berthold von Regensburg are an example. But there are other cases where the Decalogue is used by a fanatic in ways that are not only excessive but positively evil.

Girolamo Savonarola (1452-98) was educated at Ferrara by his paternal grandfather, Michele, who held rigid moral and religious principles. Girolamo intended to follow his grandfather into medical studies, but evidently he took as his first order of business correcting a wayward people. He entered the Dominican Order at Bologna in 1474; in 1482 he moved to the priory of San Marco in Florence and there attracted huge crowds as he preached against the immorality of the Florentines and the contemporary clergy. He supported Charles VIII of France during his Italian campaign of 1494-95; he saw in Charles the punishing hand of God; eventually he established a kind of theocratic democracy in Florence. He made many enemies; and after a confession was extracted from him under torture, which he later withdrew, he was hanged as a schismatic and heretic in the market-place of Florence.

Fra Girolamo used the words of Hebrew prophets to inflame his hear-ers against sin. In his sermon for Lent 1490, the words of the prophet Amos were applied to the scandalous life of Pope Alexander VI. Likewise the words of Ruth, Micah, and Ezekiel: in particular, the words of Ezekiel sug-gested, for Carnival before Lent in 1498, the celebrated "Burning of the Vanities."

To a fanatic the example of Moses in Exodus and the text of the Ten Commandments can seem to justify excesses. Although he pitted the ideal republic against the aristocratic rule of the Medicis, the puritanical friar so hated violation of sexual purity that prostitutes had to be banned; and since usury was a kind of theft, and Jews were sometimes bankers who took in-terest on the money they loaned, Jews had to be expelled.

The only positive note in Savonarola's story is that the extremes to which he went prepared the way for moderation. Under Savonarola, statements supporting the political opposition were made a capital offense; enemies were exiled; blasphemers and sodomites were put to death. In time a back-lash brought the Medicis into power.

The Ten Commandments, as Savonarola interpreted them to the nuns of a monastery in Florence, reveal a set of sins for which we are required to make a perfect confession. Savonarola taught that when you hold this holy mirror in front of you, however long your life might be extended, it would not suffice to catalogue your sins.

Following Jesus, Savonarola believed all the commandments can be reduced to loving God with one's whole heart and one's neighbor as one-self. The first three commandments require trust, reverence, and subservi-ence. Not only doing good to one's neighbor, but desiring such, is required; and since coveting one's neighbor's wife is mortal sin along with adultery, and coveting one's neighbor's goods is a mortal sin like theft, the command-ments reduce to eight.

Not all sins, however, are mortal sins; and just as it is a mortal sin to desire the act of what is a mortal sin, to desire the act of what is venial sin is only a venial sin. A mortal sin is against the love of God and one's neighbor, such as taking the Lord's name in vain or murder. But there are merely ve-nial sins, such as eating two almonds when it is not necessary, or turning into a vineyard while on the road to Rome. That is not going straight, but it's not going in the opposite direction either.

While there are some touches of balance in Savonarola, what is distinctive is his rigor; and his rigor may be judged excessive. For example, the first commandment requires true faith as the church teaches, and that true faith distinguishes true Christians from "pagans, Jews, Heretics, Schismatics, and False Christians." Savonarola argued that it is a "sin against the commandment" not to confess the articles of faith or to deny them under torture. And he makes it an obligation, especially for a bishop, preacher, doctor of the church, to vigorously oppose heretics.

With these premises Savonarola draws conclusions about Christians in relation to Jews: "It is sin against the commandment, to associate with Jews, to eat and drink with them, to receive medical care from them, to accompany them to the bath, to make anything for them, to serve them, to dwell in the same house with them. The church has forbidden it, and who is warned not to allow it, sins mortally, and deserves to suffer the ban." One can understand that faithfulness to one unrepresentable God excludes idolatry, and that taking the Lord's name in vain excludes the use of the name in sorcery, but the excess to which Savonarola uses the commandments to separate Christians from Jews goes beyond reason. "It is to sin seriously against the Commandments, for persons to take part in a Jewish service of worship, for thereby they deny Christ, as though he had not come. Women sin, who help Jews in preparation of unleavened bread, or who eat of it."

Then the text returns to superstitions, sins against the Holy Ghost, failure to keep vows, and seven damning vices. In interpreting vows, we note a touch of balance and restraint. Jephthah, who vows to God the first thing he sees on return from victory, feels obliged to devote his daughter to God. Savonarola calls him a fool to make such a vow and impious to keep it ("Fu pazzo a fare il voto, ed impio ad observario"). Savonarola enlarges the area by considering other cases, and by giving his reasons. Under the second commandment a man is not obligated to keep a promise under changed circumstances, and the example is the vow of a rich man to build a church. When his fortune changes and he is poor, he is no longer obliged to do what he cannot. Under the third commandment it is not obligatory for pregnant women and nursing mothers to fast.

With these touches of balance, it is a greater shame that his zeal led him into excesses such as an anti-Semitic interpretation of the commandments given originally by YHWH to Israel.

John Wycliffe:
A Powerful Original

John Wycliffe (ca. 1330-84), Oxford philosopher, rector, propagandist, envoy, and preacher, believed that authority came by grace, maintained the rule of secular authority over clergy, and asserted the right of every man to examine the Bible for himself. He organized a band of itinerant preachers — his "poor priests" — who continued what he had begun in 1380, a translation of the Bible into English. These became known as the Lollards, from a Dutch word for "mumble," some say. True, the Wycliffe Bible is hard reading today. Yet Wycliffe's sermons show him to be a master of contemporary idiomatic English, and considering the disorganized state of the English language at the time (England had almost as many regional dialects as it had counties), it is a remarkable achievement. Passing through the hands of several translators, the Wycliffe Bible gradually improved in dignity and grace and eventually helped create an appetite that would be satisfied almost two centuries later by the classic eloquence of the Tyndale Bible (the first Tyndale New Testament appeared in a pocket version in 1526). The Tyndale Bible set much of the text for the 1611 King James Version.

In Wycliffe's day the so-called Authorized Version was centuries away and impossible to imagine. It would be easy to underestimate Wycliffe's achievement. It was not merely social; Wycliffe's insights are enduring. After his death in 1384, his followers, living in a Lollard underworld, were hunted down and killed. Wycliffe's writings were burned and his remains disinterred and burned, the ashes cast into the river Swift. And so arose the prophetic verse:

> The Avon to the Severn runs,
> The Severn to the sea,

> And Wycliffe's dust shall spread abroad,
> Wide as the waters be.

Wycliffe's belief that the truth of the Bible was open to the heart of every devoted reader was part of a revolutionary way of interpreting the Bible. In his opposition to the monopoly held by the church on matters of interpretation (the Bible must be interpreted for the doctrine it contains), Wycliffe believed that one passage of the Bible would explain another better than any interpretation imposed from the outside. This leads to a concept of the Bible as a whole, as a self-interpreting collection of sacred writings. Christian education is based on a personal reading of the Bible. In Wycliffe's day, even the clergy did not read the Bible as a source for sermons, preferring to draw on civil and natural history, fable and mythology.

We honor Wycliffe as a powerful original. His focus is clear in the following passage:

> Hear the commandments of God read, preached, and taught, and do after them as God hath bidden. But what man is there now a days that dreadeth to break God's commandments, or setteth any price by the sweetest word or the sharpest word in all God's law? Dear God, it is a wonder of all wonders on earth, that from the beginning of our life even to our last end, we are never weary, either night or day, to labor about worldly goods, pleasing to our wretched body, which shall last here but a little while; but about the learning of God's commandments, which shall be food and nourishment for our souls that shall ever last in bliss or pain, about such things may we not labor truly to the end even one hour of the day?

In this introduction to an exposition of the Decalogue, the man who hears the Ten Commandments and lives by them gives signs of not being in deadly sin, and can trust in the "high bliss of heaven": "when a man will gladly and willingly hear the word of God when he knoweth himself prepared to do good works; when he is willing to flee sin then a man can be sorry for his sin."

On the Ten Commandments Wycliffe was a not unorthodox Catholic teacher. To obey the commandments is to honor God duly: "He must steadily believe that Almighty God in Trinity the Father, the Son, and the Holy Ghost, three persons in one God, are the noblest object that may be, so that all power, all knowledge, all wisdom, all goodness, all charity, all

mercy, is in him, and cometh from him." It is typically Augustinian to find
the first three commandments corresponding to the three persons of the
Trinity, a tradition Thomas, for one, did not follow.

Sunday is to be kept as the Holy Sabbath because of all of God's supreme attributes. The Sabbath is mercy expressed in the incarnation of Christ
and his atoning death. On Sunday it should be matter for our meditation, that
creation was completed on that day, that Christ rose from the dead on that
day, that knowledge and wisdom came to the earth by the descent of the Holy
Spirit on that day, and that on that day, "as many clerks say, shall be —
doomsday — for Sunday was the first day, and Sunday shall be the last day."

What is Catholic in Wycliffe is his trust in the mediation of grace
through the priesthood, through the merit of the saints, and through the
veneration of images. Interpreting "Honor thy father," Wycliffe places the
priest among our "three fathers": our natural father, the priest by whose
means we become the spiritual children of the church, and our Father in
heaven. By obedience to the divine will we gain a part in all the good
prayers, and good deeds, of all saints. Clearly the child of the church shares
the merits of those who have earned more than they need for their own salvation. Wycliffe does not find the reverence of images (he uses the word
"worship") to violate "Thou shalt not make graven images"; rather the laity
and especially the ignorant learn from "dead images, how they should worship the saints in heaven, after whom those images are shapen"; but it is
idolatry or having a "false god" when one "worshippeth or prayeth to an
image made of man, with that worship and prayer that is due only to God,
and his saints." All this is quite Catholic.

What is Protestant is that lay Christians can use the authority of
Scripture to rebuke delinquent priests. All Christians can confess sins "immediately to God," "should not give a penny to a pardoner," and should
scorn idle, hypocritical mendicant friars. Support of the clergy is premised
on the "ghostly father" giving good example and teaching God's law. But
when he fails, he is to be privately rebuked. If he is habitually delinquent,
then maintenance should be withheld. As for the begging friars, Wycliffe
doubted their sincerity, comparing them to the Pharisees for whom Jesus
had hard words.

Wycliffe follows the traditional Latin Decalogue. The prohibition of
making and worshiping idols is assumed in the first commandment, and
not given special place as the second commandment. This is also the case
in Luther's German version. Making a separate prohibition comes with Calvin and other Reformers who regarded images as idols, as clearly Wycliffe

and the Lutherans did not. The fourth commandment, "Worschipe thi fadir and thi moder," is expanded by adding "thi neghbore as thi self," which reflects the Johannine mystical concept of the indwelling of God in man and man in God. The prohibition of adultery also is interpreted spiritually as "avouterie, for he brekith the marriage that schude be bitwixte Crist and him." Following the expansion of all sexual sin as "luxuria" in church Latin (followed in Romance languages), the sixth commandment becomes "Thou schalt do no lecherie, bodili'ne goostli" ("goostli" meaning mental or spiritual as opposed to bodily or physical). The prohibition of coveting or desiring what is the neighbor's is divided into the two last commandments, as in Luther's version, whereas in the Calvinistic or Reformed versions, standard in English, they are combined.

> And Crist seide, if thou wolt come to blisse, kep myn commandementis:
>   I. I am Lord thi God . . .
> II. Thou schalt not take the name of thi Lord God in veyn, nether in word, nether in lyinge.
> III. God biddith have mynde to halwe thin holiday. In sixe daies thou might worchep and in the seventhe day is reste of the Lord God. In that day thou schalt do no servile werk, ne no werk of synne, thou, ne thi sone, ne thi doughter, ne thi servaunt, ne thin hand-mayden, ne thi werk-beest, ne the straunger in thin hous. For in sixe daies God made hevene and erthe, and al that is therinne, and restide in the seventhe day.
> IIII. Thou schalt worschipe thi fadir and thi moder, that thou be longe lyved upon erthe, and thi neghbore as thi self. And whoevere loveth his neighbore, loveth his God, and dwellith in God and God in him.
>   V. Thou schalt not sie thi brothir: and it is undirstonden of unskilful sheynge.
> VI. Thou schalt do no lecherie, bodily nor goostly.
> VII. Thou schalt do no thefthe, since God thy fader is treuthe.
> VIII. Christ forbideth all men to speak false witness against their neighbor.
> IX. God forbiddth thee to covet thy neighbor's house, nor no other things that be unmovable . . . [= real property, in contrast to live with power to move from one place to another].

X. Thou schalt not desire the wife of thy neighbor, nor his servant, nor his maid, nor his ox, nor his ass, nor thing that is
his.

The commandments, according to Wycliffe, are what is "boden" and
"forboden," or what God bids man do and forbids man to do. God's purpose for man is clear: "What he schulde do for to come to hevene."

The Lord "that ladde the[e] out of Egipt" is God "that brought the[e]
out of bondage where thou served men." "Thew schalt not have bifore me
alyen Goddis. Thew schalt noon ymage have, graven with mannys hound,
ne no leeknesse in hevene ne in erthe ne in watris." As for the Lord God: "I
am the Lord thi God, a stronge gelous lovere." Then comes the sanction ex-
tending to the third and fourth generation.

Wycliffe elaborates false worship by illustrating what the worship of
the flesh, the world, and the devil means. First, "What is a 'god'?" Whatever "a man loveth moost, he makith his god."

Second, "What is a 'sin'?" To love anything in place of God. Three
major types of sins which include all sins ("ennrappeth aile othere") are
"love of fleische, and love of else, and pride of life." He follows Paul as well
as John in condemning gluttons and lechers: "for gluttons make their belly
their god." Appetites go to excess, and God commands restraint ("God
biddith the[e] feede the[e] in mesure, and . . . thou passist this mesure for
lust of thi beli").

It is not only the flesh that moves us to do more than the flesh needs,
for the covetous man makes temporal goods his idol ("mawmet"). The
proud man makes the devil ("feend") his god. "Thus it is in dede, howevere
oure mouth blabre." These sins apply, Wycliffe adds, as much to priests as
to laypeople.

The conclusion about God echoes Paul: that God gives to all life and
spirit and every other thing. He cannot live in a temple built by man or be
worshiped as a thing made by man's hand. "In him we liven, and in him we
stiren, we ben also his kyn, as poetis seyn. Therefore he cannot be like unto
gold or silver or ston, of the craft of gravinge, or of manis hond-
worchynge." Idolatry is then ignorance of God: "for we knowyn him litil,
we loven him the lesse: Therefore we must think of "the might of the Fadir,
the wisdom of the Sone, and the goode wille or grace of the Holi Goost."
Then, not distracted by "bodeli thingis . . . [we] kepe him right."

The second commandment (after a good account against lying) continues the trinitarian theology, citing "Seynt Austyn" (Saint Augustine),

with trinitarian anthropology: "the name of God printid in his soule . . . : mynde, resoun, and wille, and aile ben o[ne] substance." Then it is man also who is triune: "Thou schudist . . . worschipe the name of thi God, that thou hast with thee . . . of al thi mynde."

God, worshiped as the Trinity, is worshiped by obedience, making him the end of every work. No oath is needed, except in court, and words need only be yea, yea and nay, nay. To do what man should not do is to take in vain his high and holy name. "For no man is maad but to serve God, in doynge his wille or suffrynge peyne."

The third commandment is to keep the holiday holy ("have mynde to halwe thin holiday"). Without mentioning "Sabbath," Wycliffe uses both the justification of Exodus that the Lord God rested from his six days of creation, and the reason of Deuteronomy, that all persons and animals should rest from their labor. The justification of Sunday as the day of rest involves the three persons of the Trinity: the Father made the world on Sunday, the Son rose from the dead on Sunday, the Holy Ghost descended on Sunday. The last judgment will also be on Sunday. Sundays throughout the year are holy, but four principal feasts are to be kept: Christmas, Easter, Ascension Day, and Whitsuntide.

All of the above is very Catholic, so very Catholic that we miss any mention of the Mass. But the ways in which Sunday is to be kept are so very Protestant that we could find a fit place for his precepts in a Puritan manual.

The meaning of avoiding "servile work" is to "kepe . . . out of sin," since whosoever sins makes himself servant to sin. The way to use your mind on this holiday is to hear of God, and as Paul teaches, "that freedom of his law." Christians should learn what the priest teaches: what they should busy themselves with are the study of virtues, the Ten Commandments, and seven deeds of mercy; and they must learn to speak with people of heavenly things, and to put away guile and wrong and other sins, and to love God in perfect charity.

True, the "Catholic" aspects are largely liturgical points such as we might expect of an Anglican. There is no hostility to festivals and feast days of the church. But the "Protestant" elements are very sober and serious studies of bringing life into keeping the will of God. And this also becomes an important part of the Book of Common Prayer. Wycliffe has a way of combining aspects of life that are sometimes thought contradictory and exclusive. For example, the fourth commandment is moral, mystical, and commonsensical. The moral is to expand honor to parents to "worship" their neighbor as themselves ("Thou Schalt worshipe thi fadir and thi moder and thi neghbore as thi self"). But it is also mystical in uniting this love of neighbor to the indwelling of man in God and God in man. ("And whovere loveth his neighbore, loveth his God, and dwellith in God and God in him.") Here Wycliffe cites John's first epistle in combining the two branches of charity.

Common sense enters a caution about being too charitable. Respond to people in need but help them within reason. Limit must be set to charity so that people must help themselves by their own work. Christ is Wycliffe's example of perfect charity: "For Crist cam of poore men, and leet his modir be poore, and his poore cosynes; and whanne thei askiden. . . . Richesse of the world, he denied them that . . . ; and bileve techeth us that he did al for the betere. And so schulde we serve him, if we been his children, and love him moore than the worlde or oure veyne name."

Again, in the fifth and sixth commandments we find this balance between the moral, the mystical, and practical common sense.

"Thou schalt not sie thi brothir" does not forbid legal execution for the interesting reason that the murderer's act and the law take his life. But "mansleer" names the one "that hatith his brothir," the "bac-bitere," the one that "consentith to the yvel." There is then murder by thought, murder by word, and murder by inaction. Wycliffe refers to prophets of the old law and apostles of Christ who were martyred. One can kill by default. In a sense Paul killed Stephen, the first Christian martyr, by not objecting to his execution by stoning.

At this point there is a question: What of the church that sells the permission to sin, and allows men to live in sin for an annual rent? Here the critic turns to the selling of indulgences.

The primary argument against adultery under "Thou schalt do no lecherie, bodily nor goostly" is that "ech mannis soule schlde be Cristis spouse." Faithlessness breaks the mystical marriage. Then comes common sense. The flesh is strong, therefore be a coward and flee the occasion in which you will be tested by attraction: "Fle as Godis coward the company of wymmen." Heed three examples: "For what man was strengere than Sampson? or who wiser than David? or who moore witti than Salomon his sone? And alle weren brent with fier of lust."

The seventh commandment, "Thou schalt do no thefthe," is based on God's nature as truth. The idea must be that the act of taking for your own what is another's is a falsehood, and this implies calling your own what is his.

In retrospect, what was most important here for English society was that the lord and the priest were condemned as thieves. It is extortion when lords oppress the people with tyranny. Each man in his degree is duty-bound to serve God. Titles come of obligations fulfilled through grace. He that stands in grace is true lord of things, and whoever fails by default of grace lacks title to what he claims.

Here is the denial of legitimate authority on moral grounds relevant to a Lollard. The Lollards are regarded as ancestors of Christian socialists, and it is easy to see in Wycliffe, as in Luther, seeds of social revolution. But if tyrants steal from the people, priests steal from God. Wycliffe would argue that curates of the church who steal the goods of God that come in by the roof, and not by the door (that is, Christ), are thieves by night and day, thieves of simony, of benefits, and sellers of sacraments. And therefore, according to Christ, shepherd of all shepherds, these are great thieves and cursed of God.

Of these three uses of the Decalogue — political, pedagogical, didactic — clearly Wycliffe's application of the prohibition of theft to lords and priests is political. The eighth commandment, against false witness, springs from concern that society should live under laws applied justly. Indeed, we have not found another Christian as deeply concerned with the truth of evidence presented as testimony in courts of law. Wycliffe's argument is comparable to the argument of Philo Judaeus. Christ forbids any man to bear false witness against his neighbor. This is needful to execute laws, for God's law and man's law ask witnesses, and from such witnesses comes human judgment; and false witness makes false judgment, and so error in witness stretches very far. For many are disinherited and hanged by such false witnesses; and thereby there come to be many false heirs. Who so bears false witness, bears witness against truth, and since God himself is truth, the false witness opposes God. And so, when he bears false witness, he takes God to witness that thing he says is true and of God, and since that thing is false, as much as in him is he makes his God false, and brings himself to naught; for God may not be, except he be true. Hence no one bears false witness except he oppose God. And all the saints in heaven and all creatures witness that God is against the one who lies. And here wise men say by witness of saints, that the craft of lying is even more unlawful, for it comes only from the devil, the father of lies ("but from the feend, that first made lying"). For if it were lawful, it would honor Christ, the person of God that is the first truth. And therefore, Wycliffe argues, nothing opposes God more than does lying. If a man might by a private lie save all this world that otherwise would be destroyed, he still should not lie.

From this concern with public justice and courts of law, Wycliffe turns to the root of all evil: covetousness. The ninth and tenth commandments show the pedagogic use of the Decalogue, for keeping the commandment against coveting requires recognizing what should be "fully quenched." Hence the didactic conclusion that "Christ prevent in us such evil will."

Wycliffe concludes that the Ten Commandments are the surest law of all, of greatest authority, and of greatest use ("eke of moost nede"). Our Lord teaches that all his will and laws should be kept. Other laws may be despised if not grounded in divine law. Even if these others be of the emperor and the pope, it is a thousand times worse to do their laws rather than God's.

10

Martin Luther:
A Decalogue of Faith

In the spirit of that original, John Wycliffe, a century later Martin Luther (ca. 1483-1546) encouraged laypeople not only to repent of their own sins but to observe and rebuke priests and monks, and particularly the pope among prelates, for *their* sins. Born in Eisleben, Germany, to a family involved in leasing the copper-mining businesses of the region, Luther, at age twenty-four, contrary to his family's wishes, entered the house of reformed Augustinian eremites. Less than ten years later he was delivering twice-weekly sermons and teaching theology at the university at Wittenberg. His thought matured rapidly. In his autobiography (1545), he gives an account of the famous but undatable "tower experience" in which he understood, in a flash of insight, what would become the cornerstone of his critique of Christian tradition: God's righteousness as revealed in the gospel does not refer to God's condemnation of sin but to his gift of innocence to the unworthy sinner, who receives it through faith. Luther would later argue that all Christians are equally spiritual, that the church has no monopoly on righteousness, that communities should govern their own religious life without reference to pope or hierarchy. His own translation of the Bible and his hymns became and remain immensely popular.

Yet Luther's Ten Commandments, like Wycliffe's, are those of traditional Catholic moral instruction. Neither Wycliffe's followers nor Luther replaced the Decalogue of medieval catechetical instruction with a strictly accurate translation from Exodus 20 or Deuteronomy 5. The version spread most widely among Protestants by Luther's small and large catechisms is the same in ordering as the Latin Catholic Decalogue.

The commandments are moved to first place in Luther's catechisms, preceding rather than following the creed. With Luther, faith, the central tie of man to God, is an act of trust rather than an assent to propositions. In this shift of meaning he recovered the usage of the Gospels: in New Testament Greek the verb "to put trust in," "to have faith," is the common form, and "the faith" in the sense of statements held to be true is rare. For Luther the commandments are specific ways in which we are to "fear and love God."

A religion based on the Ten Commandments will not allow a theologian to deal only with how God works in man. Luther also has his role in sustaining public order. He is the leader of a religious movement; he owes support to princes; he acknowledges that Christians live in social, political, legal, and economic institutions. He must then consider the complex relations of man to man. Luther is a teacher and pastor, and in private life a husband and a father. In the cure of souls, and judgment of conscience and conduct, as well as in the rearing of children, he is obliged to correct excess and to restore persons to health and balance. The theologian may despise good works, but the moralist defines evil works and does what he can to prevent and punish them.

Thomas Aquinas and Martin Luther

When we read Luther, and keep Thomas Aquinas's interpretation of the Ten Commandments in mind, we can recognize both deep agreement and deep divergence. Thomas did not teach that persons, by obeying the commandments and developing good habits, could earn salvation. He explicitly denied that man could earn salvation or that God owes man the reward of eternal life. It is by God's grace that man is saved. Moreover, he laid emphasis on love as the motive of genuinely good acts. Like Luther, Thomas stressed the spontaneity and joy of genuine spiritual response to God.

The age of Thomas contrasts with the time of Luther, when God had come to seem distant, beyond ordinary contact — unless in anger he were punishing human sin by sending the Turks. And Thomas had the freedom to welcome the pagan wisdom of Aristotle, while Luther regards Aristotle as a diabolical threat.

Where Luther calls "reason the devil's whore," Thomas believes in the support that reason and the evidence of the senses can give to the doctrines of the church. Luther asserts a faith that must accept what God has revealed. With Aquinas humans can know what is good and right to do. Happily these are the very acts that God has commanded: we can know that

God has commanded them because he also knows these are good and right. But with Luther, because of man's perverted passions, his sinful and rebellious nature, God must will some acts to be good, others evil; man must obey, even if he cannot; and God must overrule human will, even replace human will, as man becomes passive and allows God to act in him.

Thomas has confidence in his reason, and encourages others to use theirs, to know what is, and how events are caused, and to what ends we act. Luther has no confidence in reason: in faith he throws himself on God's mercy. He discourages others from vain efforts to save themselves and promises God's help to the repentant and humble.

Thomas was a most successful Dominican friar. He took and fulfilled his vows without struggle and seems to have developed a harmonious spiritual and intellectual life. Luther entered the Augustinian monastery in spiritual crisis, found that the regimen left him in despair, and having discovered a way of faith, left the monastery to marry a nun (1525). Psychologically Thomas and Luther are as far apart as the "once born" and the "twice born" discussed by William James. As a man who developed gradually, Thomas is always confident that harmony will emerge from apparent contradiction. Luther, with his strong sense of the divide between "before" his conversion and "after," sees the world in terms of his own inner struggle.

The contrast between Thomas's synthesis and Luther's polemics has sometimes led comparativists to picture Thomas as one who constructed what Luther set out to destroy. Thomas thought faith and reason, in principle one, had been reconciled: that the discoveries of science must harmonize with Scripture and Catholic tradition. But the "modern world," if so general a term has any meaning, is built on the divergence between the religious and the scientific; and in both method and conclusions, it is the scientific that has overcome the religious and replaced the God-centered world with a nature- and man-centered world.

Luther on the Sixth Commandment

In one dramatic gesture Luther rejected both the ecclesiastical exaltation of virginity and the limitation of the clergy to celibates. And in principle Luther rejected the superiority of celibates to married people. Exceptional cases occur, but celibacy he rejects as unnatural. "Remember that marriage is not only an honorable but also a necessary estate, earnestly commanded by God, so that in general men and women of all conditions, created for it, should be found in it. Yet there are some exceptions, al- though few, whom God has especially exempted, either because they are unfit for wedded life or because, by reason of extraordinary gifts, they have become free to live chaste lives unmarried. To unaided human na- ture, as God created it, chastity apart from matrimony is impossibility." This is the advice given to youth.

Luther was not just an ex-monk who married a nun, he was ada- mantly antimonastic. Consider the vows of "poverty, chastity, and obedi- ence": Luther urged breaking vows and leaving the convents, not only holding property in place of total renunciation of goods, and bearing arms in self-defense; the most drastic reversal is to declare that celibacy and elected virginity are sinful. All this is clearly based on a reinterpretation of the fifth, sixth, and seventh commandments. Luther's revolt against the Ro- man Catholic tradition was less intellectual than existential.

Another irony attending Luther's interpretation of the sixth com- mandment ("Thou shalt not commit adultery") is that he erases much Christian tradition — about fifteen hundred years' worth — and brings Protestants closer to Jewish practice. Ministers of religion in the Protestant churches marry, as do rabbis. Yet in nearly all other respects, and we have seen this particularly for the prohibition of idols and commanding the Sab- bath, Luther accepts these restrictions only for Jews.

There are various ways of showing that Luther is not as inconsistent as he first appears. One way is to point out that he has followed the method of seeking the meaning of the Decalogue in what is permanent and univer- sal. If he rejects the Jewish necessity of the seventh day, it is because what is natural to him is to rest sometime, though not necessarily on the Sabbath. And if he rejects the Catholic requirement of a celibate clergy, it is because it is unnatural to him for an ordinary man (of "flesh and blood") to live without a woman.

What is most interesting in Luther's method is the way he finds oppo- sites in conflict, sometimes choosing sides and sometimes reconciling op- posites.

There is a dialectical movement that requires, once the theology of faith has been stated, that the mind adjust to the political necessity of order and to the moral necessity of balance. That Luther requires three uses of the Decalogue is not arbitrary, nor is it any development toward a highest synthesis in a reconciling third. Because God is the first principle, political order and moral balance are always subject to God. Within each use we shall see opposition between faith and the pride of the flesh, the world, and the devil. From obedience to authority and maintaining order comes the battle against the disobedience of anarchy. From the search for the good comes the necessity of limiting excesses — of lust, for example — to attain balance.

Faith

The first use of law explored by Luther is soteriological (*soteria* is ancient Greek for "salvation"). The question of salvation may seem to have Christ's answer: obey the commandments of Moses. This is the mistake of those who look upon the ten as rungs in a ladder that we may climb to heaven. For Luther the commandments show men what they ought to be inwardly as well as what they ought to do outwardly; and when a person uses them as a mirror, he comes to know that not only has he not done what they command and has done what they forbid, but he cannot satisfy these requirements. Luther therefore uses the Ten Commandments pedagogically to convict his listener or reader that he is sick, that he is damned, and that he has been duped in trusting in good works.

What does it mean when, at the foot of Mount Sinai, the Israelites turn to idolatry? Luther has little interest in the golden calf as such. But idolatry of conceit is a great sin. Man sets up himself as the great idol to be worshiped in the search for honor. The goals that lure us are pleasure, power, and pride, for we easily yield to the lusts of the flesh, the world, and the devil. These "sham gods" are very attractive. They are painted in alluring colors and we see them in stained glass.

Yet Luther recognizes that each of us develops by stages, that like children we must be rewarded quickly and sensuously for doing what we ought. Weak minds need to be coaxed. The danger of remaining at a childish level is that we are tempted to follow wolves in sheep's clothing.

For Luther "trust" is often coupled with "faith," and to "trust God" is an act rather than a proposition a person professes. The *Large Catechism* uses the Ten Commandments as a step leading to learning the set of propositions of the Apostles' Creed, and faith does rule out doubt. But the single word signifies the agency of the whole person, "thought, word, and deed" directed toward God and even, in its most advanced development, directed by God (especially at the beginning and end of the exposition of the third commandment). "Thou shalt put all thy confidence, trust and faith on Me

alone" is developed to include "faith, hope, and charity." The other amplifications are "faith, trust, confidence, hope, and love," and specifically it is
fervent faith that is intended, for "when faith perishes, love grows cold,
God's word is neglected." The key to the coupling of love and faith is that
to be truly good an act must be done "cheerfully" and "freely."

Luther's theological coherence comes out best when we observe that
all genuine religious acts strengthen faith. The point of sermon and Eucharist is to strengthen faith. This is true also of prayer; and in contrast to good
prayer, bad prayer is selfish prayer. Good prayers in a pigsty are preferred to
petty prayers in "high, big, and beautiful churches [with] towers and bell."
The Lord's Prayer corresponds in its first petition — "Our Father which art
in heaven" — to

> [t]he first work of faith, which according to the First Commandment,
> does not doubt that it has a gracious Father in heaven. The second:
> "Hallowed be Thy Name," in which faith asks that God's Name, praise
> and honor be glorified, and calls upon it in every need, as the Second
> Commandment says. The third: "Thy kingdom come," in which we
> pray for the true Sabbath and rest, peaceful cessation of our works, that
> God's work alone be done in us, and so God rule in us as in His own
> kingdom, as He says, Luke xvii, "Behold, God's kingdom is nowhere
> else except within you." The fourth petition is "Thy will be done" in
> which we pray that we may keep and have the Seven Commandments
> of the Second Table, in which faith is exercised toward our neighbor;
> just as in the first three it is exercised in works toward God alone.

What would be the answer to such prayers of faith? It would then be God
and Christ who work and live in such a person.

Order

For the political and moral uses of the Ten Commandments we must move
from the first table of the law to the second table. The importance of honor
in Lull's proverbs on the Ten Commandments, and the hierarchy of fathers
in Thomas, can serve as a background for Luther's respect for political authority. The fourth commandment — "Thou shalt honor thy father and thy
mother" — means to Luther that there are no better works than to obey
and serve all those who are set over us as superiors.

Why does Luther in the *Short Catechism* command that "We are to fear and love God, that we do not despise nor anger our parents and masters, but reverence, serve, obey, love, and honor them"? Why in the *Large Catechism* does he say that this is the "first and greatest" duty? Why is the "obedience, humility and reverence [owed] as if we were pointed to some sovereignty hidden there"?

Luther's first use, his theology of faith, proclaims freedom from the law. Each Christian is equally free before God by grace.

> If every man had faith, we would need no more laws, but every one would of himself at all times do good works, as his confidence in God teaches him. The law is not made for a righteous man (Paul, I Timothy, 1:9) that is, for the believer, but believers do what they know and can do, only because they firmly trust that God's favor and grace rests upon them in all things. . . . All works and things are free to a Christian through his faith. . . . Faith [is not] a work among other works [but is] . . . above all works. For it is the highest work for this very reason, because it remains and blots out these daily sins. . . . God is so kind to you as to wink at such daily transgressions and weakness. Aye, even if a deadly sin should occur yet faith rises up again and . . . its sin is already gone. . . . Act [with] unconquerable confidence. . . . Whatsoever ye do, do all to the glory of God (Colossians, 3:17) . . . if we were to observe this work, we would have a heaven here on earth . . . as have the saints in heaven.

The quotations above are excerpted and presented without qualification, but the first and the last contain the all-important "if" to show that freedom from the law is hypothetical, only for the highest type of human, and that "Love God and do as you please," as Augustine expressed spiritual freedom, is not for everyone. Some heard the message of anarchy in Luther's vision of "heaven on earth." Luther was appalled by the excesses committed in his name. Even today some Calvinists still caution people to beware of Lutherans as dangerous anarchists.

Luther must prove that his total position is not as it sounded to enthusiasts, but a sober doctrine supporting political authority by preaching loyalty. Generations of Lutheran children learn Paul's doctrine "All power is of God" (Rom. 13:1-3).

The doctrine of all-but-absolute sovereignty of "princes and magistrates" is developed in the *Large Catechism*. These statements were needed to overcome the anarchy of a theology of free grace, but they give rise to the opposite warning against Lutherans, that they are friends of tyranny.

> All authority has its root and warrant in parental authority. All who are called masters stand in the place of parents and from them must obtain authority and power to command. Through civil rulers as through our parents, God gives us food, home and land, protection and security. Therefore since they bear this name and title with all honor as their chief glory, it is our duty to honor them and to esteem them as we would the greatest treasure and the most precious jewel on earth. . . . Although the duty of superiors is not explicitly stated in the Ten Commandments, it is frequently dwelt upon in many other passages of Scripture, and God intends it even to be included in this commandment, where he mentions father and mother. God does not purpose to bestow the parental office and government upon rogues and tyrants; therefore he does not give them that honor, namely the power and authority to govern, merely to receive homage. Parents should consider that they are under obligation to obey God and that, first of all, they are conscientiously and faithfully to discharge all the duties of their office; not only to feed and provide for the temporal wants of their children, servants, subjects, etc., but especially to train them to the honor and praise of God.

Luther praises magistrates who serve God by doing "superabundant good works." The theological condition under which rulers exercise power granted by God is that "these works should be done in faith." Clearly, then, the ruler to whom Christians give honor, as to God, is a Christian ruler. And such a ruler is to use the temporal power to carry out the punishments due to those who break the commandments.

Would the first three commandments require establishing Christianity as the religion of the state and people? This is not clear, but certainly not if only "to punish thievery, robbery, and adultery." The Pauline justification of power is that "it beareth not the sword in vain; it serves God with it, to the terror of evil doers, and to the protection of the good" (Rom. 13:4).

Luther then formulated the theory for Protestant established churches, not only in German states whose rulers rejected Roman Catholicism but also in the Scandinavian states. A parallel is the Anglican Church with a similar theory. The coronation oath of the present queen of England, as of past queens and kings, requires that she carry out the laws of God.

But what if there is a bad ruler? What if the king himself breaks the commandments? Does this in any way modify or diminish the obedience the subject owes the ruler?

Luther laid down the duty of the subject as absolute. "There are no better works than to obey and serve all those who are set over us as superiors." The reason given is that "disobedience is a greater sin than murder, unchastity, theft and dishonesty, and all that these may include." The obvious implication is that the obedient subject should not refuse to kill, steal, commit adultery, bear false witness, etc., if commanded by the ruler. Does Luther not foresee the corruption of the whole state and society?

This is an extreme case, and should never occur. And Luther, with all due humility, reminds rulers that duties are reciprocal. The king is a father to his people, and owes them all what a father owes his children. When Luther rebukes popes and bishops for failing to do justice for "the poor and fatherless . . . the poor and needy" (Ps. 82:3), he denounces kings and princes also. But a bad ruler is still a legitimate ruler who derives his power from God.

What does "legitimate" mean if the ruler breaks all the fundamental laws?

While Luther urges the layman to rebel against the rule of the pope in spiritual matters, why should he urge subjects not ever to rebel against the rule of a bad king? He equips the layman with the law of God to judge bishops, priests, monks, and to mock their hypocrisies, yet he denies the subject the right to criticize magistrates and princes. Can one comprehend such incoherence?

Luther had a practical political problem. He could turn only to the civil authorities to protect him from punishments meted out by the Roman Church. He could reform churches only with the support of the civil rulers. After denouncing the pope's servants as "knaves and whores; to the destruction of our souls," he addresses the civil rulers, urging them to rebel against Roman Catholic leaders: "Lo! These are the true Turks, whom the kings, princes and nobility ought to attack first."

Yet no discussion of the political order required by God's law should neglect his observation that the basic social order is the family. Early in the *Large Catechism* Luther celebrates the blessings of faith in faithful love: "When a man and a woman love and are pleased with each other, and thoroughly believe in their love, who teaches them how they are to behave, what they are to do, leave undone, say, not say, think? Confidence alone teaches them all this, and more. They make no difference in works: they do the great, the long, the much, as gladly as the small, the short, the little, and vice versa; and that too with joyful, peaceful, confident hearts, and each is a free companion of the other."

It is the family responsibility to teach the commandments to children, as did Luther himself to little Hans and his sister Lena. The family is then the moral center of all society:

> O how perilous it is to be a father or a mother, where flesh and blood are supreme! For, truly, the knowledge and fulfillment of the first three and the last six Commandments depends altogether upon this Commandment; since parents are commanded to teach them to their children, as Psalm LXXVIII, says, "How strictly has He commanded our fathers, that they should make known God's Commandments to their children, that the generation to come might know them and declare them to their children's children." This also is the reason why God bids us honor our parents, that is, to love them with fear; for that other love is without fear, therefore it is more dishonor than honor.

We should not avoid commenting on the ambiguity of relations between husband and wife. On one hand, the priest-husband allows his wife to do all the worrying about money, so that he can attend to spiritual matters. He holds the power and makes decisions, which she is to carry out, but she is treated as a child to be indulged. "The masters and mistresses should not rule their servants, maids and workingmen roughly, not look to all things too closely, occasionally overlook something, and for peace' sake make allowances. For it is not possible that everything be done perfectly at all times among any class of men, as long as we live on earth in imperfection." The problem of social order is then best solved by a man and wife whose work is done for love and faith in one another. This is the best model Luther knows of faith producing good works, which are done with no reward expected. Then it is reasonable to hope that from this center come children instructed and trained in obedience to the commandments. The householder-master and his mistress can achieve balance between strictness and laxity in managing the servants. Obviously a balance has to be found between extremes. But it is the political realm where there is an unresolved tension between anarchy and tyranny.

Balance

The third use of the Decalogue, the moral, brings us to Luther's most difficult problem. The model of balance taught with every commandment of the Ten Commandments in the *Short Catechism* is the balance between "fear and love." Not fear without love, or love without fear, but the two opposites in balanced union in the relation of honor. We have now seen the first use of the Ten Commandments, that with primacy of faith as the inner motive it is faith with works, not faith without works or works without faith, that counts. With the second use we saw the threat of anarchy driving Luther toward tyranny and failing to counterbalance order, the submission of servant to lord, with any recourse of dissent, protest, civil disobedience, or revolt. But the ideal of balance rests in the loving and faithful man and wife, and their relation to servants; in short, the ideal of balance is the order of discipline coupled with kindness and tolerance of mistakes.

A virtue, according to Aristotle, is a mean of excellence between two excesses which are too much and too little — temperance between overeating and starving, or courage between rashness that ignores danger and temerity and cowardice that shrinks from danger. It was Aquinas who adapted Aristotle's *Ethics.* Luther, although he had lectured on the *Ethics,* never refers to "the philosopher" in *Good Works,* and elsewhere makes only typically vulgar rejections. Thomas was induced by pagan philosophy to consider the commandments virtues. Luther the theologian will make no such error. The commandments of God are to induce a man to trust faith.

Luther explicitly corrects such a scholastic ethics as that of Thomas Aquinas:

> Men have followed blind reason and heathen ways, and have set faith not above, but beside other virtues, and have given it a work of its own, apart from all works of the other virtues, although faith alone makes all other works good, acceptable and worthy, in that it trusts God. . . . Indeed, they have made it a Habitus, as they say, although Scripture gives the name of a good, divine work to no work except to faith alone. Therefore it is no wonder that they have become blind and leaders of the blind. And this faith brings with it at once love, peace, joy and hope. For God gives His Spirit at once to him who trusts Him.

As taught by Luther, the Ten Commandments are clearly a set of moral rules. The three duties to fear and love God in thought, word, and deed lay a theological basis in the fourth commandment of the greatest and all-inclusive duty of obedience. If in conforming our wills to God's we overcome, with God's grace, our pride and disobedience, then the last six commandments develop further various duties toward our neighbor. Not to kill him requires of us meekness and gentleness, not to commit adultery with the neighbor's wife or husband requires of us chastity and temperance, not to steal requires of us benevolence, not to bear false witness requires of us truth telling or honesty, not to covet requires respect for what is our neighbor's. Thus we can from Luther's exposition draw up a table of virtues.

Clearly also, this set of moral rules teaches us what the vices are. Each commandment listed above specifies various "passions and lust of man that these also be killed." These are anger and revenge (dispelled by meekness), lust (killed by chastity), robbery (replaced by benevolence), and lying (refuted by truth telling). Also to be conquered are desire, envy, and vices of the flesh. In other places Luther lists anger, greed, hatred, and malice.

The human heart depicted by Luther is the battleground between the virtues and the vices. There is the great warfare between God and the devil, and if Luther omits the traditional medieval list of seven deadly sins and seven virtues, what he interprets the commandments to mean comes to much the same conclusion.

Luther's language is more biblical than philosophical; he does not talk of Thomas's "irascible" and "concupiscial faculties." Still, there is in human nature as we find it something perverse, what Kant later called a "root of radical evil." The theological understanding is that man has fallen and that children of men in every time and place inherit original sin.

Now if human depravity includes human reason and will as well as the flesh, then it is reasonable to write, as Luther does, "For this reason we pray: 'Thy kingdom come, that Thou rule us, and not we ourselves,' for there is nothing more perilous in us than our reason and will." It may seem paradoxical to present "reason" to a being with a perverted intellect, but here we have the clue to why "faith" is the faculty which comprehends God's commandments.

Luther has no place for the development of the "pagan" virtues — temperance, courage, prudence, and justice. Luther's faith is coupled with hope and charity and certain other virtues that may serve as little bridges over the gap between nature and the Christian virtues. Yet both Thomas and Luther grade persons. Thomas grades according to degrees of intelligence, from the dimwit who doesn't grasp the implications of first moral principles and must be taught the derivative rules, up to those whose grasp is of the good itself, truth, beauty, God. Luther has persons of weak faith, who when tested outwardly give up, and middleweights who can take what defeats the puny. But then in "the highest stage of faith . . . God punishes the conscience not only with temporal suffering, but with death, hell and sin, and refuses grace and mercy." Luther found this agony expressed in the Psalms.

As for moral types, the worst kind are the wicked who are "always ready for sins; these must be constrained by spiritual and temporal laws: like wild horses and dogs, and where this does not help, they must be put to death." Then there are the "lusty, and childish in their understanding of faith and of the spiritual life, [who] must be coaxed like young children and tempted with external, definite and prescribed decorations, with reading, praying, fasting, singing, adorning of churches, organ-playing . . . until they also learn to know the faith." Then there are the lazy who "want to abuse their freedom because of false confidence, and use their liberty for a cloak of maliciousness." There are a few "who need no law. . . . God's favor and grace rests upon them in all things."

In conjunction with the commandments is the creed, whose practical function is to tell the penitent that there is "grace" by which he is strengthened, and the Lord's Prayer, which "teaches him how to ask for this grace."

The process of seeking and finding the strength required inwardly to convert a wicked person into a good person must begin with trust. The meaning of the first commandment is such a beginning, that of "a child [who trusts] its father. For nature teaches us that there is one God, Who gives all good and helps against all evil." "Thou shalt have no other gods." In the process each "Thou shalt not" is interpreted positively: "Benefit and help [the neighbor] when he is in need" (fifth commandment); "put no shame upon ['the neighbor, his wife, his child, his friend'], but to preserve their honor, so far as he is able" (sixth commandment); "aid [one's neighbor] in increasing [his 'temporal possessions']" (seventh commandment); "increase and guard ['one's neighbor's worldly honor and good name'] (eighth commandment); "consider the natural law [knowing no act here commanded that each of us would not wish to have done to himself, if he were God, or in God's place or his neighbor's]" (ninth and tenth commandments).

The last commandments are not those about which a priest may ask questions, because the question of a person's desire is between that person and God. And the positive goal implied by "Thou shalt not covet" is to be free from "wicked inclinations . . . until the flesh turns to dust and is *new created*" (emphasis mine).

The hope of Luther is not that reason can be enlightened and limit the excesses of the passions. Reason is "blind," and evidently part of our perverted nature; as we've noticed, Luther often says "kill reason" and will and appetite. Only when "we let our reason and will be idle" can God take over and rule us. When the unruly heart of man opens itself to Christ, then he comes to "live, work and speak in us."

John Calvin:
The Logic of the Law

John Calvin (1509-64) used the Ten Commandments in his catechisms, sermons, and commentaries. As a member of the second generation of Reformers, he worked from a secure base of power in Geneva and could write systematically on the law of Moses. His *Institutes of the Christian Religion,* which went through five editions between 1536 and 1559, remains the standard of excellence in Protestant theology. One hesitates to cite any other systematic presentation of the Ten Commandments for comparison.

We turn first to his sermons on the Ten Commandments, which he preached in Geneva in 1555. There had been great hope in the thirty-five years after Luther's sermons in Wittenberg that the Catholic reformers south of the Alps could secure papal recognition of the need of reform, but with the Council of Trent leaders such as Ignatius Loyola were preparing to win back the heretics and schismatics.

In lining up lay troops of reformed Christians in Geneva, Calvin and his fellow theologians used the Ten Commandments as discipline. If the law of Moses prescribed death for blasphemy, then the Spanish freethinker Servetus had to die to preserve the integrity of this people of the covenant (1553). If vices are not permitted among Christians, then the blasphemies of a passerby are not to be endured. There were to be many casualties on both sides of the battle line before toleration of religious differences became the teaching of seventeenth-century leaders such as John Locke, and people moved by the horror of burning heretics relaxed the zealotry.

Since a twentieth-century reader is appalled by the conclusion of Calvin's practical syllogism — Servetus burned at the stake — let us use an example from his rigorous study of the law of Moses which helped produce our economic world. It is now incredible to modern Protestants that the great reformer Calvin was an inquisitor who employed the death penalty; it is also incredible that for many centuries it was a violation of "Thou shalt not steal" for a Christian to lend money to a Christian under conditions of interest.

One of the most extraordinary works by a Christian on the law of Moses is Calvin's *Commentary on a Harmony of the Last Four Books of Moses*. The problem seriously divides Jews. Why with a vast sum of legislation ascribed to Moses, usually counted 613 laws, should just these 10 be considered *the* law of Moses? Philo took these to be the heads under which all other laws can be subordinated. The basis of Reform Judaism is that by "law of Moses" is meant the ten. Is this judgment an arbitrary simplification, as Orthodox Jews tend to say? Calvin took very seriously the charge that Christians fail to keep the whole law. Calvin's argument, to sum up sixty pages of analysis, is that the ten, "the moral law," states the end and use, and all others are "exposition" of the ten, or ceremonial supplements or political supplements to the law.

Is a moneylender violating the commandment "Thou shalt not steal"? Christian theologians for centuries had seen lending with interest as a hard-hearted denial of charitable help to the indigent. But Calvin pointed out that this does not apply to lending to the affluent. The condemnation is of "unjust exactions . . . whereby the creditor, losing sight of equity, burdens and oppresses his debtor." Further, such legislation was made for circumstances different from our own, and usury is not now unlawful; except when it contravenes equity and brotherly union, usury is no worse than purchase. It is important to note that when persons are in need, they should not be forced to borrow money. What is meant by the text (Exod. 22:25) is that "What charity dictates should remain, i.e., that our brethren who need our assistance are not to be treated harshly."

Calvin's legal skills are sometimes those of a constitutional lawyer, and he is clearly worthy of his seat, along with Moses Maimonides and Thomas Aquinas, on a kind of Mosaic supreme court. He is perhaps better known as a trial lawyer, pressing the correctness of Protestantism against Rome's decrees of the Council of Trent. But the basis for his dissatisfaction with Catholicism has already been made clear in our account of Thomas's high estimate of human reason in knowing and practicing God's law. Calvin, as God's lawyer, must tell man, his accused client, that he must plead guilty and throw himself upon the mercy of the court. Calvin is an unusually honest lawyer: he tells his client that his case is utterly without merit. This is, of course, the pedagogical use of the law, close in spirit to Luther's appropriation of Saint Paul's leading the sinner to Christ. Only in this theological context can we then proceed to the political use of the law, of which the condemnation of Servetus and the justification of lending money at a just rate of interest are aspects. Then we shall conclude with the didactic use, the moral life.

Calvin and the People of the Covenant

Opening his series of sermons on the Ten Commandments, Calvin brings his congregation to Mount Sinai. It is they who have escaped from bondage in Egypt, which means slavery to sin and the devil. It is they who have been guided by the Lord to the great event of the giving of the law. And they must wait at the foot of the mountain because none are chosen to know God as was the prophet Moses.

Why should we enter into covenant with God? Calvin recognizes that the law pales in comparison to the idols we make and shape to our liking. Calvin knows we are lazy and "so asleep in the world that we cannot be awakened to magnify God," and that when awakened to our misery we hate God. Thus Calvin begins with the "malice in our selves which prevents us from serving God." Yet attractive as our idols are, and as demanding as it is to obey the law of the covenant, God offers us a perfect law which covers everything. "Now it is admirable that God goes to such pains to teach us and further declares that he omits nothing."

Why, finally, should we enter into covenant with God? The final reason is not what we should expect: that the majesty of the omnipotent requires obedience. No, it is God who humbles himself to enter into covenant with us; this is not only the old covenant of Moses but a new covenant of Christ, whereby "God has given us his heart in the person of our Lord."

Calvin the prophet reports what he has heard God say to the people. Now if God has humbled himself, offering his heart to his people in "enter[ing] into covenant, article by article, and to pledge myself to you," how can mere creatures respond in any way other than by entering into covenant with the Creator?

The second sermon develops the most important point about Moses. In spite of the "infinite distance between you [human] and me [God]," God speaks to Moses "as friend . . . face to face." When we read Calvin on Moses, it is as if we were reading a Jewish writer rather than a Christian writer. We have seen even in Thomas that the law of Moses was contrasted unfavorably to the law of Christ, as one of fear to one of love, as the condition of bondage to that of freedom, as the external observance to the inner response. But what Calvin develops is the gratitude we all owe to Moses for deliverance from slavery in Egypt. When God says, as all Jewish writers stress, "I am the Lord," this is the Creator making himself "*our* God," whose purpose it is to win us over by revealing his majesty to us in an acceptable way. This is the God who humbled himself in an infallible testimony of mercy.

Calvin's Moses enjoys the status of an intermediary between God and men. Calvin writes of humility before the Word of God brought to us by Moses. According to Isaiah, the seraphim in the temple "hide their eyes when God reveals himself," and so should we. Moses could not "see the face of God without perishing." But if God is said to have shown Moses only "his back," Calvin argues that this is a case of "*as if.*" The symbolic meaning of the "figure of Seraphim" is that we must not presume to approach God or rise that high. The Word to be preached to us and presented in writing shows God making himself available to us in our weakness.

The manifestation of God to Moses was so unique, matched not even by Isaiah, that Moses was elevated beyond the company of men. Then Calvin goes further. From the biblical account of Moses' forty days and forty nights on Sinai without food and drink, Calvin deduces that Moses became an angel. Somehow he regained his human body when he descended to Israel at the foot of the mountain. And he remained humble — so humble that when he wrote, he added nothing of his own. The Scripture he wrote was the pure word of God. Moses is then the model of the prophet, and ministers ought to follow his example of proclaiming all that God has commanded and adding nothing of his own.

Protestants may reject Catholic interpretations of the Ten Commandments because, as with Thomas Aquinas, in them tradition and reason share authority with Scripture. Calvin believes he has not corrupted God's Word with the traditions of men who have only vain imagination. But if it can be shown that he has himself depended on traditional interpretation of Scripture, then his polemic against "papists," as he says contemptuously, applies to his own reading, and any dependence of Moses on "wisdom of the Egyptians," which he is said to have mastered, becomes an occasion to modify the claim to infallibility.

But Calvin, as we have seen, is not a biblical literalist. Most statements of Scripture should bear only plain natural sense, but at many points the meaning can be grasped only as allegory. "Liberation from Egypt, the house of bondage" is not only a singular event in Israel's history, but the universal truth that God through Moses liberates us from bondage to sin and the devil.

There is, however, a moral basis for gratitude for the covenant and trust in the law of Moses. The commandments fit the human condition. We have "a wretched inclination" to make images. We are of "a perverse and evil nature." Without the Decalogue we would never be able to worship God in true purity or even conceive of him correctly. If "Thou shalt not kill" teaches us what we already know — that anger, hatred, and violent destruction are vices — we might just as well go on studying Seneca (as did Calvin), or some other Stoic moralist. But the teaching of God gives us the deeper insight into human nature, that moral evil is rooted in the creature's revolt against his Creator.

Cicero restored piety to the list of cardinal virtues, so not only temperance, courage, prudence, and justice, as in Plato and Aristotle, but also piety make up the *five* pagan virtues. Calvin's case against Catholic moral philosophy is that it neglects the virtue piety. Civil constitutions, for which Calvin has the greatest concern, must be covenants of a people with God. The obedience that is basic in society, not only in ceremony but in a pure conscience, must point toward God's throne on high. When in the *Institutes* Calvin argues that the first concern of government is piety, he supports this by appealing to all philosophers and the consent of all nations.

Calvin enters into the debate in the way that has made him famous. Although it seems unjust, children suffer because of the sin of Adam. Children are not innocent and are included equally with their parents in generic condemnation. Since the whole human race is "vicious and perverse," God owes us nothing. If he acts kindly toward us, it is out of pure grace.

Everyone works with some indemonstrable premises, and we can credit Calvin with great candor in showing us that he has assumed as a matter of faith that God is good, and that God's goodness is in his justice and loving-kindness. The judgment he has passed on Adam and Eve and all their descendants for transgressing his one command is not just by our standards, and his mercy shown in rescuing only some from the abyss is not totally merciful by our standards; but it is not for us, creatures, and fallen creatures, to judge our Creator. He is our Judge and our Redeemer.

And what can we learn of God's blessing? Contrary to the sociological view of the Protestant ethic, riches, health, and similar things are not signs of salvation; such signs are when he corrects and purges us of our iniquities in order to restore us to his image. One cannot know directly or indirectly whether one is among the elect who will escape the abyss. If one is saved, it is by pure grace, for no one can deserve to be saved. Our only assurance of salvation is in the loving-kindness that must constitute our refuge.

The Pedagogical Use of the Law

If we turn to Calvin as a legal counselor and ask him about the ultimate basis of obligation, we find a meticulously careful answer. Calvin's reasoning is linear, in contrast to the zigzagging between opposites of Luther. By linear is meant that a well-formed argument begins from the premises, takes care to state all of them, and then shows that the conclusions follow.

No theologian ever gave a clearer and more comprehensive answer to the basic question: Why should man obey God's law? In the *Institutes* he says:

1. To the Creator belongs the authority to lay down the law.
2. The creature owes everything to the Creator, and the basic obligation is to obey the divine will in every way.
3. Conscience is "an internal witness and monitor of the duties we owe to God, show[ing] us the difference between good and evil. . . . [It] accuses us when we deviate from our duty."
4. But "Man, . . . in a cloud of errors, scarcely obtains from this law of nature, the smallest idea of what . . . is accepted by God; but is . . . at an immense distance from a right understanding of it."
5. Therefore "The Lord gave us a written law," especially since in our "arrogance and ambition, . . . blinded with self-love that he cannot . . . learn to submit and humble himself, and to confess his misery."
6. From the law we learn of God and all that we owe him. He is lawgiver and judge, among many other attributes, and we learn his will, that righteousness is a "delight, but iniquity and abomination to him."
7. "Unless we will with impious ingratitude rebel against our Maker, we must necessarily spend our whole lives in the practice of righteousness."
8. "There is no other legitimate worship of him, but the observance of righteousness."
9. We are obliged, "like insolvent debtors," to pay the debt, but unable, yet our "want of ability is no excuse: our inability is our own fault."

10. We "are therefore unworthy to retain a place among his creatures, much less to be numbered among his children."
11. There is nothing we can say, and nothing we can do; "the divine judgment cannot be perceived without inspiring a dread of death."
12. Hence we are dejected and feel "nothing but despair."
13. Yet he is Father and we throw ourselves on "the Divine mercy, as to the only port of salvation."
14. God "subjoined promises [as well as] threatenings, in order that our hearts might imbibe a love for him, and at the same time a hatred to iniquity."
15. To the obedient "he promises also the blessings of the present life, as well as eternal felicity."
16. Because there is "divine benevolence" which rewards our obedience, no number of "good works" can merit any reward whatsoever; we must act toward him "spontaneously as if it were not a duty."
17. There is no "evangelical law" replacing the old law. Since the original "Law of Moses" is perfect, nothing should or could be added to it, and nothing taken away diminishing it. All Christ did was "restore it to its genuine purity."

Many of these assumptions may seem dubious and unnecessary, but Calvin accepts the whole Bible as a plan of salvation. Everything in the Old Testament as well as the New Testament has a necessary place, and we must not pick and choose what pleases us.

Calvin knows his client well. The human, all too human, tendency is to deny the charges and plead innocent. When man is told that his only hope is to plead guilty, he is true to human nature. Calvin is trying to tell us the truth about ourselves: we are responsible for our own unhappiness.

Calvin's interpretation of the Ten Commandments is a short course in ultimate jurisprudence. But does his use of Scripture omit the allowances made by Christ for human frailty? Does it pass over the inability of a limited creature to fulfill unlimited demands? Does such a demand that we face the Judge on the ultimate day reduce us to a paralyzed state of inaction? Is it only the logic of the law that motivates the lawyer to the extreme of reducing man to total helplessness? Are such questions as inevitable as they are unanswerable? We may put to Calvin the philosophic objection that a person has duties that he ought to fulfill as he can, but no duty to do what he cannot. Perfect he cannot be; therefore, Calvin's divine command ethics is incoherent in its demands. But Calvin's system has already rejected human judgment as a norm by which to judge divine judgment. The system does what it is intended to do: make one utterly secure within the system and impervious to objections from outside.

Political Use of the Law

Calvin is as much concerned with honor as had been the knight Ramón Lull writing in the thirteenth century. Just as Thomas and Luther, Calvin extends "Honor thy father and mother" to all in authority over us. The fifth commandment requires that honor be given by us to those to whom God assigns it.

We might have been bewitched by historians' talk of "ages" into expecting that a Protestant Reformer would set out to defend individuality and a classless society against a knight's concept of social order as a hierarchy. It might seem that since Protestants rejected ecclesiastical layers of pope, cardinals, archbishops, bishops, priests, and deacons, and talked of a priesthood of all believers, that they would also deny degrees in secular society. On the contrary, all may be equal in the sight of God, but "the Lord God desires the preservation of the order He has appointed."

Why should the Lord command us to submit to authority? It requires of us "a habit of submission." All lower degrees share in the supreme dignity of God. The titles of Father, God, and Lord are so eminently applicable to him that those on whom he bestows them are touched by a ray of his splendor and rendered honorable in their respective stations.

But there comes great responsibility with this derived authority and legal power. Calvin begins with parents' rule over children, but goes from the particular case upward in the hierarchy. The one source of power is never in doubt. Calvin may be a defender of legitimate government, be it monarchical or aristocratic, but the authority of all superiors is only derivative and conditional. God's authority is absolute, earthly kings' relative. Relative, that is, to God's law: and since God has given us his law, we are in position to judge whether obedience to superiors conduces to obedience to him.

It is perhaps unnecessary to point out that in peoples deeply influenced by Calvinist doctrine — Dutch, English, Scottish, and New Englanders — the seeds of revolution were planted. Hierarchical thought of the theocratic variety may be forced by the logic of the law to become revolutionary.

Didactic Use of the Ten Commandments

It was Calvin who departed from the medieval Decalogue of the catechisms continued by Luther in both his small and large catechisms. The Ten Commandments taught by all Protestants except Lutherans is that from Exodus 20 and Deuteronomy 5. The division is significant because, unlike in the Catholic Decalogue, here the prohibition of making and worshiping idols is not subordinated under the exclusive loyalty to the one Lord under "other gods." The significance of a separate prohibition is that Protestants of the Reformed camp rejected images, as Luther had not; thus the example of Moses smashing the golden calf became the iconoclastic destruction of statuary, paintings, stained glass. In the time of Queen Elizabeth many churches were stripped down to the bare walls, which the queen then employed to display, along with the royal arms, the tables of the law, the creed, and the Lord's Prayer. The proper place for the worship of the God of the Book was a meetinghouse, in which the pulpit for the preaching of the word took priority over the altar or replaced it altogether. Pure worship of God did not require an appeal to the senses. Vestments, crucifixes, incense, and candles were abandoned; often pipe organs and bells were smashed along with other "idols."

Luther, we saw, had retained in his teaching of the commandments the hallowing of the "festival day," which included holy days such as Easter, Pentecost, and Christmas; but he came to think that perhaps, since all days are holy, only one day in the seven was necessary for public worship. With Calvin's Ten Commandments, faithful to the Mosaic prescription, it was the Sabbath that we are to remember to keep holy. Under Puritan rule in New England, "Six days shalt thou labor" was not to be breached, even upon such a papist holy day as Christmas.

Calvin goes further than Luther went in his interpretation of "Thou shalt not commit adultery." Luther himself had abandoned the celibate life of a monk and married a nun (1525), after having spoken in ecstatic terms of the love of man and wife (1520). For Calvin marriage was a sacred covenant, ordained of God. He joined Luther in preaching that all should marry because God has commanded it to reduce the temptations of the flesh. He confessed himself to be ashamed of sexual intercourse, and warned married couples against excessive affection that would make them adulterer and adulterous. Quite consistently with the effort to reduce lust, dancing was condemned as lewd conduct.

Calvin taught the Ten Commandments on many levels — in

catechetical instruction, in sermons, and in his systematic theology. Notably in catechisms, though he began his first catechism with the law, then the creed, following Luther he reverted to tradition by placing the doctrine of God before the statement of God's will in relation to God and our neighbor. He did not, as Luther, prefer a Christian restatement of the Decalogue, as found in the Gospels or the teachings of Paul and Peter. The Old Testament versions in Exodus and Deuteronomy are perfect. The law of Moses is already the law of Christ. The covenant with Abraham remains the same covenant under Moses and through Christ, an eternal covenant of God with mankind. The changes from the "old" to the "new" covenant are not changes in substance but only in form. What we have through revelation and through conscience is the universal principle of all law. In this respect Calvin's theological ethics is a philosophic ethics, and although he and his followers constantly reproach the "papists," there is a continuity in Calvin with Philo and Thomas Aquinas. On the level of jurisprudence, Calvin's restatements of God's will is a statement of justice and equity.

The ten "Thou shalt's" and "Thou shalt not's" become, in the *Institutes,* ten propositions about what God is, what God has done, what God hates, what God loves, what God wills that man should do. Almost the only basis for all these statements about our duties is Scripture.

When we examine these propositions, we notice a double subject, God and man. All the duties that are commanded theologically — gratitude and giving thanks for benefits, honor to those who are excellent, "spiritual obedience of the conscience," trust arising from knowledge of perfections, "wisdom, righteousness, power, truth, and goodness" — apply to relations between humans. The pedagogy used by Calvin to lead the penitent to Christ can also be viewed from the perspective of man as the virtues of a good person.

Similarly, from the perspective of the second use of the law, the political, there is a most important imperative embedded in the text: "Let all things be done decently and in order" (1 Cor. 14:40). The commandment "Be orderly!" was a strong impulse in Calvin, preserving the church of Geneva from "convulsion and ruin," and by implication applying to each life, family, society, and nation. We have already seen that the divine command of honoring parents extends to reverence to all in authority. One application of doing things in order applies to courts of law. Since oaths are the guarantee of true witness in the legal order, they must be sustained.

Calvin gives the appearance of a cold logician bringing out from every particular commandment a general principle from which it can be deduced. He states his distinctions with icy clarity. His intent is to state the will of God, or man's chief end, with purity and clarity. Because he inspired iconoclasts to rid the churches of the artistic products of man and to stamp out dancing — and, as we find in seventeenth-century English Puritans, theatrical performance — we have been blinded to the singular beauty he exemplified, the beauty of purity and clarity, which is akin to the bare beauty of mathematics.

Reading Calvin on the Ten Commandments, one has the experience of discovering, as did the hymn writer, that there is behind the "frowning countenance" of God a "smiling face." Calvin's cold logic, discerning through the Bible the mind of the Creator, discovers a warm heart.

He coolly dismisses as a principle of moral good "avoid evil!" by pointing out that rocks and trees abstain from evil! We would expect him to subscribe to Aristotle's principle of justice: "Render each his due" and "Render . . . to each what is properly his." We would expect him to recommend for us as runaway horses to be bridled, and he does subscribe to moderation: "All immoderation is unlawful." We would expect him to warn us to know our humble place, under God, to honor all in authority over us.

But Calvin also urges, following the Deuteronomic reminder to Israelites that they were once strangers and slaves in Egypt, that we should show sympathy to those in the same need as our own. Justice means more than claiming what is your own and rendering his own to every one; it means also to "protect each other's rights." Finally, since all humans are of one flesh, and all we have is God's gift, we ought to do what is natural to our kind and help one another.

Those who share in the covenant find in the laws of God happiness and glory. Is there joy in the law? It is far easier for us to understand Luther's joy in being free from the law. The law restricts, condemns, and punishes, and Luther's spirit felt liberated by Saint Paul's teaching of Christ's forgiveness and saving grace. Whereas Luther's story of his discovery was publicized, Calvin was extraordinarily reticent about his conversion. Perhaps Calvin had an experience of the revelation of the law of God that he could not tell in his own case, but which was sufficiently like Moses' on Mount Sinai that led him to communicate himself by interpreting Moses. Moses, according to Calvin, climbing Sinai, was turned by God into an angel who received the tablets and, when his body was restored, brought them to the people at the foot of the mountain. Calvin gives no source for this in his sermons, but he was a man learned in the teaching of the Greek as well as the Latin Fathers of the church, with a special fondness for the Cappadocians (Saint Basil and his younger brother Gregory, and Saint Gregory Nazianzus, whose poetic version of the Decalogue inspired verse in the Latin West).

In Saint Gregory of Nyssa's *Life of Moses* we read that Moses was inducted into the great mysteries on Mount Sinai. To enter into the presence of the invisible, Moses himself became invisible. Calvin could not, following Saint Paul, talk about his own mystical experiences. As the apostle said, "whether in the body, or out of the body, I know not. God knoweth."

∽ 12 ∽

Paracelsus:
Commandments without Stone

Theophrastus Bonbastus von Hohenheim (1493-1541) renamed himself Paracelsus to indicate his desire to go "beyond" the Roman physician Celsus. A Swiss physician educated at the University of Basel, Paracelsus, after his studies in alchemy and chemistry, was appointed city physician, but his open opposition to the systems of medicine prevailing there forced him to leave Basel in 1528. The balance of his life was spent moving from place to place. He coined the word "alkahest" for the hypothetical universal solvent sought by alchemists. It seems his work in science and theology had a striking unity. He believed that the principles of medicine were to be derived from the study of nature and not from scholastic disputations. He made new chemical compounds, encouraged research, and revolutionized medical methods. He was the first to describe silicosis and to connect goiter with minerals found in drinking water. He improved pharmacy and therapeutics and established the role of chemistry in medicine. We note that his empiricism did not prevent him from developing interpretations of God and man. Paracelsus believed that just as we know nature only to the extent that we are ourselves nature, so we know God only insofar as we are God.

The intellectual and moral courage he showed as a scientist is also evident in his interpretation of the Ten Commandments. Paracelsus follows the traditional Catholic order continued by Luther but reverses the ninth and tenth commandments: first, "Thou shalt not desire the spouse of another," and second, "Thou shalt not desire the property of another." This is significant because Paracelsus is deeply concerned with the meaning for Christians of woman and man created by God so that two become one body. What is significant in the story of Adam and Eve is that marriage is commanded by God. "He wills that we should be united, together, united, joined, thou mine, I thine, and not; thou mayest go, when thou wilt, I also; but remain inseparable in a bond." We saw Luther celebrate a good marriage of mutual love, and Paracelsus is close to this, and to Calvin's interpretation of marriage as a sacred contract. Paracelsus is perhaps even more opposed to divorce than the Orthodox theologians.

In one respect he is more Augustinian than either Luther or Calvin. The God who commands is the Father, the Son, and the Holy Spirit. What the law was for Israel's monarchy is no longer important: our ability to carry out the commandments is through Christ. For "Christians and mankind who will to enter the Kingdom of God . . . we have another teacher in our monarchy." Though Israel knew only the Father, it is eternally true that there are three persons in God.

As Paracelsus runs through the Ten Commandments, we are commanded, for example, not to take God's name in vain, but also not to swear using the name of the Son and the Holy Ghost. With regard to obeying each commandment there is a refrain: *Wir auch, und mehr,* "We also, and more."

The meaning of idolatry is not, as with Israel, the prohibition of images of God but that "the devil has set up idols in us, . . . and further, makes man into an idol."

Paracelsus takes sides with Luther and Calvin against the Catholic multiplication of holy days, but, as developed later, following Luther, he keeps four significant days of remembering great events of the history of salvation: Christmas, Good Friday, Ascension, and perhaps most significant, Pentecost.

Paracelsus departs from both Catholic and orthodox Protestant traditions chiefly in what we have called the "political use" of the Ten Commandments: the application to society and state. We have seen that in the tradition of Lull, Thomas, Wycliffe, Luther, and Calvin, "Honor thy father and thy mother" means to submit to the magistracy, prelates, preceptors, and so on. Paracelsus protests that besides our bodily parents, "There is only one father, who is in heaven." Therefore the tradition *"is false."*

The commandment "Thou shalt not kill," says Paracelsus, forbids use of authority to take life; and, he adds scornfully of capital punishment and war, in taking a life we act "as though we have done God a service."

Adultery is a most serious breach of the commandments (six and nine), and Paracelsus scorns the church's prescription — the mere penance of lighting a candle in church.

Stealing rules out "feeding yourself on the property of another, and living without working with your hands."

In short, Paracelsus says no to the tradition of obedience to civil and ecclesiastical authority, no to capital punishment, no to war, no to any exception to strict monogamy, no to living by any other means than one's own labor.

Paracelsus does not call himself a "Reformer," nor identify himself with any group, but he takes as strong a position against clerical celibacy as did Luther and Calvin — and, as we have seen, against penance. However, he ignores the other Catholic and Protestant sacraments. In this respect he resembles Schwenckfeld, and in the next century George Fox.

Let us now follow the pattern of the *triplex usus legis* that we know from our study of Luther and which was shared by Calvin with Melanchthon and eventually accepted by the Anglican divines. We shall consider first the pedagogical use, second the political use (traditionally the "third use"), and last the didactic use. Paracelsus's pedagogical use will enable us to examine a theology and anthropology with hardly any of the inner struggle of Luther over faith and works or the pedagogy of Calvin to bring depraved man to confess his hopeless state. (This is illuminating because many Protestants, especially since the Enlightenment, have no patience with such pessimistic views of the worthlessness of works for salvation. Paracelsus is perhaps the preeminent example of anti-Calvinistic optimism.) As for the rejection of the traditional political use, many Protestants view religion as completely separate from government. The didactic use is developed by Paracelsus to show how demanding are the requirements for entry into the kingdom of God.

Pedagogical Use of the Ten Commandments

The aim of Paracelsus's pedagogy is to lead the thinking reader from the stage of mere reason to that of understanding and thence on to wisdom. On the low level of mere reason we find the false ("false prophets, false Christians, false apostles, the scribes and pharisees, those who sit in Moses' seat"). The writer assumes a reader who needs only to be reminded of how he has been misled by superstitions, by inflated claims of church authority ("councils, synods, etc."), and who seeks, beyond human wisdom, divine wisdom.

Our very bodies come on three levels, the elemental, the visible, and the sidereal. This is "God living in us as a Trinity." From God the Father comes all that we are on the plane of existence, subject as Adam to death.

But God the Son "makes us from his blood and flesh" and liberates us from death. "Through the Holy Spirit we will be taught and enlightened."

There is then a ladder by which we may ascend. Luther, who needed faith to unite man to God, is generally thought to have failed to discover this ladder. Paracelsus denies an "infinite distance between man and God" — any such consequence of the fall of Adam is "total depravity." If we know only God the Father, as did Israel, then we may reach the Orthodox conclusion, for "God the Father who made us from limbo [the original stuff of the world] therefore is not in us, but in his Kingdom." Luther and Calvin, then, think chiefly or only of God as in heaven, another world, and not sufficiently of God in us, in this world.

Paracelsus is most distant from Calvin, for whom the covenant under Moses at Sinai bound Israel to the Lord. Paracelsus hardly refers to Moses, and never to the tablets of stone. For Christians "the Law of the Father . . . is understood through Christ, Who interprets them, and Christ is understood through the Holy Spirit, who makes Christ understandable to us."

If, then, we know only God the Father, we may think ourselves fallen and depraved ("der in Gott den Vatter glaubt, der veracht sich und sein menscheit selbs"). It is not sufficient to take one's wisdom only from the Son. By moving up to the level of Spirit, one gains divine wisdom.

History develops in three stages, as Joachim of Fiora (1132-1202) had taught. Paracelsus adapts the symbol of the tree: "Without earth, nothing, without the tree, nothing, without the fruit, nothing." The three are all one — one thing and not three. The pedagogy is to repeat history in the growth of the individual person; begin with what was before us, without beginning, then the thousand years of the Son, and now "The Holy Ghost will teach us all." What we are preparing ourselves for is the coming of the kingdom. "Christ has invited us to his table in the Kingdom of God. There we will be as the Apostles of earth, marvelously all with [fiery] tongues we will speak and be full of the Holy Ghost."

Paracelsus's high estimate of human nature is clear from the first paragraph of the exposition of the fifth commandment. I paraphrase and condense: What on earth is more noble than the life of man? This then is given to all men equally, rich and poor, small and great. We have on earth time to live in which to fulfill our purpose. That is, we are made and become men so that we grasp life and consume divine things during our life on earth. Therefore we are in our life obliged to know through our own experience of Scripture itself what we have not learned from father and mother and to find out what we are: namely, sinners. Furthermore, the whole Bible, up to Christ and beyond Christ, establishes and teaches everything that is necessary to know of Christ. All men are in this school; no one is to be left out, no sect, no name, no creed not yet on earth. In the Bible we discover what kinds of creatures we are; and in the New Testament we discover what good God has done us through his Son; and thereby we will discover ourselves drawn to Christ and taken into his blessedness. And so we must recognize at the last judgment that we have had time and hour sufficient, also Sabbath, festival, celebration, which we could have occupied with useless toil, to discover the Scripture of our origin, departure and loss of paradise, salvation through the Son of God.

Thus Paracelsus proclaims the way to salvation, but it is not universal salvation. Some choose death rather than life, and rather than search the Scriptures some "play, drink, go whoring, fight and indulge in other such sensuous excess [*Üppigkeit*]."

Absence of Political Use

In Paracelsus's interpretation the Ten Commandments give no support for the civil order. Just as Luther had used them as a norm by which to show that pope, bishops, priests, and monks were not following God's law, so Paracelsus applies the norm to civil rulers. Emperor, kings, and knights might claim that their power is of God, but at best this could only be the power of God the Father. By the authority of God the Son they violate the very equality of persons in their hierarchy and clearly base their power upon murder, theft, and false witness.

Particularly in interpreting "Honor thy father and thy mother," Paracelsus denounces the extension beyond parents and God. It is a natural understanding that we should honor father and mother. The basis supplied by Paracelsus is the dignity of every man, for every man is given a goal to fulfill on earth.

No one lives so short a life as not to carry out his striving to do his spontaneous work and to gain peace. ("Niemandt zu kurz, denn was zu gnugsamer erforschung bis auf die tod zu reichen gnugsamb ist" and "Sabath, die feier, die fest, darinn wir wol hetten mügen stillstehn mit unnötiger arbeit.") Now murder, as in the cases of Peter and Paul, may cut life short and apostolates go unfulfilled. Christ's life was cut short; given fifty, sixty, or seventy years, who knows how many would have been converted?

Paracelsus mentions lives highly regarded by Christians and passes over in silence the orthodox argument that it was the death of Christ that broke the devil's hold on mankind or atoned for the fall of Adam. Without a fall of mankind from God's grace, no restoration through sacrificial death is needed. Nor does the meritorious death of a saintly martyr figure in Paracelsus's concern.

The next argument is that he who "takes the life, takes all" the man has; and further, not only is this a violation of "Thou shalt not steal," but it breaks the commandment "Thou shalt not covet what is someone else's." Paracelsus is appalled by the finality of death, and he expresses the idea in Christian language: "Christ never waked from the dead anyone murdered, martyred." If Christ didn't restore the life of a martyr, Paracelsus suggests, who could bring one back to life? The argument runs substantially as follows: The purpose of life is to know God, and you would take that from him? In life we should search the Scripture, and you would take that from him? We are the children of God and God is our Father, and you would strangle the son or daughter of God? We are all saved from death through God and are all called by God unto death, and you would introduce another death, would make yourself a judge and lord over God and against God?

Paracelsus extends the argument to include criminals. Terminating their lives deprives them of the opportunity of "repentance, atonement, and improvement, and therefore makes [those who joined in] condemnation guilty [along with the criminals]." Further, those who execute criminals carry the criminals' unforgiven guilt, for they were deprived of the opportunity to repent. Paracelsus's reasoning is compelling: It is presumptuous for any man to claim the "right to kill and so to break God's commandment." Not an iota of the commandment can be changed. Whence comes the "authority to kill"?

Paracelsus is not usually presented as a Christian. Sometimes readers try to fit him into the pattern of belittling Christianity and glorifying pagan antiquity. Clearly, on the issue of capital punishment, the error of Justinian was to be, like Pilate, an agent of Caesar. Pilate "judged not following the authority [*Gewalt*] that is of God, but after the law of Caesar." As judge, he failed to understand *the sense* in which Christ called himself a Son of God, *the sense* in which he was called king: so the law required his death. Pilate failed to interpret Jesus aright. Paracelsus stands or falls by his interpretation of the commandments and of pagan alternatives.

Commenting on the stoning to death of the first Christian martyr, Saint Stephen, Paracelsus carries further his analysis of the pagan mentality. The heathen considered Christ's claim only with reason, which is trivial. Stephen was killed by the emperor who responded to his jurists who were pagan teachers. Stephen understood this and said, "Forgive them: they know not what they do."

For Paracelsus the words "Let him that is without sin cast the first stone," by which Christ silenced the angry crowd ready to stone the woman taken in adultery, yield much to interpretation. First, that stoning, which was to be in fulfillment of a law against adultery, is such an evil that we say the commandment "Thou shalt not kill" now cancels this horror. Second, all turned away and no one would cast the first stone, which means no one could be judge and executioner of another. "In the case of spilling human blood, we all should go away." Third, who is qualified to be jurist, judge, or hangman? No one. Fourth, he who is our ruler, Christ, did not condemn the woman, hence we, who are under him, should also say, "Go, and sin no more."

But even worse than killing the body is killing the soul. That is the "sin against the Holy Ghost, therefore it can never be forgiven, neither here nor there."

Killing includes making war and all sorts of violence; "Where is there greater murder than in wars?" Killing in war springs from desire for "fame, wealth, pride, authority, and power, arrogance, etc.," and these things all make killing and murder the more serious, for accompanying are "theft, lies, and coveting what is another's: [these commandments are] broken over and over." Along with war, Christ condemned what was based on misunderstanding what he meant by "kingdom." This kingdom cannot be protected by fighting the Turks, and only "false Christians" lead crusades. "Knighthood is nothing but murder-mongering" ("Ritterschaft nichts dann Mörderei").

Christ made no exception for self-defense. Paracelsus quotes from Matthew 5, the Sermon on the Mount, called traditionally "Counsels of Perfection" (the idea of "perfection" suggests standards beyond the commandments): "He who will take your coat, let him, and give him also your mantle." Christ said nothing about taking him to court. Paracelsus concludes that Christ teaches that there should be no court of law or jurists. The Christian then does not accept the protection the state provides. If the pacifist dies for his belief, "So we shall suffer death, in that we die in Christ, in which purpose the Apostles died."

What approach then does the lover of peace use? "So we have also from Christ this commandment, that through his word we should make the unfaithful faithful."

Paracelsus has given a most complete argument against capital punishment and war. Pacifism, to name only the latter part of his argument in favor of protecting every human life, has a long history with distinguished representatives among radical reformers. Among all the lines of argument, the most distinctly Paracelsan is that each life needs and ought to be allowed all possible experience and learning so that it may be fulfilled. Providing the conditions and opportunities for this development clearly requires a new age.

Didactic Use of the Ten Commandments

In explaining why Paracelsus lacks the political use of the Ten Commandments, we have already had to present his didactic use. Because he is a Christian perfectionist taking Christ's counsel of perfection as conflicting with the death penalty, war and use of arms, and all civil law and courts, we are confronted with a very clear and coherent, and most difficult, ideal of the kingdom of God. It transcends the political order, in principle undermines its authority, and apparently is intended in a future age of the spirit to replace existing institutions. Since all political and ecclesiastical hierarchy is denied by the equal nobility of all persons, it would be fair to classify this utopia as "anarchistic," but only if all allusions to license are stripped from the word.

We need then to examine the distinctive moral teachings of commandments other than the first, fourth, and fifth. In his second commandment, "Thou shalt not curse," we are given a unique piece of analysis of the absurdity of cursing. Cursing someone, as saying "God damn you," is cosmic stupidity (or mischief, *Unfug*). The words imply that when we act out of "envy, hate, scorn, arrogance," our judgment of another person can effectively coerce the universe to destroy that person. This superstition is coupled with the attempt of a mere creature to control the divine agency of punishment, thus making God into our "hangman-servant" (*henker-knecht*). The conclusion is to recognize the wisdom of Christ: "Let your yea be yea, and your nay nay" (Matt. 5:37).

Regarding "Thou shalt not steal," he insists that each person should live by his own labor. Yet he is not a pure individualist. But in discussing the sixth and ninth commandments he conveys profound respect for the love of man and woman. His ideal institution, the family, rests on freeing the man and the woman from making their alliance one between their parents' interests.

How can Paracelsus's interpretation of the Ten Commandments be summarized? The end of the commandments as a whole is to encourage the soul to do its work. To observe a holy day is to quiet motives like greed that would drive one to make money every day. Indeed, before one gets down to work each day one should ground one's happiness by thinking about the kingdom of God. Work is to be such that it does not interfere with following what "nature gives" — the principle to follow "God who is bodily in us." We can know God through the Spirit interpreting what we are given in Scripture.

The pedagogical use may be summed up in the imperative, "Let the Spirit ascend from reason to understanding to wisdom!" The nonpolitical use of the commandments is "to forgive all that may experience and learn and fulfil a spiritual destiny!" The moral use is "live so as to be ready, by observing counsels of perfection, for the coming of the Kingdom of God!"

The statement by Paracelsus is far fuller than others from the radical reformers. There are many differences between them, and they deserve comparison. What seems to be the common theme is, in the words of John Milton, the progress "up to a better cov'nant"; and this project entails concentrating on the individual spirit and on growth in satisfying the highest and most difficult commandments. The radical shift is to strengthen the kingdom of God by turning away from concern with kingdoms of this world.

❧ 13 ❧

Joseph Waite:
Ecstasies of the Puritan Heart

A mong the Puritans the study of the Ten Commandments was pursued in the home; mother and father were trained as decalogic teachers. In cooperation with church leaders, parents combined education and religious instruction. It would be wrong to limit this fierce instruction to children; reading them now, accepting the danger of hypocrisy as a given, one naturally feels the stiffening of the parents before the sting of the law and the lash of this interpretation. The duty of self-examination, after all, is pertinent in proportion as one has self to examine.

As guides to parents, then, three dialogues were published by Joseph Waite in 1681. The full title is suggestive:

> *The Parents Primer and the Mothers Looking Glasse or,*
> *counsel for parents in the education of children for their*
> *temporal, Spiritual, and Eternal Happinesse,*
> *In a Dialogue between a Minister and a Father*
> *to which is added a Second Dialogue and to that*
> *a Third Dialogue concerning the Sabbath-day.*

The treatise begins with an imperative: "Parents are Commanded to teach their children" the moral law, or Ten Commandments. Mr. Waite has heard it said that only Jews have the law, but he rejects the implication that "Gentiles are Lawlesse," that they "may worship idols, takes Gods name in Vain, prophane the Sabbath, dishonour Parents, Kill, Steal, commit Adultery, what the Devil and We will." Waite tells the parents to teach the Decalogue whenever possible. "Thou shalt teach [these words] diligently unto thy Children, and shalt talk of them when thou sittest in thine House, and when thou walkest by the Way, and when thou liest Down, and when thou risest Up."

Waite addresses his dialogues to both parents, together with their children. According to Scripture, husband and wife are "one flesh" and a child, in Hebrew, is named as one who comes from the mother who bore him. Education is "our dutie." Waite quotes verses by a classical author famous for rectitude, Cato: "give your children Learning." The first word of the Latin is emphatic and loaded with meaning:

> Instrue praeceptis animum,
>   nec discere cesses:
> Nam sine doctrina vita est
>   quasi mortis imago.

These lines may be rendered: "With principles stock thy mind, cease not to learn; without doctrine life is the virtual image of death." *Instruo* means, says the minister, "a setting in order." Like "to build," "to instruct" is based on the assumption that children need to be set in order. "Children are Out of order, both in Heart and Life" — "every faculty, such as imagination, memory, understanding, will, affections, and every part of the body." Waite does not say children are little devils, but to think them innocents or even angels would be, for him, simply perverse. "The Soul in Every Faculty, is out of order. The Imagination, Deviseth evil. The Memory, Retains evil. The Understanding, is Dark: and Misjudgeth evil, and good. The Will, is opposite to the Will of God. The affections, Love evil, and Hate good. And the disordered Soul puts the Body out of order in Every Part, e.g. The Eye, Beholds vanity. The Ear, Hears it. The Tongue, Talks it. The Hands, Work it. The Feet, Follow it."

What Augustine stated on the basis of his observations of children and of his own self-reconstruction prior to conversion is explained as the work of the devil and the disobedience of Adam and Eve: "God set All in good order by Creation: but the Devil put All out of order by Temptation: and all into Confusion and Desolation."

The divine image of God may be found in Adam and Eve, but "[t]his Stately Structure which God set up by Creation: Satan hath pulled down by Temptation." The image of God is best expressed by Adam's being "with God in Paradise." The image of God is replaced by the "image of the devil," which debased man — man who, "being Drove out [of Paradise] is Without God in the World. . . . He was made but little lower than the Angels: Sin hath debased Man, to a Hog, a Dog, a devil."

What is sin? "Sin is . . . the transgression of the Law. . . . Transgression is a going beyond the Bounds of the Law. Or doing any thing Contrary to the Command: in Deed, Word, or Thought." The Puritan ignores the distinction between venial and mortal sin: for the Puritan there are no "small sins." Men are deceived who deny that "[s]mall Sins will bring them to Hell."

Then follow "Six Titles of Sin," which are six similes, building up an ever more repulsive likeness. Sin is "[a] Mire that makes the Soul like Swine: so wallowing"; "A Fire that consumes . . . Goods, Good Name, Body, Soul and all"; "A sepulchre full of dead mens bones, and All uncleanness"; "the Dog Vomit, i.e. stinking Carrion, that the Stomach of a Dog cannot endure"; "the Poyson of asps . . . an Oath, a Lie, a Wicked Word in the mouth: is worse than a Toad under the Tongue." "The plague of the heart, a dreadful disease! If the Plague be in London a Year, we think it a Long Time for such a Dismal Disease to Last. But this Plague of Sin hath been in the World, between five and six Thousand years."

To project the severity of the disease of sin, which is "a Contradiction to the Will of God," is to argue for the importance of the Ten Commandments, which are the cure. Teaching by word alone is not sufficient; it must also be by doctrine and by example — where "doctrine" means inculcating belief in God and his twenty attributes, ending with "God as a Creatour, not as A Father, in a State of Nature, and themselves as Creatures; no Children of God, before they be Born of God."

The contrast between man in nature, ever deeper and deeper in debt to God until damned in hell, and man redeemed by Christ could scarcely be more pointed. It is faith that gives man "Right to the Tree of Life." God's law is: "He that believes shall live. He that believes Not, shall Never live, but Die for Ever." Faith alone, without works, justifies, but good works are "fruits of Faith."

So much is quite faithful, in its brusque manner, to the doctrine of Luther and Calvin. Perhaps a new touch, certainly for Luther, who pictured the father alone instructing his household, is that the man's wife is present at the dialogue with the minister. She never speaks, because "she learn[s] in silence, as best becomes, with an intent to ask her Husband at home" — which cannot endear Waite and the Puritans to feminists. Yet "the Law of God is called the Law of the Mother. And she commanding her Child. According to that Law, Her Law is the neglect of which Duty, let the Mother take heed: lest there come a Time, when Torment makes her Tare the Hair off her Head."

He who would obey the commandments must first, through God's grace, become his instrument. "Let your Tongue be the Pen in Gods Hand, to write them There, if the Lord Please." The child is trained to obey and imitate his or her father and mother, who are instruments of instruction at home. There are also great leaders of Israel, among them Moses, against whom the children of Israel "murmured, while they live, but mourn for them when they are Dead." To be an instrument of God is to be like Christ. "Magistrates and Ministers [are] called Saviors. Magistrates to save the Body, Ministers to save the Soul." They are only "a Type of Christ, the Savior: Alpha and Omega." The child's early piety is a training to become an instrument of God's will. The sinner must repent, and repent instantly, not putting off repentance. The sinner "can No more Repent, himself, than he can Pardon himselfe."

If God enables the sinner to repent, it is difficult to see in what sense the sinner shall repent unless there be a new creature through Christ.

Waite's second dialogue shows what variety of matter the Decalogue could yield to a Puritan interpretation.

The Decalogue is both the primitive perfect law written in Adam's heart and the natural law which is universal. It applies to unbelievers as well as to believers. Still, Adam broke the tablets of law, and the image in our corrupted state is dim. The form in which this original law was given by God is conditional, "If thou do, thou shalt live," with a conditional threat, "do thou not, thou shalt die." The contrasting imperative mode, "do this," is here called "a peremptory precept." We would call it categorical or unconditional. It is distinctly Puritan in its obliviousness to the principle of interpretation and the adjustment of rules to circumstances through equity.

The Decalogue of Moses, carried on tablets of stone from the hand of God on Mount Sinai, is different in form from the natural law. Through it God declares himself to be our God, and we, as his people, must obey. God took the initiative and gave us the covenant. "It is not, Do this and I will be thy God: but I am thy God therefore Do this."

The Decalogue as a covenant of works might be conceived as a contract: "God require[s] and Man consent[s]." But the covenant is a covenant of grace. Those of the new covenant of Christ hold that this is the same as that delivered at Sinai: "The covenant is One and the Same in Substance."

For Waite the Decalogue is the moral law and to be distinguished from the ceremonial law and the judicial law. Israel alone was under all three laws. Under the moral law it was a humane society, under the ceremonial law a church, and under the judicial law a civil society or common-wealth. Israel was the only national church. Christ's covenant of grace replaces the ceremonial law, which is abolished. And the judicial law no longer is our law. The moral law, however, is basic to all forms of law: the Decalogue is the root of law.

Was the Decalogue, as given to Israel, a covenant of works? In Waite's dialogue the father reads biblical texts that way but is corrected by the minister. Salvation depends on faith, not works, and from Luther's perspective, represented by the minister, the layman is slipping back into Catholic error. Yet good works must flow from faith.

For Waite the story of the giving of the covenant is significant in every detail. The exodus from Egypt is the escape of the redeemed from the bondage of sin. The tablets signify the heart on which God writes his law. The tablets placed in the ark signify the coming of Christ. These meanings are emblems of salvation through Christ. All the ceremonies have mystical significance. Putting the sins of Israel on the head of the goat has a higher meaning: Christ bears the sins of the world. What Christ revealed is the root of the law, which is love. The moral law is branched throughout the whole Bible. Although some commandments are positive and most are negative, every negative commandment implies a positive, and every positive commandment implies negative. This analysis also points out that every negative implies other negatives, every positive other positives. "Thou shalt not kill" condemns "all kinds of Murder, . . . Battles, Quarrels, Blows with hand or heart, to hurt in any part." The result is inclusive law. "Thy law is exceeding broad" (Ps. 119).

The most elaborated of the ten is "Remember the Sabbath to keep it holy." God willed it to have a special importance. It is characteristic of the Puritan interpretation, although each commandment is worthy of expansion into a whole sermon, to devote a third dialogue to the Sabbath.

Between the Decalogue written in the Bible and the Decalogue written in the heart there is no contradiction. They who think grace is sufficient for them to live without the written law — the antinomians — are a very great source of evil. "A good work-man will have his Rule ready at his Back, to try his work, so let a Christian have the Law: not only in his Heart and Head, but also under his Eye in the Bible: that standing Rule, that Sure word, more to be regarded than what is spoken with an audible voice out of Heaven. The commandment is a Lamp, and the law is Light. The Sun is not more necessary by Day, nor the Moon by Night, nor a Candle in a Coalpit, or dark Dungeon, than the Law: without which the world would be a Hell."

The Puritan method of interpretation draws from the Decalogue simile after simile. Deprived of all forms of pictorial idols, condemning the stage as idolatrous, without music and dance, with no frivolity, the Puritan heart could celebrate the law, turning a discourse on rules into ecstatic poetry.

The most elaborated metaphor is the tree of life. "Expounded, and Branched out in the Bible these ten words with more than Ten thousand words: to prevent this Pretense also for ignorance: viz, this Brevity is Obscurity, this Shortnesse is Darknesse: a Word is for the Wise, we are Weak."

The root is love. The moral law is "the fountain of all laws . . . they all belong to . . . the Root." "Moral, Ceremonial, judicial" laws are "the branches." The root is love.

Waite took preaching most seriously: the model of a great sermon was God himself declaring the Ten Commandments. The preacher has a duty to God to preach, and the words he preaches are God's own words, and therefore are to have effects. "English Heathens who let their children Loose to serve Satan" deserve, as did Jews long in Egyptian darkness, a "rousing lecture" such as God gave them. The preacher has collected stories of crime and classified them under each of the Ten Commandments. Why are there "so many Murders, with Heart, Hand, and Tongue"? "It's because the sixth commandment is not preached." He then goes on to more sad stories of consequences of adultery, "because the Seventh commandment is not preached."

The greatest of sins is left for the climax. As an example of pride he picks "a preacher who appears in the pulpit in a monstrous Periwig! A crown of Pride." This makes him "liker a courtier than a preacher." The conclusion is an exhortation containing the command: "Glory in legality."

~ 14 ~

Thomas Hobbes and John Locke

The interpretations of three major philosophers of the seventeenth and eighteenth centuries in England and New England show the relevance of the Ten Commandments in the revolutionary period. They are among the most distinguished political and metaphysical minds of the times: Thomas Hobbes (1588-1679), John Locke (1632-1704), and Jonathan Edwards (1703-58).

We could scarcely ask for stronger presentation of the familiar three uses of the law, taken in the order of the *political*, which Hobbes used almost exclusively, and for whom the tablets are "the law of sovereignty"; the *moral*, which Locke stressed almost exclusively, and for whom the tablets are "the law of virtues"; and the *pedagogical*, which concerned Edwards, the most theological of the triad, almost exclusively, and for whom the tablets must be summed up in "the law of love." That these three major Protestant minds clarify for us the three uses of the law may be explained by the continuity of intense concern with prioritizing the uses in the revolutionary period.

There are different ways we can compare and contrast the three. The one most faithful to the Lutheran and Calvinist commandment to bring repentant sinners to confess their depravity and throw themselves upon the tender mercy of God is Edwards, to whom we devote the next chapter. The one most concerned with the authority of the ruler to establish peace and end civil strife is Hobbes. The one who shows the deepest concern with the moral development of the individual is John Locke. It is to Hobbes that we first turn.

Political and intellectual life in this period, which was marked by the rivalry of Anglican and Puritan, was deeply permeated by the Ten Commandments and the doctrine of their three uses. Hobbes was the son of an Anglican priest. It is said that, deeply eager that some power prevail in the Civil War, at first Hobbes made the ruler in his *Leviathan* to resemble Oliver Cromwell; but then, as Cromwell's cause faltered and Hobbes joined Prince Charles in France, where he waited to be crowned King Charles II, Hobbes made him resemble his Royal Highness. Hobbes's views of Scripture influenced Spinoza, whose unorthodox views of the divine nature may have provoked his excommunication by the Jewish community of Amsterdam in 1656; modern historians recognize Spinoza as the chief philosophic challenger of revealed religion. Hobbes's books were banned by both the Catholic Church and Oxford University. There was talk of burning not only his books but Hobbes himself.

Hobbes, a layman, is no less pessimistic about human nature than Edwards, a Puritan minister best known for his deeply felt warning to "sinners in the hands of an angry God." While the Puritan turns exclusively to God to change the person internally, Hobbes, a classical scholar who translated Thucydides and Homer, regards the dutiful citizen as obliged to follow the religious forms commanded by the sovereign. As to worship, Hobbes would rebuke Edwards for concentrating on conversion and ignoring public institutions, while Edwards would rebuke Hobbes for neglecting the inner life of religion and the ultimate destiny of the soul.

Sharp opposition between Hobbes and Locke exists on certain topics: human nature, the social contract, and powers of the government specifically in regard to religious groups. If, as Hobbes argued, the state of nature — roughly, human life without society and state — is like that of unrestrained predation, in which each tries to rule and possess all, and the result is life that is "poor, solitary, nasty, brutish, and short," then it is wise for all to vest their powers and all rights save life itself in a sovereign. The transfer by contract produces peace, and justifies the authority of the ruler over the whole of society. The king authorizes what is the law. The *Leviathan* is the best justification in English of the authority of the king over the religion of his people. But if, as Locke argued, human nature contains seeds of reasonable cooperation and mutuality, then the contract out of which society, in his view, emerges involves no such transfer of liberties to the ruler. People retain their natural rights, and the powers of the ruler must be limited to respect them. Individuals therefore should be encouraged to develop their virtues and find occasions to use their abilities to make wise decisions. Among these opportunities is forming associations for the purpose of worship, although there are certain limits within which sects may be tolerated.

A reading of Hobbes and Locke is most helpful in grasping what is involved in an established and state-supported church as opposed to the "disestablishing" that took place in the American colonies when they formed the United States. The process was more gradual than we like to imagine. Article 1 of the Bill of Rights did not forbid the "establishment" of the Congregational churches of New England, which was legal for a generation. The Constitution forbids *Congress* to make any law regarding an establishment of religion. This is the rejection of Hobbes's position and not a restriction on local hegemony. The guarantee of "free exercise" is an endorsement of Locke's idea that churches are voluntary associations.

Certainly the orthodox Protestant Reformers — Lutheran, Calvinist, Anglican — would have thrown their warnings of anarchy against any such resolution of the problem of church and state. But some reformers, such as Paracelsus, would have welcomed the virtually unlimited toleration of religious sects, which inevitably means great latitude for moral variation. The problem then becomes: Is morality to set limits to variety? If there is no institution setting those limits, as an established church once did, is there any consensus in society among the variety of sects? If so, does the Decalogue represent that common understanding?

Thomas Hobbes's Decalogue: "The Law of Sovereignty"

Hobbes's *Leviathan* is the most famous treatise in defense of the sovereignty of the ruler. There must be a way for men to pass beyond the misery of life in the state of nature, where each man lays claim to everything and seeks to dominate every other man. There the condition of man is that of beasts; each man is to every other as a wolf of prey (*homo homini lupus est*). We recall Hobbes's description of life in nature: "poor, solitary, nasty, brutish, and short."

Peace comes out of civil war when there is a contract, by which each cedes all the claims except life itself to the sovereign. One of the choices the king is to make for his people is the choice of a religion. For Hobbes, wars between Huguenot and Catholic kept France in turmoil for most of the sixteenth century. In Germany peace was sought according to the principle that each ruler might decide whether his people be Catholic or Lutheran or Reformed. "Whose the rule is, his is the religion" (*cuius regio est, ejius religio*), Hobbes concludes.

Book 3 of *Leviathan* gives the argument basic to the "Christian commonwealth." What should be the law of such a kingdom? God has made his Son, Christ, his vice-regent on earth.

The paradigm of Christ's kingship on earth is the kingship of Moses over Israel in the desert. Christ "is to be king then no otherwise than as subordinate or vice regent of God the Father, as Moses was in the wilderness, and as the high priests were before the reign of Saul, and as the Kings were after it" (*Leviathan* 3.41). The textual proof is God's promise to Moses: "I will raise them up a prophet like unto thee, and will put my words into his mouth" (Deut. 18:18). Sixteenth- and seventeenth-century paintings, most prominently Tintoretto's "Sequence," make visible the "similitude" of events from the life of Moses to that of Christ. Hobbes shows the political significance: it gave the king divine status as vice-regent and identified the king's law with the law of God.

Hobbes quotes and interprets the Ten Commandments in part 3 of *Leviathan*.

> That part of the Scripture, which was first Law, was the Ten Commandments, written in two Tables of Stone, and delivered by God himselfe to Moses; and by Moses made known to the people. Before that time there was no written Law of God, who as yet having not chosen any people to bee his peculiar Kingdome, had given no Law to men, but the Law of Nature, that is to say, the Precepts of Naturall Reason, written in every mans own heart. Of these two Tables, the first containeth the law of Soveraignty;
>
> 1. That they should not obey, nor honour the Gods of other Nations, in these words, *Non habebis Deos alienos coram me,* that is, *Thou shalt not have for Gods, the Gods that other Nations worship; but onely me:* whereby they were forbidden to obey, or honor, as their King and Governour, any other God, than him that spake unto them then by Moses, and afterwards by the High Priest.
>
> 2. That they *should not make any Image to represent him;* that is to say, they were not to choose to themselves, neither in heaven, nor in earth, any Representative of their own fancying, but obey Moses and Aaron, whom he had appointed to that office.
>
> 3. That *they should not take the Name of God in vain;* that is, they should not speak rashly of their King, nor dispute his Right, nor the commissions of Moses and Aaron, his Lieutenants.
>
> 4. That *they should every Seventh day abstain from their ordinary labour,* and employ that time in doing him Publique Honor.

5-10. The second Table containeth the Duty of one man towards another as *To honor Parents; Not to kill; Not to Commit Adultery; Not to steale; Not to corrupt Judgment of false witnesse; and finally, Not so much as to designe in their heart the doing of any injury one to another.* The question now is, Who it was that gave to these written Tables the obligatory force of Lawes. There is no doubt but they were made Laws by God himselfe: But because a Law obliges not, nor is Law to any, but to them that acknowledge it to be the act of the Soveraign; how could the people of Israel that were forbidden to approach the Mountain to hear what God said to Moses, be obliged to obedience to all those laws which Moses propounded to them? Some of them were indeed the Laws of Nature, as all the Second Table; and therefore to be acknowledged for Gods Laws; not to the Israelites alone, but to all people: But of those that were peculiar to the Israelites, as those of the first Table, the question remains; saving that they had obliged themselves, presently after the propounding of them, to obey Moses, in these words (Exodus 20:19.) *Speak thou to us, and we will hear thee; but let not God speak to us, lest we dye.* It was therefore onely Moses then, and after him the High Priest, whom (by Moses) God declared should administer this his peculiar Kingdome, that had on Earth, the power to make this short Scripture of the Decalogue to bee Law in the Commonwealth of Israel. But Moses, and Aaron, and the succeeding High Priests were the Civill Soveraigns. Therefore hitherto, the Canonizing, or making of the Scripture Law, belonged to the Civill Soveraigne.

The Judiciall Law, that is to say, the Laws that God prescribed to the Magistrates of Israel, for the rule of their administration of Justice, and of the Sentences, or Judgments they should pronounce, in Pleas between man and man; and the Leviticall Law, that is to say, the rule that God prescribed touching the Rites and Ceremonies of the Priests and Levites, were all delivered to them by Moses onely; and therefore also became Lawes, by virtue of the same promise of obedience to Moses. Whether these laws were then written, or not written, but dictated to the People of Moses (after his forty dayes being with God in the Mount) by word of mouth, is not expressed in the Text; but they were all positive Laws, and equivalent to holy Scripture, and made Canonicall by Moses the Civill Soveraign.

So for Hobbes Moses is the archetype of the ideal ruler for an unideal world.

John Locke's Decalogue

John Locke was as deeply involved in politics as was Hobbes. Hobbes, the tutor of Charles II, hoped for an end to civil war by the reestablishing of royal sovereignty, and he remained in exile until he could return with the prince who was restored as Charles II. James III went to Rome. After the last of the Stuarts came the Glorious Revolution. Locke had a hand in the plot to bring a Protestant prince, Dutch William, William of Orange, to rule with Mary the queen. Limited monarchy under a constitution replaced absolute rule, and the efforts to coerce religious dissenters were relaxed, though several further steps beyond those taken in 1690 were required before toleration could be extended to Roman Catholics, Jews, and freethinkers. The English Bill of Rights served to check political power, and Locke, the intellectual genius of the English Revolution, became the mentor of several generations of American colonists preparing the way for the American Revolution, which eventually led to the Constitution of the United States.

Locke is the best known of all English philosophers, particularly because of the empiricism of his *Essay concerning Human Understanding.* Empiricism involves submitting beliefs to the test of evidence, for and against. Beliefs are held by individuals. Locke's political theory starts with individuals and free consent, which implies that the state is formed by contract and churches by voluntary covenant between individuals. Locke went beyond his *Letters concerning Toleration* in the constitutions he wrote.

For his interpretation of the Ten Commandments we turn to Locke the biblical commentator and Locke the theorist of education. Like Hobbes, Locke had a well-thought-out theory of the Decalogue. While Hobbes's use of the Decalogue was exclusively political, Locke's was exclusively moral. Hence the contrast between Hobbes's "law of sovereignty" and Locke's "rules of virtue." Between them they cover the first and third uses of the Decalogue and leave to Jonathan Edwards the theological use. (In the next chapter we shall examine Edwards and see if he includes the other uses.)

Locke professed a Christian duty to study the Bible, "receiving with stedfast belief, and ready obedience, all those things which the spirit of truth hath therein revealed." The purpose was practical: "to obey the will of God." He had taken account of the Gospels in his *Reasonableness of Christianity,* and was challenged to interpret the epistles of Paul. His final writing was the *Paraphrase and Notes on the Epistles of St. Paul.* Among those who saw the manuscript in 1702-3 was Sir Isaac Newton, a close acquaintance.

The philosophical assumption on which the interpretation is based is that if "God chose Paul as Apostle to the Gentiles, he chose a man who was capable of convincing argument." The reader must then "see how the scatter'd Parts of the Discourse hang together in a coherent well-agreeing Sense, that makes it all of a Piece." In assuming that all the Bible "says" is true, he concentrated his attention on the "moral laws." The ceremonial and civil laws are abrogated, and thus the Ten Commandments would remain authoritative. Divine revelation communicates "the invisible things of God" and makes known "the natural and eternal rule of rectitude." Although such truths are above reason, they are yet subject to the scrutiny of reason. Philosophy must confess its limitation, and not even the greatest system of morality compares with the teachings of Jesus.

Man, as Locke interprets the biblical view, was created immortal. But the disobedience of Adam, contrary to the commandment of God, cost him immortality. "Through sin Adam earned Death." The descendants of Adam do not share his guilt, as Calvin held, but do have a sinful tendency in their flesh, the source of "deviations from the strait rule of rectitude."

We read in Locke's paraphrase of Paul's letter to the Romans: "That by Adams transgression sin entered into the world and death by sin and soe death reigned-over all men from Adam to Moses. That by Moses god gave the children of Israel (who were his people i.e. ownd him for their god and kept them selves free from the Idolatry and revolt of the heathen world) a law which *if they obeyed they should have life i.e. attain to immortal life, which had been lost by Adams transgression*" (emphasis added). We should point out that this renders the Ten Commandments hypothetical rather than categorical, and presupposes human freedom to enter into contract with God. Locke's standards of empirical proof extend to revelation, which afforded belief, not certain knowledge. In general, Locke's practice of empiricism allows only for degrees of belief proportionate to the quality of the evidence pro and con.

Unlike most interpretations of the place occupied by Christ in mankind's schemes of salvation, Locke's Christ did not die as a sacrifice, to pay for the sin of Adam. By his sinless life Christ "extinguished or suppressed sin in the flesh" (paraphase of Rom. 8:38). By conquering the devil once and for all, Christ initiated a new covenant of grace.

The meaning of Christ's resurrection is that "all humanity was restored to life. This restoration does not save them from physical death but is the promise of a resurrection in the future." Those who have faith in Jesus as the Messiah "are accepted by God into the Kingdom of Christ, have their sins forgiven, and are made righteous and capable of eternal life."

Obviously, again, Locke's reading of the human situation is far more optimistic than Hobbes's, and more generous than that of the Puritans, who limited salvation to those whom God chose, the elect. And compared with the creeds required by the orthodox, Locke's profession of faith is very simple.

According to Locke, the command of the covenant is "Do this and live." What is to be done is not merely "an initial act of sorry but . . . 'doing works meet for repentence' and 'a sincere obedience to the law of Christ,' the remainder of our lives." Locke's emphasis was not on the experience of salvation or on some pietistic rebirth but on being moved to agreement by rational deduction; for Locke, as for Hobbes, geometry was the touchstone of proof. In philosophic terms Locke's was a "divine command theory" of morality: an act is moral because it is commanded by God. But God's existence was the first point in a deductive chain of reasoning which eventually should include all the commands that would lead to happiness. Late in his life, Locke admitted that try as he would, he could not work out a deductive system of ethics, but he continued to believe in it.

Locke's concept of church reflects his individualism and still sounds "enlightened." In civil law, he notes, a church is "a voluntary society of men, joining themselves together of their own accord in order to the public worshipping of God, in such a manner as they judge acceptable to him, and effectual to the salvation of their souls." But in the context of salvation, for Locke the church is "the people of God."

In the *Reasonableness of Christianity* there is a near identity between "the natural rule of rectitude, the law of Moses, and the law of Christ." For Locke "a natural and eternal rule of *rectitude* . . . is made known to men by the light of Reason." Thus Locke paraphrased Paul (Rom. 2:26). The moral precepts of the law of Moses (excluding the "carnal ordinances . . . abrogated" by Christ) are so clear that everyone can understand them without trouble. (This again is the language of Locke's empiricism.) The role of Jesus was to renew the Decalogue, adding "his own Divine Authority" and making "Knowledge of the Law more easy and certain than it was before" (paraphrase of Eph. 2:15). Thus Jesus plays a role in meeting standards of certainty acceptable to Locke's empiricism.

As we might expect by now, "The rectitudes of the law," made by God "to be the moral rule to all man kind," are eternal and unmovable. This may echo Newton as much as Saint Thomas and Paul. "The rectitudes of the law" are then not arbitrary but in harmony with the nature of things and "discovered by the light of nature." They are the "very foundations of all order and moral rectitude in the intellectual world" (paraphrase of Rom. 8:7).

Locke's distance from the early reformers is obvious from his insistence on the ease with which Christian truth is apprehended. But he is not an anarchist. Is the Christian to follow Luther's interpretation of Paul's obedience to "higher powers"? Unlike Hobbes, Locke rejected the Anglican interpretation of the divine right of kings, on the ground that the gospel should not meddle with civil law, determining the office of the magistrate. In what sounds like a prudential move during repressive times, Locke argues that the Christian has no special privilege in civil law and is not to neglect civil duties. Men "have a right to prefer freedom to slavery if they can obtain it" (paraphrase of 1 Cor. 7:21).

To sum up: For Locke moral laws are objective, there in the nature of things as "the will of God." They are not only revealed to Moses and Jesus, but to Paul also, and these communicate to us moral truths. Such truths are "eternal" and apparently universal. Independent of time and space, they are "invisible things of God." Our reason grasps the evidence of a moral truth much as it grasps a mathematical truth — and also comparably can demonstrate it.

Locke's empiricism had ramifications for education. Locke outlined three steps involved in arriving at certainty — collecting evidence, weighing the probability of propositions in light of the evidence, and placing confidence in those propositions in direct proportion to their probability — and these had to become habitual if students were to replace bad habits.

Locke defined morality as acquiring "habits," which is doing what persons "have to do." Morality is "taught . . . more by Practice than Rules." It should be taught to children, but as "wisely adapted by Nature to their Age and Temper," and in "all that they have to do, Sport and Play too." It is not memorizing a rule but practicing an action, and therefore whenever done "awkwardly, [the teacher makes] them do it over and over again, 'till they are perfect." The tutor should beware of doing what is easy, that is, merely commanding, and likewise expecting the wisdom of years.

What is Locke's example of good habits? It comes from the area of courtesy: "Thus bowing to a Gentleman, when he salutes him, and looking into his Face when he speaks to him, is by constant Use as natural to a well-bred Man, as breathing; it requires no Thought, no Reflection." On the level of a child's learning the right and good act, the opposite, discourtesy, is called a "fault" (rather than the far stronger terms "wrong," "sinful," "evil," or "criminal"). Good habits are learned "one by one" as faults are cured, until bad habits are weeded out and good ones planted in place of them. When children are cured of faults, they are preserved "from Transgression, and the Rebukes which follow'd it." Therefore "ill Customs" should not be neglected. Parents bring up the infant in the "nurture and admonition of the Lord": "Train up a child in the way he should go: and when he is old he will not depart from it" (Prov. 22:6).

Locke does not give any list of rules, such as those King James is supposed to have taught his son Charles. He rejected the wisdom of his day, which emphasized memorization of rules. "For if you burden him with many *Rules*, one of these two Things must necessarily follow; that either he must be often punish'd, which will be of ill Consequence, by making Punishment too frequent and familiar; or else you must let the Transgressions of some of your Rules go unpunish'd, whereby they will of course grow contemptible, and your Authority become cheap to him."

Does Locke think of the Ten Commandments as sufficiently few? He does not tell us what he thinks specifically of the order in which they should be introduced. He does say, "I know not whether he should read any other Discourses of Morality but what he finds in the Bible." Clearly, from what we have seen of extensions of the fifth commandment, "Honor thy father and mother," the good habit of "bowing to a Gentleman . . . and looking into his Face when he speaks to him" would be such an extension.

Locke has a contemporary-sounding belief about how good habits are successfully inculcated. "The mode," as Thomas would say, of teaching morality is *kindness*. Once again Locke is a psychologist of education: "[K]eep them to the Practice of what you would have grow into a Habit in them, by kind Words, and Gentle Admonitions, rather as minding them of what they forget, than by harsh Rebukes and Chiding, as if they were wilfully guilty."

Exactly how biblical commandments were taught systematically in Locke's day can be learned from the *Whole Duty of Man*. David Hume mentions that his moral thought went on from this popular anonymous work to Cicero's *De officiis*. (This would have been years after Locke's death in 1704 — Hume was not born until 1709.) Locke advises this same Latin classic, "Tully's Offices," not as a schoolboy text used to learn Latin but "as one that would be informed in the Principles and Precepts of Virtue for the Conduct of his Life." Thus there is a long period of moral education by practice, with the motive of "the Love of Reputation, instead of satisfying his Appetite."

A Ciceronian theory of virtues, with strong emphasis on piety in ad-

dition to the classic four virtues — temperance, courage, justice, and prudence — was brought by Locke into harmony with the Mosaic commandments. But the Puritan would rebuke Locke for motivating the child to
please men rather than to serve God. And we cannot ignore that, on the basis of biblical morality and classical ethics, the structure of an important
modern doctrine has been erected, the doctrine of the "natural Rights of
Men" and international relations "grounded upon Principles of Reason."
Locke cites the classics of his century — Grotius and Pufendorf — by
which we shall "be instructed in the natural Rights of Men, and the Original and Foundations of Society, and the Duties resulting from thence." In
our terms, political science was taught as part of moral philosophy.

With this foundation the student (whom Locke assumes to be "an
English Gentleman") goes on to learn "the *Law* of his Country." This is necessary for every level of society, not merely for lawyers. Locke speaks scornfully of the common practice of the law: "I do not mean the chicane or
wrangling and captious Part of the Law: A Gentleman, whose Business is to
seek the true Measures of Right and Wrong, and not the Arts how to avoid
doing the one, and secure himself in doing the other, ought to be as far
from such a study of the *Law,* as he is concerned diligently to apply himself
to that wherein he may be serviceable to his Country."

Whether Locke knew that Alfred the Great had prefaced his code of
Saxon law with the Ten Commandments, we cannot ascertain. But he continues in the same tradition, to approach the English Constitution "in the
ancient Books of the *Common Law,*" getting the history of laws made under
every king. The moral inquiry, "the right Way . . . to study *our law,*" is to
gain "an Insight into the Reason of our *Statues* . . . and the true Ground
upon which they came to be made, and what Weight they ought to have."

In many ways Thomas Jefferson was a fine example of the gentleman
Locke would want his friend's son to become when he wrote *Some Thoughts
concerning Education.* Jefferson read Scripture, taking from the teachings of
Jesus his maxims, and in this sense thought he was a "Christian." He was
learned in ancient languages and refers to the ethical theories, which he
compared in their specific ranking of virtues. And in studying constitutions
and laws he was concerned to be clear about their reason and grounds. This
clarity is a very valuable extension of the decalogic reason of the Mosaic
covenant — the simplicity of the Ten Commandments — into American
political life. To this theme we shall return in a later chapter on Jefferson.

$\smile$ 15 $\backsim$

Jonathan Edwards:
The Commandment of Love

It is evident that Hobbes regarded the legitimacy of government and law to rest in the power of the king. But Locke rested law on moral principle, and urged resting our acceptance of authority on morality. Locke is a deep critic of Hobbes, and in turn Jonathan Edwards (1703-58), American Puritan, urges us to study the Decalogue in a way that transcends Locke's morality. The theological principle is: "No true virtue without supreme love to God and making God our supreme end."

The human spirit Edwards describes in his fifteen-sermon series *Charity and Its Fruits* is not pretty: "an envious spirit," "a selfish spirit," "an angry spirit," "a censorious spirit," to name only four vices that occur in his titles. The bleakness of this view equals anything Hobbes considered in his state of nature. For Edwards the problem of creating society out of self-seeking individuals cannot be solved in Hobbes's or Locke's way. Conformity to the religion of the ruler is hypocrisy, and as sermon 3 argues, "Nothing can make up for want of sincerity in the heart." What is needed is more and other than Locke's "reasonableness." It is "supernatural grace infused into the human heart." Sermon 2 addresses "love more excellent than extraordinary gifts of the Spirit." It is grace that makes us "long-suffering and kind" (sermon 4) and counters envy, pride, selfishness, anger, censoriousness (sermons 5-9). This is the powerful motive that "tends to holy practice" (10), enables us to "undergo . . . sufferings" (11), is "never overthrown" and "lasts eternally" (13-14). The ideal to which all these "Christian graces concatenated together" is "heaven [as] a world of love" (13 and 15). There is something of Locke's simplicity and clarity in Edwards's thought, and something of his empiricism in Edwards's comparison of religious experience with the supernatural gift of a new sense.

Edwards's originality was in part the gift of circumstances. After taking his degree at Yale, he served under his liberal grandfather in Northampton, Massachusetts. After twenty-three years of ministry in Northampton, where he opposed his grandfather's position on the Great Awakening, Edwards was dismissed. The next, very productive six years were spent in the frontier settlement of Stockbridge. Here, at the western edge of Massachusetts, he wrote his major philosophical works and hoped to produce a more systematic account of Christian doctrine. Yet he answered the call of another kind and accepted, reluctantly, the presidency of the College of New Jersey in Princeton. Edwards died a few weeks after his induction as president.

Edwards moved beyond Locke's empiricism by clarifying the mind's active role in the knowledge process. He developed the idea of habit, which we've seen in our discussion of Saint Thomas, so that habit constitutes the pattern of events and is itself a principle. Physical laws — say, the law of gravity — are not mere descriptions but explain the tendencies in things. Edwards's philosophical originality can be seen in his use of the idea of law as essential to understanding entities as such, and his grasp of existence as both defined by law and constituted of relationships. As they enter the mind, simple ideas are not just "givens"; they are prone to certain relationships. They are parts of networks of potentials. They are perceived as such by the imagination; for Edwards it is the imagination that determines how one perceives and acts.

Edwards does not refer to these philosophic ideas in so many words in his sermons. Indeed, from the sermons it may seem that he proposes a philosophical theology of grace that seems to have nothing to do with law generally, or with the Ten Commandments particularly. Yet Edwards's philosophy and his theology are branches of one trunk and root. In his first sermon we learn the relations between the law, the Word, and love:

> 1. The Scripture teaches this of the Law and Word of God in general. By the law in Scripture is sometimes meant the whole of the written Word of God. So in John 10:34, "Jesus answered them, Is it not written in your law, I said, Ye are gods?" But there the passage quoted is taken from the book of Psalms. And sometimes by the law is meant the five books of Moses. So it is to be understood where we meet with the distinction of the law and the prophets. Acts 24:14, "Believing all things which are written in the law and the prophets." Sometimes by the law is meant the Ten Commandments, as containing the sum of the duty of

mankind and all that is required, as of universal and perpetual obligation. But whether we take the law as signifying the Ten Commandments, or the whole written Word of God, the Scripture teaches us that
the sum of what is required is love. So when by the law is meant the
Ten Commandments, Romans 13:8, "He that loveth another hath fulfilled the law," and therefore several of the Commandments are re-
hearsed. And thus again in the tenth verse the Apostle says, "Love is
the fulfilling of the law." Now unless love was the sum of what the law
requires, the law could not be wholly fulfilled in love. A law is not fulfilled but by obedience to the sum, or whole of what it contains. So the
same Apostle again in I Timothy 1:5, "Now the end of the commandment is charity." Or if we take the law in a yet more extensive sense for
the whole written Word of God, the Scripture still teaches us that love
is the sum of what is required in it, as in Matthew 22:40. There Christ
teaches that on those two precepts of loving God with all the heart, and
our neighbor as ourselves, hang all the law and the prophets. That is,
all the written Word of God. For that which was then called the law
and the prophets was the whole written Word of God which was then
extant.

2. The Scripture teaches this of each table of the law in particular.
That command, "Thou shalt love the Lord thy God, with all thy heart,
and with all thy soul, and with all thy mind," is given as the sum of the
first table of the law, in the twenty-second chapter of Matthew, in answer to the question of the lawyer, who asked him, "Which is the great
Commandment in the law?" Verses 36-38, "Master, which is the great
commandment in the law? Jesus said unto him, thou shalt love the
Lord thy God with all thy heart, and with all thy soul, and with all thy
mind. This is the first and great commandment." And in the next verse,
the loving of our neighbor is mentioned as the sum of the second table,
as it is in Romans 13:9, where the precepts of the second table are re-
hearsed over in particular. "For this, thou shalt not commit adultery,
thou shalt not kill, thou shalt not steal, thou shalt not bear false witness, thou shalt not covet; and if there be any other commandment, it
is briefly comprehended in this saying, viz. thou shalt love thy neighbor as thyself." And so again Galatians 5:14, "For all the law is fulfilled
in one word, even in this; thou shalt love thy neighbor as thyself." The
apostle [James] seems to teach the same thing in James 2:8, "If ye fulfill
the royal law according to the Scripture, Thou shalt love thy neighbor
as thyself, ye do well." Hence love appears to be the sum of all that vir-

tue and duty which God requires of us; and therefore must undoubtedly be the most essential thing, or the sum of all that virtue which is
essential and distinguishing in real Christianity. That which is the sum
of all duty is the sum of all real virtue.

It may be well to address the narrower concern: Edwards's position
seems to rest only on the words of the Gospels and Epistles of the New Testament.

Edwards's answer is very clear: the rules of Christ are the same rules
given by Moses, but Christ gave a "new commandment" in the sense of
supplying the motive to fulfill the same old commandments.

> Another remarkable description which the Scripture gives us of a gra-
> cious love to others, which shows how contrary it is to selfishness, is
> loving others as Christ hath loved us, as in John 13:34, "A new com-
> mandment I give unto you, That ye love one another; as I have loved
> you, that ye also love one another." It is called a new commandment in
> contradistinction to that old one in Leviticus 19:18. Not that the duty
> of love to others, which is the matter of this commandment, is new; for
> the same kind of love was required of old under the Old Testament
> which is required now. But it is called a new commandment in this re-
> spect, that the rule and motive annexed, which we are now more espe-
> cially to observe in these days of the gospel, are new. The rule and mo-
> tive which was especially set in view of old was love to ourselves, that
> we should love our neighbor as ourselves. But the motive and rule
> which is more especially set in view now in the days of the gospel,
> since the love of Christ has actually been so wonderfully manifested, is
> the love of Christ to us; and so the commandment in these Gospel
> days, or the new commandment, is that we should love one another as
> Christ has loved us. It is here called a new commandment. So in John
> 15:12 Christ calls it his commandment emphatically: "This is my com-
> mandment, That ye love one another, as I have loved you." That we
> should love one another as we love ourselves is Moses' commandment.
> But that we should love one another as Christ has love[d] us is Christ's
> commandment. It is the same commandment which Moses gave as to
> the substance of it, with a new enforcement and light annexed. For this
> rule of loving others as Christ has loved us does more clearly and in a
> further degree show our duty and obligation with respect to our neigh-
> bor, than as Moses revealed it.

Interpretations of the Decalogue do not ignore the social and political dimensions of human existence. So a third concern is that Edwards is thinking only of salvation, bringing sinners to confess their sins, in the hope of being rewarded in heaven. What does this have to do with the other two uses of the Decalogue, the political and the moral?

Edwards would reply that "Faith . . . produces good works," and these good works include obedience to political rulers and establishing harmony between husbands and wives, parents and children, masters and servants.

> The truth of the doctrine appears from what the Apostle teaches in Galatians 5:6, even that faith works by love. A truly Christian faith is what produces good works. But all the good works which it produces are by love. . . .
>
> That love is an ingredient in true and saving faith, and is what is most essential and distinguishing in it. Love is no ingredient in a merely speculative faith; but it is the life and soul of a practical faith. A truly practical and saving faith is light and heat together, or light and love. That which is only a speculative, is only light without heat. But in that it wants spiritual heat or divine love, it is vain and good for nothing. A speculative faith consists only in assent; but in a saving faith are assent and consent together. That faith which has only the assent of the understanding is no better faith than the devils have, for the devils have faith so far as it can be without love. The devils believe and tremble. Now the true spiritual consent of the heart cannot be distinguished from the love of the heart. He whose heart consents to Christ as a Savior loves Christ under that notion, viz. of a Savior. For the heart sincerely to consent to the way of salvation by Christ cannot be distinguished from loving the way of salvation by Christ. There is an act of choice or election is true and saving faith, whereby the soul chooses Christ for its Savior, and accepts and embraces him as such.

Civil harmony comes from accepting one's station and its duties:

> "In lowliness of mind let each esteem other better than themselves." Love will dispose to contentment in the station in which God hath set him, without coveting anything which his neighbor possesses, or envying him any good thing which he has. Love will dispose men to meekness and gentleness in their carriage towards their neighbors, and not to treat them with passion or violence, but with moderation and calm-

ness. Love checks and restrains a bitter spirit. For love has no bitterness in it. It is altogether a sweet disposition and affection of the soul. Love will prevent broils and quarrels, and will dispose to peaceableness. Love will dispose men to forgive injuries, which they receive from their neighbors. Proverbs 10:12, "Hatred stirreth up strifes; but love covereth all sins." Love will dispose men to all acts of mercy towards our neighbor who is under any affliction or calamity. For we are naturally disposed to pity those whom we love when they are afflicted. This would dispose men to give to the poor, and bear one another's burdens, to weep with those that weep, and rejoice with those that rejoice.

Love would dispose to those duties which they owe one another in their several places and relations. It would dispose a people to all the duties which they owe their rulers, to give them all that honor and subjection which is their due. And it would dispose rulers to rule the people over whom they are set justly, sincerely seeking their good. It would dispose a people to all proper duty to their ministers, to hearken to their instructions and counsels, and submit to them in the house of God, and will to support them. And it would dispose ministers faithfully and earnestly to seek the good of the souls of their people. Love would dispose to all suitable carriage between husbands and wives; and it would dispose children to obey their parents; parents not to provoke their children unto wrath; servants to be obedient to their masters, not with eye service, but in singleness of heart; and masters to exercise gentleness and goodness towards their servants.

And in fine, love would dispose men to do to others as they would that others should do to them, if they were in their neighbor's circumstances, and their neighbor in theirs. Thus love would dispose to all duties, both towards God and towards men. And if love will dispose to all duties, then it follows that love is a root and spring, and, as it were, a comprehension of all virtues. It is a principle which, if implanted in the heart, is alone sufficient to produce all good dispositions; and every right disposition towards God and men is, as it were, summed up in it.

Although as a theologian Edwards must follow Scripture in ascribing the commandments to God as author and judge, and describe righteousness as pleasing to God and sainthood as the gift of grace, rewarded with eternal bliss of heaven, as a philosopher he describes the basis of goodness as "being in general, simply considered," and true virtue as love of being and beings. In this unity, Edwards argues, is found beauty.

Instead of part of the covenant of Sinai, a revelation establishing the faith, the Decalogue need not be considered but as a philosophical proposition about human happiness. The truth of the commandments may be translated from theological into metaphysical language. And therefore the subject is not only the scriptural will of God but the ideas, associated one with another, in moral philosophy. What the apostle calls "gifts of the Spirit" can then be critically considered as the fabric of human virtues. The crucial text of the moralist and aesthetician is: "Method, show how all the virtues are derived from pure benevolence."

The basis of morality in human nature is "the love of happiness." Edwards did not conclude from the fall that all desires of the human heart were excessive, because love of happiness cannot be too much. This love necessarily means love of one's own happiness. But to love one's own happiness only is too confined. For, being general, it is love of whatever is "grateful and pleasing," and we often find others pleasing. Therefore self-love should not be condemned. It is our nature, necessary to each human, and therefore common to all. "For it is undoubtedly true that whatever a man loves, his love may be resolved into his loving what he loves. . . . It is a general capacity of loving, or hating; or a capacity of being either pleased or displeased: which is the same as a man's having a faculty of will." What he means is to distinguish us humans as moral agents from "stones and trees, which love nothing and hate nothing."

Those who affirm "that all men are created equal" and have a "natural right to life, liberty and the pursuit of happiness" are usually not as clear as Edwards. His expression is that humans do not differ in degree to which they love happiness. "Saints and Sinners," for a Puritan the starkest of human contrasts, "love happiness alike, and have the same unalterable propensity to seek and desire happiness." This is generic to the extent that it is true both in this life and the next. He deduces therefore that the holy saints in heaven still love their own happiness. If this were not so, heaven "would be no happiness to them; for that which anyone does not love, he can enjoy no happiness in."

It is through the theory of self-love and of benevolence that the Ten Commandments can be assimilated into natural law. Edwards draws on the traditions of Philo Judaeus, of Thomas Aquinas and other Catholic scholastics, and of the Protestant Reformers who continued the natural law tradition. Indeed, it is remarkable to find so traditional a theory stated with such freshness and innovation. The divinely created and sustained laws include what Edwards called "moral constitutions." The principle running through both levels is causal regularity: a "new effect is consequent on the former, only by the established laws, and settled course of nature: which is allowed to be nothing but the continued immediate efficacy of God, according to a constitution that he has been pleased to establish." Scholastics had differed on whether the commandments and ordinances of the Creator depended on God's will, which Scotus argued against Thomas, who saw them as expressions of God's reason. Edwards neatly combines them, and although common or natural morality is called "immediate arbitrary constitution," Edwards adds, "When I call this an arbitrary constitution . . . I mean that it depends on nothing but the divine will; which *divine will* depends on nothing but the *divine wisdom.*"

Jonathan Edwards has been called the father of American theology *and* philosophy. In his double role as theologian of the Decalogue and philosopher of the Decalogue he resembles Thomas Aquinas in the high Middle Ages. As an American philosopher, he stands alone looking back and looking forward.

~ III ~

MODERN

16

Montesquieu:
The Decalogue of a Philosophe

M ore than any other single figure, Montesquieu represents the
eighteenth-century search for moral wisdom underlying the body
politic. He believed that by comparing various religious and moral codes
we could know which of them, in belief and practice, demonstrate greater
and which less good results. But no theory could upset the accommoda-
tions of time. This pragmatism is the method of the writers of the American
Federalist Papers (1787-88). In that regard Montesquieu's conception of the
balance of power in the three branches of government — executive, legislative, and judicial — influenced the founding of the presidency, the Congress, and the Supreme Court of the United States. To have made this contribution to a constitution which has served for over two hundred years
makes Montesquieu a father of Founding Fathers.

Baron de La Brède et de Montesquieu was the title of Charles-Louis
de Secondat (1689-1755), the political *philosophe* of the Enlightenment. In
the present context it would seem that Montesquieu's career was shaped by
the very difficulty faced by every act of interpretation. His efforts to state
his philosophy were interrupted by unpredictable events until he concluded that his philosophy would never pronounce a final program but
rather could offer an orientation which adapted itself to unpredictable
events in light of permanent principles.

Indeed, Baron Montesquieu reminds the reader of his great work *The
Spirit of the Laws* (1748) that he writes not as a theologian but as a politician. Although he happens to be a Christian, as a politician his question
must be, *which religion is best for a good commonwealth?* The purpose of religion is its usefulness: "Religion ought to humanize the manners of men."
It is easier to study different religions by studying how they teach the "vari-

ous duties of life," and to leave to others the question of determining which, if any, is "true." But it is not the case that he follows Pierre Bayle (1647-1706) in regarding all religion as false. Montesquieu seems to have been not a religious skeptic but a religious pragmatist.

Still, his approach may appear external and not that of personal conviction. Yet he appreciates the zeal of religious people; he believes *their true* religion couples well with love of country. Indeed, from the political viewpoint there are distinct advantages to the religious motivation of duty. Religious rules are not limited to securing the minimal permitted conduct, but rather to securing "not what is good, but what is better; not directed to what is right, but to what is perfect." Even without God's authority and a prophet's revelation, primitive religion guards society by teaching universal norms: "not to commit murder, not to steal, to avoid uncleanliness."

Montesquieu does not quote the Ten Commandments, but like many modern commentators (see chap. 18 on Jefferson), he may have been influenced by the decalogic model in his use of codes or lists of principles of behavior. For example, he cites the seven precepts of the Essenes (which, we note, resemble the seven laws of the Noachites). These precepts are:

1. To observe justice to mankind
2. To do no ill to any person, upon whatever account
3. To keep faith with all the world
4. To hate injustice
5. To command with modesty
6. Always to side with truth
7. To fly from all unlawful gain

There are also seven principles in the moral tradition of the Roman Stoics. For Montesquieu the value of these rules lay in the achieved results: "Never were any principles more worthy of human nature, and more proper to form the good man."

Here Montesquieu comes close to declaring his personal faith, but he does so in a hypothesis contrary-to-fact. "If I could for a moment cease to think that I am a Christian, I should not be able to hinder myself from ranking the destruction of the sect of Zeno among the misfortunes that have befallen the human race." These seven Stoic principles are:

1. To carry to excess only those things in which there is true greatness
2. To despise pleasure and pain

3. To be a citizen, a great man, a great emperor
4. To regard riches, human grandeur, grief, disquietudes, and pleasure as vanity
5. To labor for the happiness of mankind
6. To exercise the duties of society
7. To honor that sacred spirit which dwells within us as a favorable providence watchful over the human race

These two lists of seven principles express Montesquieu's civic religion. The theology is minimal. The creed is relatively activist — that is, compared to the religion of the monks. Montesquieu then not only anticipated the bicameral Constitution of the United States of America, he shows a harmonizing of various codes of mankind, and finds such codes in the several traditions constituting a pluralistic society. For Montesquieu a constitution was not a contract but a labyrinth. Society was the beneficiary of a range of laws — natural, divine, legal, political. The head of state was a ship captain negotiating shifting forces on the high seas of history. Finally, virtue is the quality most important in a democracy, but only if it is *political* virtue, that is, "the renunciation of oneself."

The Stoic ethic of finding happiness inwardly by "labouring for the happiness of mankind, and exercising the duties of society" is not at odds with Jewish and Christian morality. Echoing perhaps his liberal philosophy, Montesquieu says a religion influences the heart with its "many counsels, few precepts." The result of living within the boundaries of restraint is to "behave with gentleness and compassion to the unhappy."

From Montesquieu's approach we can draw at least six arguments for the Judeo-Christian ethical scheme, always remembering that for Montesquieu himself the benefits flowing from any such scheme derive from it already being in place.

The first is that a religion of the heart bridles the evil intents, such as envy and jealousy, covered in the ninth and tenth commandments (Catholic numbering) against coveting what belongs to one's neighbor. This argument extends to the various admonitions against hatred, anger, greed, lust, and revenge stressed in the teachings of Jesus. Montesquieu writes: "The Pagan religion . . . which prohibited only some of the grosser crimes, and which stopped the hand but meddled not with the heart, might have crimes that were inexpiable; but a religion which bridles all the passions; which is not more jealous of actions than of thoughts and desires; which holds us not by a few chains but by an infinite number of threads; which, leaving human justice aside, establishes another kind of justice . . . ought not to have inexpiable crimes."

The second argument follows from the first, namely, that breaking the law of God is to be confessed and the sinner is to seek divine forgiveness. Those who are sinned against are also to forgive the sinner. Religion of the heart

> is so ordered as to lead us continually from repentance to love, and from love to repentance; which puts between the judge and the criminal a greater mediator, between the just and the mediator a great judge. . . . But while it gives fear and hope to all, it makes us sufficiently sensible that though there is no crime in its own nature inexpiable, yet a whole criminal life may be so; that it is extremely dangerous to affront mercy by new crimes and new expiations; that an uneasiness on account of ancient debts, from which we are never entirely free, ought to make us afraid of contracting new ones, of filling up the measure, and going even to that point where paternal goodness is limited.

Montesquieu does not elaborate his ideas of repentance and modes of expiation beyond the principle: "Penances ought to be joined with the idea of labor, not with that of idleness; with the idea of good, not with that of supereminence; with the idea of frugality, not with that of avarice."

The third advantage in a system of religious laws, control of sins, and prescription of penances is that the more humans are restrained by religion, the fewer are the crimes to be punished in the civil system.

Montesquieu presupposes that what is a sin in religion is also a crime in civil law. "When a religion condemns things which the civil laws ought to permit, there is danger lest the civil laws, on the other hand, should permit what religion ought to condemn. Either of these is a constant proof of a want of true ideas of that harmony and proportion which ought to subsist between both." One example of disharmony instilled by a religion, such as among the Tartars of Genghis Khan, is not to "believe it to be any sin to break their word." Montesquieu's society depends on traditional prohibitions such as we find in the Decalogue. There is a legitimate oath against lying, an oath not prohibited by the second commandment and required by the eighth (Catholic numbering): "Thou shalt not bear false witness." Montesquieu writes: "As both religion and the civil laws ought to have a peculiar tendency to render men good citizens, it is evident that when one of these deviates from this end, the tendency of the other ought to be strengthened. The less severity there is in religion, the more there ought to be in the civil laws." This is the asymmetry between severity and relaxation between the two systems. But there is also a symmetry between them. "When the doctrine of necessity is established by religion, the penalties of the law ought to be more severe, and the magistrate more vigilant; to the end that men who would otherwise become abandoned might be determined by these motives; but it is quite otherwise where religion has established the doctrine of liberty."

Is this a reference to Calvinist or Jansenist predestination that might lead to such moral despair in one convinced that he is doomed to hell that he, discouraged, neglects effort? Several times Montesquieu deplores "inactivity of soul."

How church and state adjust their systems to each other Montesquieu does not suggest. Somehow a good society must avoid "laws which render that necessary which is only indifferent [because they] have this inconvenience, that they make those things indifferent which are absolutely necessary." The rhetorical balance of Montesquieu's style suggests something of the prudential balance of his thought.

There are several ways in which "religion may support a state when the laws themselves are incapable of doing it." One way is to go beyond the punishments of criminals under civil law: this is the punishment of sinners in hell. Hell is more useful to the state than rewards of heaven. Montesquieu writes: "The idea of a place of rewards has a necessary connection with the idea of the abodes of misery; and when they hope for the former without fearing the latter, the civil laws have no longer any influence. Men who think themselves sure of the rewards of the other life are above the power of the legislator; they look upon death with too much contempt. How shall the man be restrained by laws who believes that the greatest pain the magistrate can inflict will end in a moment to begin his happiness?"

It is then in the interest of government to support religion, which keeps people in a state of anxiety over their ultimate destiny. This would count as a strong argument in favor of Calvinism as the best religion for a state.

A way religion can support the state that is more congenial to secular reason, which has discarded punishment of hell along with reward of heaven, is its ability to replace war with peace. Montesquieu writes that religions in ancient Greece provided "the Eleans, . . . priests of Apollo, lived always in peace. In Japan, the city of Maeco enjoys a constant peace, as being a holy city. . . . Every year all hostility ceases between the Arabian tribes for four months. . . . In former times, when every lord in France declared war or peace, religion granted a truce, which was to take place at certain seasons."

Society is benefited by religion when religion can make peace between states engaging in war. States that exempt ministers of religion from military duty seem to recognize the need for a countervailing power. "When a state has many causes for hatred, religion ought to produce many ways of reconciliation," writes Montesquieu, again delighting in formal patterns of thought while eschewing utopian goals. When there is no form of reconciliation, feuds between families go on to extinction. This observation suggests Montesquieu would consider it an abusive religion that encouraged vengeance and provided no way to forgive past wrongs.

Religion may also be seen as useful to society by applying to it the pragmatic test: whether its principles may be applied in beneficial ways. "It is not so much the Truth or Falsity of a Doctrine which renders it useful or pernicious to Men in civil Government, as the Use or Abuse of it."

Montesquieu may well consider the immortality of the soul a true belief, yet those who deny it, such as Confucians and Stoics, may yet "draw . . . from their bad principles consequences, not just indeed, but most admirable as to their influence on society . . . [yet] those of the religion of Tao . . . believe in the immortality of the soul; but from this sacred doctrine they draw the most frightful consequences." Happily, concludes Montesquieu, from observing Christian priests, we believe they are a practical lot. Whether the doctrine is true or false, "the Christian religion performs in the most admirable manner."

Montesquieu's hypothesis is that ecclesiastical history is one of the successes of pragmatic reason. "When Constantine ordained that the people should rest on the Sabbath, he made this decree for the cities, and not for the inhabitants of the open country; he was sensible that labor in the cities was useful, but in the fields necessary." The degree to which pragmatic reason dominates is beyond the scope of *The Spirit of the Laws,* but the conclusion favors adapting a few principles to many changing circumstances: "It follows . . . that it is almost always proper for a religion to have particular doctrines, and a general worship. In laws concerning the practice of religious worship there ought to be but few particulars; for instance, they should command mortification in general and not a certain kind of mortification. Christianity is full of good sense; abstinence is of divine institution; but a particular kind of abstinence is ordained by human authority, and therefore, may be changed."

Montesquieu has no formal obligation to cover all the Decalogue systematically. He has given a method of considering the uses and abuses of religious rules. The criterion is teaching good manners. Obviously the third commandment (Catholic numbering), to keep the Sabbath, which means in Christian tradition to celebrate holy days, is part of decent civil life. And the fourth commandment, extended from honoring father and mother to paying respect to all in authority, is essential to this end. Without these there is no civil life of the community, no discipline in the family and education, and no six days of labor in the workplace.

Are there then no abuses of the rules of religion? When one studies the wisdom of the ancients, Plato's *Laws,* Cicero's *Offices,* and Philo's *De Decalogo,* one has high standards. There are admirable models, such as regarding "the man who involuntarily killed another [as] innocent" deserving sanctuary in the tabernacle, as Moses taught in his "laws [which] were perfectly wise," writes Montesquieu. Christians are human, subject to moral self-delusion, and typically hypocritical. "Men who are knaves by retail are extremely honest in the gross; they love morality. And were I not treating of so grave a subject I should say that this appears remarkably evident in our theatres: we are sure of pleasing the people by sentiments avowed by morality; we are sure of shocking them by those it disapproves."

Among the abuses of the church founded by one who drove the money changers from the temple are the clergy who use their rights as privileged nobles to amass possessions. When there are established abuses, these rules should be broken — that is, when priests are avaricious, monks lazy, and people superstitious.

Probably the commandment that has led to the gravest abuses is the one that forbids taking the Lord's name in vain, and which was extended to the prohibition of blasphemy. This was interpreted to condemn as mortal sin and gravest danger to Christian society the thinking, speaking, or publishing of anything judged by divines to be heretical.

On this point Montesquieu would deprive the church of the assistance of the state hunting down those who diverge from orthodoxy. "Penal laws ought to be avoided in respect to religion." The argument is interesting: the fear of God differs from the fear of civil punishment. To link them is to confuse our judgment.

However Montesquieu justifies his own professed Christianity, it is the judgment of a person coldly and analytically considering the pros and cons. The faith of a Luther or a Calvin is missing. The speculation of the Lord's lawful cosmos of Newton is absent. There is no beginning with the ultimates of justice and mercy in an effort to deduce the moral law. The theological and metaphysical dimensions are all subordinated to the calculations of use and abuse within the human scene of thoughts, words, and deeds.

When we ask after the first table of the Decalogue, we find only an appendage to his justification of the commandments of the second table. We leave to the end of our account what Montesquieu adds about the first and second commandments.

As for "I am the Lord thy God which brought thee out of Egypt, out of the house of bondage," the cool interpretation is: "When an intellectual religion superadds a choice made by the deity, and a preference for those who profess it over those who do not, this greatly attaches us to religion."

And what of "Thou shalt have no other gods before me" and "Thou shalt not make unto thee a graven image to worship it"? Montesquieu says: "We look upon idolatry as the religion of an ignorant people, and the religion which has a spiritual being for its object as that of the most enlightened nations."

What had been articles of faith with the Reformers, principles of the cosmos with the natural theologians, are, with Montesquieu, opinions of enlightened people. And yet from the distance provided by the disturbed twenty-first century, Montesquieu's opinions seem almost visionary.

17

Immanuel Kant:
A Critical Decalogue

The great rationalist Immanuel Kant (1724-1804) did not ignore the problem of radical evil — the evil assumed by the Ten Commandments. For him radical evil is the root of our innate tendency to prefer our happiness to our duty. To overcome this tendency we need God's help. In Kant's terms: if we *ought* to obey the commandments, we *can*. Ultimately, Kant argues that we can fulfill our duty only through God's grace, but up to that point he argues for the inescapability of duty. Doing one's duty is rewarded by happiness, but we cannot do our duty in order to gain happiness: our happiness comes by the grace of God. Kant's rationalism is not optimistic; it is a response to, rather than a supplement of, the necessity of faith.

This interpretation of Kant is prompted by seeing his philosophy in light of the Decalogue. He is most often read as a champion of reason. At first a student of the rationalistic system of Leibniz, Kant was in his own words "awakened from his dogmatic slumbers" by the shock produced in him by the skeptical empiricism of the philosophic genius of the Scottish Enlightenment, David Hume. What if pure reason, deduction from self-evident principles such as the law of identity, A = A, has no content, no reference to fact? And what if matters of fact, gained through the senses, have no logical necessity? How, then, is such a science as physics possible? Is the necessity of such a principle as gravity built on an illusion? How can one be sure that future cases of attraction between bodies will be directly proportional to their masses and inversely proportional to the square of their distance?

Kant's own system is based on a kind of knowledge never before conceived. It has content, and was therefore "synthetic" and not merely analytic (analysis refers to an affirmative statement such as A = A in which the predicate concept is contained in the subject concept: "all red roses are red"). Yet it was gained a priori, independent of any sense experience, and all minds can grasp it in intuition. The whole structure of natural knowledge rests on this foundation of the mind's categories. What is given to the senses must conform to this order. This discovery was compared by Kant to the Copernican revolution. Whereas previous rationalism rested reason on nature, for Kant nature rests on reason. As Copernicus argued that we could understand our observations of the movement of heavenly bodies as a function of our own movement, so Kant's a priori principles of human knowledge are a function of the limits to which our sense experience has to conform.

Kant grew up among Lutherans and believed that we have no natural ability to destroy the root of evil in our souls, and that the natural instincts, while not to be trusted, may be trained to serve God. But he also argued that "to claim that we *feel* as such the immediate influence of God is self-contradictory, because the Idea of God lies only in reason."

What then of the moral order? Traditional rationalism is based on deducing justice and benevolence from God's nature: what God must command as right for man follows from what God is. But what if the skeptical side of Hume is correct and we cannot know God? We cannot even prove that he exists, according to Philo, the skeptical character in Hume's *Dialogues concerning Natural Religion* (1779); Kant's *Critique of Pure Reason* (1781) continues to demolish traditional proofs of the existence of God. Has the moral order no knowable foundation? If man cannot know God, then the claims of Moses, Jesus, and Muhammad are, as some radicals argued, the claims of impostors.

As we have seen, the method of Montesquieu — to study history and anthropology and laws — might seem to be a sounder rationalism, since it is empirically grounded in customs and judgments and has ascertainable good or evil results. But a skeptic could quickly point out that by looking for similarities to support his presupposed Noachite natural law tradition, Montesquieu quietly overlooked all the dissimilarities. What is called "demonstration" is no more than assuming that the conclusion is true and illustrating it in interesting anecdotes that seem to fit, and then, having enlarged the circle, proudly claiming at the end of the process to have gained some new knowledge! To humbly admit to be professing a faith, with no evidence, would be intellectually more perspicacious and more honest.

Not everyone was as deeply involved in the methods of Newtonian science as was Kant, but almost everyone can grasp the implication for society of moral skepticism. One simple conclusion is libertinism: "There is no God, therefore everything is allowed." Minds raised on Montaigne's essays, such as "Cannibalism," recognized the extraordinary range of customs and judgments among mankind.

While theologians have sometimes felt the strong resonances between Moses and Kant, Kant scholars, for the most part, have not commented on the relationship between the lawgiver of Israel and the philosopher of the categorical imperative. Those who should know best, Enlightenment Jews who founded Reform Judaism, recognize the continuity and harmony. The clearest pages by Kant on the Decalogue — he quotes the summary of the law, "Love God above everything, and thy neighbour as thyself" — are in *The Critique of Practical Reason.*

On "I am the Lord thy God that brought thee out of Egypt, out of the house of bondage," we have Kant's statement of man's status as creature subject to a sovereign yet independent in the moral kingdom: "*Duty* and *obligation* are the only names we must give to our relation to the moral law. We are indeed members of a moral kingdom rendered possible by freedom, and presented to us by reason as an object of respect; but yet we are subjects in it, not the sovereign, and to mistake our inferior position as creatures, and presumptuously to reject the authority of the moral law, is already to revolt from it in spirit, even though the letter of it is fulfilled."

Doubtless Kant, brought up by a Pietist Lutheran mother, had heard at home and in church that "Love is the fulfillment of the law." So the gospel of Christ was contrasted to the law of Moses, supported by the text from Saint Paul: "The letter killeth, but the Spirit giveth life."

> The commandment of love is possible because it requires respect for a law . . . and does not leave it to our own arbitrary choice to make this our principle. Love to God, however, considered as an inclination (pathological love), is impossible, for He is not an object of the senses. The same affection towards men is possible no doubt, but cannot be commanded, for it is not in the power of any man to love anyone at command; therefore it is only *practical love* that is meant in that pith of all laws. To love God means, in this sense, to like to do His commandments; to love one's neighbour means to like to practice all duties towards him. But the command that makes this a rule cannot command us to *have* this disposition in actions conformed to duty, but only to *endeavour* after it.

This illustrates the unusual effort often made by Kant to be clear about ambiguous meanings. What we *like* to do need not be commanded at all. It is better that we do what we ought to do gladly, rather than grudgingly; this is called by Aquinas, as we saw, "the mode of virtue," and is usually attributed by theologians to grace, as in Luther.

Religious morality aims, Montesquieu pointed out, at perfection rather than at the good. Kant's observation is more subtle.

> That law of all laws, therefore, like all the moral precepts of the Gospel, exhibits the moral disposition in all its perfection, in which, viewed as an ideal of holiness, it is not attainable by any creature, but yet is the pattern which we should strive to approach, and in an uninterrupted but infinite progress become like to. In fact, if a rational creature could ever reach this point, that he thoroughly *likes* to do all moral laws, this would mean that there does not exist in him even the possibility of a desire that would tempt him to deviate from them; for to overcome such a desire always costs the subject some sacrifice and therefore requires self-compulsion, that is, inward constraint to something that one does not quite like to do; and no creature can ever reach this stage of moral disposition. For, being a creature, and therefore always dependent with respect to what he requires for complete satisfaction, he can never be quite free from desires and inclinations, and as these rest on physical causes, they can never of themselves coincide with the moral law, the sources of which are quite different; and therefore they make it necessary to found the mental disposition of one's maxims on moral obligation, not on ready inclination, but on respect, which *demands* obedience to the law, even though one may not like it; not on love, which apprehends no inward reluctance of the will towards the law.

Kant then continues the Reformers' emphasis on "depravity," which Kant renamed the "root of radical evil" in human nature. What we seek is the satisfaction of our appetites, and since we are not saints, or what Kant called "holy wills," the good will must *respect* the law of duty and restrain the passions. The positive commandments are to *respect* the holy day and *honor* one's parents, and the other eight are prohibitions beginning in Hebrew with "Lo" or "not." Kant's moral man is moral because he chooses a higher motive, which is to do what is right because it is right. Sometimes when we do what we like, or what pleases us, it is also the right thing, but it has no moral merit. Only when we do what we do not like, because it is right, can we know that we have acted as good wills. Only acting from the motive of duty has merit.

The counterintuitive quality of Kant's argument may flow from his concept of maxim. Maxims are general rules followed by rational agents in specific circumstances. Kant would test maxims by universalizing them — the categorical imperative — to see if they could be followed by all agents in such circumstances. But principles, such as we find in the Decalogue or the Noachite code, are stripped of circumstances. Principles assume interpretation according to given and unforeseeable situations. The distinction between the maxim and the principle may account for the flexibility of the Decalogue and the contrasting arbitrary or hypothetical aspect of Kant's maxims.

The critical rationalism of Kant defines the inner principle of the good will as freedom or autonomy. Sometimes Kant is represented as rejecting Judeo-Christian morality, because the tradition is theonomous as opposed to autonomous. It is true that God's law is often contrasted to man's law, particularly when it is declared that the sovereignty of God is opposed to the wicked ways of man. Man is sometimes said, as by Luther and Calvin, to be in revolt against the divine will. But by identifying the commandments of God with the dictates of conscience, theonomy *is* autonomy. If the will of God is concerned with human happiness, as Thomas Aquinas affirms, then to obey God is equivalent to fulfilling the highest needs of human nature. Particularly if the commandments are the duty side of the rights of persons in community, there is yet another way in which Kant's kingdom of ends is saying philosophically what Christian moralists say the Decalogue means.

The critical rationalism of Kant offers to fulfill the promise of the gospel to make plain the duty of man. The advantage of the philosophical version of the gospel is that it avoids both religious *and* moral fanaticism. By this Kant means that the good will cannot by virtue of a *militant* moral disposition claim to be a holy will. The pretension of a holy will is to be in "fancied *possession* of a perfect purity of the disposition of the will." The philosophic ethic avoids such hypocrisy, and does not "permit [men] to indulge in dreams of imaginary moral perfections." Kant argues this on grounds that are integral to Christ's teachings: humble avoidance of self-love and self-conceit.

As we have seen, the categorical imperative is the maxim by which a good will wills its acts. Another way of putting a purely moral question is: What act ought everyone do? In judging an act right, would I will that everyone without exception do the same? The only rational answer is "act only on that maxim which thou canst at the same time will to be law universal." This philosophical principle, within its own rather severe limits, is of the same form as versions of the Golden Rule, and has the beauty of form required of a test called "generalizability." The good will is good in itself, even if it accomplishes nothing, says Kant, like a jewel that shines by its own light.

Kant's principle takes two other forms. One brings out the autonomous status of moral law: "a principle of morality is binding if and only if it is one which I impose on myself." Another form seems formed on the model of "the kingdom of God," a purely moral community of wills: "Thou shalt treat all rational beings, including thyself, as an end, never as a means."

Theologians sometimes question the promises and warnings contained in the Decalogues cited from Exodus and Deuteronomy. Are these not extraneous promises? It is morally irrelevant for the observant and his descendants to live long "in the land which the Lord thy God giveth thee." Is it not compromising to the purity of a categorical imperative to add *if thou violate God's law, God will punish thee and thy family?* These are hypotheticals, and take the form, *if I do not obey, a curse will come upon me,* or *if I obey, a blessing.* While clearly indifferent to actual cultural differences such as we have accounted for throughout this historical study, this may seem good logical criticism. In the light of it, we find this celebration of duty alone: "*Duty!* Thou sublime and mighty name that dost embrace nothing charming or insinuating, but requirest submission, and yet seekest not to move the will by threatening aught that would arouse natural aversion or terror, but merely holdest forth a law which of itself finds entrance into the mind, and yet gains reluctant reverence (though not always obedience), a law before which all inclinations are dumb."

With a few simple changes Kant's moral philosophy can be adjusted to satisfy the usual Jewish and Christian criticisms. These are that it is purely formal, and lacking properly synthetic aspects of bonds to others in community. Basically, reason and duty and the categorical imperative are Kantian equivalences replacing faith and love and the divine imperative. That Kant's moral philosophy is a version of the Decalogue, with its summaries and principle of benevolence, appears more likely if we draw some parallels. Simply substitute for Kant's "good will" the concept of *the loving and forgiving, as well as righteous, will,* along with the concept that the right act is in imitation of divine justice, charity, and forgiveness.

Kant's critical reason aimed at an ethics that was "pure," that is, at the principle of a good will that does what is right with no fear of punishment for disobedience and no hope of reward for obeying. The good will is good without qualification. That comes close to the tautological self-evidence of "the good will is good." But Kant's good will is full of specific commandments, such as *keep promises* and *always, under any circumstances, tell the truth*. The content makes the Kantian conscience very like that of the strict Lutheran he was trained to be.

Although the imperative is not the commandment of the Lord, as with Luther and Calvin, God is still there waiting silently in the wings of the stage of moral struggle. Suppose a particular good will acts on the principle of the categorical imperative, but in this world, as far as we can observe, the consequence of doing good is misery. Is this the absurdity protested by Job, that righteousness is not rewarded? Kant's reason revolts, as does that of Job. There must be good consequences from a good life. With this certainty Kant's moral reason postulates a just God who rewards persons in the next life. Arguments for God's existence, from the order and purpose of creation, reduce to the ontological argument, which is circular. In cosmology the reason must remain skeptical of God. But in ethics, in the end practical reason justifies belief. Many Protestants have read Kant as a theologian who understood the meaning of faith.

⸺ 18 ⸺

Thomas Jefferson:
The Decalogues of a Civil Religion

"Every religion," wrote Jefferson, "consists of moral precepts, and of dogmas. In the first they all agree. All forbid us to murder, steal, plunder, bear false witness, & ca. and these are the articles necessary for the preservation of order, justice, and happiness in society." For Thomas Jefferson (1743-1826), as long as there is a core of moral agreement, the sects can differ completely in dogma.

Let us explore in greater detail how Jefferson came to his civic religion, which is essentially universal civic morality.

Jefferson discovered all the main points of his philosophy that bear on the Ten Commandments when he was young; he wrote them down in his *Literary Commonplace Book*. Even as a youth, Jefferson was a practical moral philosopher; he was less concerned with the history of moral ideas than with their power to shape the future. Contemptuous as he remained of metaphysical speculation, he was confident of finding true moral norms, the Creator's law made self-evident in conscience.

From the passages he copied from Henry St. John Bolingbroke (1678-1751), it is easy to understand why he was Jefferson's favorite philosopher. Bolingbroke drew on wide practical knowledge of affairs in and out of power. His brilliance as an orator and writer was compromised by his egotism and rakishness. For over a decade he was a leading Tory statesman; when George 1 succeeded Queen Anne, he fled to France where he did most of his writing. In Bolingbroke's view the monarchy must stand above faction and represent the nation.

Jefferson's *Commonplace Book* contains fifty-four entries from Bolingbroke, six times as many as from any other author. Bolingbroke challenged the young Jefferson to rise above the "vulgar notions" of sacred authors. Indeed, Bolingbroke presented this new morality as superior to the old because it conformed to the new vision of nature opened up by Newton.

Thirteen years later, in a letter to the Philadelphia scientist David Rittenhouse (1732-96), Jefferson refers to "the decalogue of the vulgar." The error of "the vulgar" is to believe that "man is . . . the final cause of the whole creation." Though this argument would never be made today, it apparently moved the young Jefferson. "I combat the pride and presumption of metaphysicians in a most flagrant instance, in the assumption by which man is made the final cause of the whole creation; for if the planets of our solar system are worlds inhabited like ours, and if the fixed stars are other suns about which other planets revolve, the celestial phaenomena were no more made for us than we were for them."

We may smile as we remember that Alexander Pope's (1688-1744) *An Essay on Man* (1734) was dedicated to Bolingbroke ("Up, St. John . . . !"), but we can also see why it was a good first course in philosophy. It taught the fundamentals, such as a warning against assuming that every word stands for some "phaenomenon." It gave the student the distinction between material substance, noted by "primary qualities" of "solidity and extension," and the thinking necessary for perception. It gave him the fundamental epistemological distinction between things known and proved as "self-evident truths" — things known a priori — and things known from perception rather than from thought alone — that is, a posteriori. It gave the student the common way of disproving a hypothesis, namely, the discovery of a fact that contradicts it.

For his *Commonplace Book* Jefferson chose passages which put philosophy to work correcting the errors of theology. First, belief in the devil is contradictory. "It is absurd to affirm that a god sovereignly good, and at the same time almighty and all wise, suffers an inferior dependent being to deface his work in any sort, and to make his other creatures both criminal and miserable." Second, God cannot coherently say "vengeance is mine, I will repay" or "I am a jealous god" for the following reason: "A monotheist, who believes that there is but one god, and ascribes to this god, whom he should conceive as an all-perfect being, the very worst of human imperfections, is most certainly ignorant of the true god, & as opposite to true theism as the atheist: nay he is more injuriously so." It were better for a person to believe in many gods than in a God having "the very worst of human imperfections."

Did Jefferson absorb the doctrine of the universal code of the

Noachites? He doesn't mention the Noachites by name, but the idea is clearly expressed: "The knowledge and worship of the one true god must have been the religion of mankind for a long time, if the mosaical history be authentic, and was not therefore confined from the beginning to the family of Sem, nor to the Israelites who pretended to be of it."

From the perspective of the religion of reason, to entrust the truth of the unity of God to one people "could answer no imaginable design of a divine economy, preparatory to the coming of Christ; since the Jews who had it, were not better prepared than the Gentiles." Here Jefferson subverts the biblical plan of salvation, both the Jewish and the Christian version.

Similarly, Bolingbroke exactly reverses the reported mystical experience of Pascal which is memorialized in the phrase "the god of Abraham, Isaac, and Jacob, not the god of the philosophers." The freethinking rationalist concludes that "the god of Abraham, Isaac, and Jacob, cannot be that glorious supreme all-perfect being whom reason shewed them, and whom they discerned with their naked eyes." Pascal regarded Israel as preserving faithfully their revealed truth; but in Bolingbroke's judgment the true God was among Jews "degraded into the rank of a local, tutelary divinity, the God of Abraham, of Isaac, and of Jacob, the god of one family, and one nation."

Jefferson learned from Bolingbroke that there are two traditions of moral thought upon which to draw: Athens and Jerusalem. This perennial contrast — or cliché — was by no means original in Bolingbroke. Jefferson held to the superiority of Greco-Roman classics from the time of reading Bolingbroke, about 1765, until 1803.

Jefferson's Classical Morality

Jefferson learned to distinguish Christian moral teachings from Christian dogmas. He copied out the brief table summarizing Christian morality. It distinguishes between the duties of natural religion and the duties added to it by two authorities: the gospel and the church.

Jefferson had no problem with the first class of duties, which is illustrated by the Creator's command in Genesis, "Be fruitful and multiply and replenish the earth" (Gen. 1:22). Since "'increase and multiply' is the law of nature, the manner in which this precept shall be executed with greatest advantage to society, is the law of man."

Jefferson questioned the connection between the law of Moses and the gospel. First, the choice of what is to be included in the canon appears to be arbitrary. Second, much of Christianity is tradition, and "tradition furnishes very precarious anecdotes to those who write at great distances of time, so it may become difficult, nay impossible, to ascertain [their] authority." Third, scriptural prohibition in marriage of incest or certain "degrees of consanguinity" had to be violated by the descent of mankind from one common father. Fourth, Moses gives an absurd account of the creation. Fifth, it is stated without qualification that crimes are punished in the afterlife, but in the covenant "the conditions of obedience and disobedience were not fully, nor the consequences fairly, stated. The Israelites had better things to hope, and worse to fear" than punishment after death.

The conclusion is that it is absurd as well as impious to attribute such laws to God. A millennium of argument has vanished. But if Christian theology was no longer alive to Jefferson, morality was necessary. If the scriptural basis had eroded and virtually disappeared, still the Greco-Roman tradition seemed solid and sound.

Not surprisingly, then, there is no commentary on the Ten Commandments from Jefferson, in spite of his deep interest in moral duties of very specific relations of persons to one another.

Jefferson's Christian Morality

Between when he adopted Bolingbroke's rationalism and when he rewrote the morality of Jesus, several momentous events occurred: the American Revolution, the French Revolution, and the rise of Napoleon. The events in France disillusioned Jefferson. In them he witnessed the incapacity of rationalists to replace the old order of throne and altar, which he as a republican so despised. Certainly his belief that progress in science would automatically produce progress in morals was shattered.

Certainly also came a new respect for the conscience of the common man: "State a moral case to a plowman and a professor: the former will decide it as well and often better than the latter, because he has not been led astray by artificial rules."

Although Jefferson expressed his deepest beliefs only to his close friends and concealed his views from the public, nevertheless he was attacked by the clergy as an infidel and an atheist.

In his early twenties his question was, "What propositions can I believe?" In his fifties, now a political leader, he had a different problem:

"What religion and moral code could aid in preserving the new republic and keep it from disintegration?" Jefferson's thinking had moved from his project to make himself an enlightened man to the problem of protecting society from degeneration. As we have seen, the idea that religion can be useful to the social order was reflected in Montesquieu's *Spirit of the Laws* (1748). Montesquieu, like Bolingbroke, was personally convinced of the intellectual superiority of Stoicism, and made a strong case that it had served ancient Rome well; but for a modern state, Christianity provided an irreplaceable system of repentance and penance, forgiveness and reconciliation.

Just how President Jefferson's position now differed from his youthful one can be seen in his comments on Joseph Priestly's "Little Treatise," "Socrates and Jesus Compared," in a letter to Benjamin Rush in 1803. There he argues that Christian morality is superior to classical morality. It's enough to make one think he had undergone a second conversion, this time not a philosophic but a Christian one. Which is not to say that he believed "the divine mission of the Savior of the World" or even that Jesus was "the Son of God." It was the moral teaching and only the moral teaching that he now embraced.

Specifically, his interpretation of the Sabbath seems to show that he knew the Ten Commandments in the Deuteronomic version: "He believed," wrote his friend Benjamin Rush, "in the divine institution of the Sabbath, which he conceived to be a great blessing to the world, more especially to poor people and slaves." Jefferson wrote to Rush:

> In some of the delightful conversations with you, in the evenings of 1798-99, which served as an anodyne to the afflictions of the crisis through which our country was then laboring, the Christian religion was sometimes our topic; and I then promised you that, one day or other, I would give you my views of it. They are the result of a life of enquiry & reflection, and very different from that anti-Christian system imputed to me by those who know nothing of my opinions. To the corruptions of Christianity, I am indeed opposed; but not to the genuine precepts of Jesus himself. I am a Christian, in the only sense he wished any one to be; sincerely attached to his doctrines, in preference to all others; ascribing to himself every *human* excellence; & believing he never claimed any other. At the short intervals since these conversations, when I could justifiably abstract my mind from public affairs, the subject has been under my contemplation. But the more I considered it, the more it expanded beyond the measure of either my time or infor-

mation. In the moment of my late departure from Monticello, I received from Doctr. Priestley, his little treatise of "Socrates & Jesus Compared." This being a section of the general view I had taken of the field, it became a subject of reflection, while on the road, and unoccupied otherwise. The result was, to arrange in my mind a syllabus, or outline, of such an estimate of the comparative merits of Christianity, as I wished to see executed, by some one of more leisure and information for the task, than myself. This I now send you, as the only discharge of my promise I can probably ever execute. And in confiding it to you, I know it will not be exposed to the malignant perversions of those who make every word from me a text for new misrepresentations & calumnies. I am moreover averse to the communication of my religious tenets to the public; because it would countenance the presumption of those who have endeavored to draw them before that tribunal, and to seduce public opinion to erect itself into that inquisition over the rights of conscience, which the laws have so justly proscribed. It behoves every man who values liberty of conscience for himself, to resist invasions of it in the case of others; or their case may, by change of circumstances, become his own. It behoves him, too, in his own case, to give no example of concession, betraying the common right of independent opinion, by answering questions of faith, which the laws have left between God & himself. Accept my affectionate salutations. Th. Jefferson.

Jefferson enclosed a copy of his *Syllabus of an estimate of the merits of the doctrines of Jesus, compared with those of others.* The cover letter saying that he had behind him "a life of enquiry and reflection" is credible. We know that his *Commonplace Book* (1765) had passages comparing Jewish and Christian principles unfavorably to those of ancient Greece and Rome. In the forty years since, he has learned to admit "the corruptions of reason among the ancients, to wit the idolatry and superstition of the vulgar," as well as "the corruptions of Christianity."

In his *Syllabus* Jefferson attempted to construct, as did Immanuel Kant (1724-1804), a religion and a morality "within the limits of reason alone." God is still there — Creator, Lawgiver, and Judge — to provide for the moral requirement that justice be done, if not in this imperfect world, then in "a future state." Both Jefferson and Kant sought a morality that was universal. Both had had difficulties with the commandment of love, yet their result is a morality of universal benevolence. In Jefferson's case, rather

than an abstract good will, there is Jesus' "moral doctrines, relating to kindred & friends . . . more pure and perfect than those of the most correct of
the philosophers . . . and they went far beyond . . . in inculcating universal
philanthropy, not only to kindred and friends, to neighbors and country-
men, but to all mankind, gathering all into one family, under the bonds of
love, charity, peace, common wants and common aids."

Jefferson partly overcame his prejudice against theologians by discovering Joseph Priestley (1733-1804). Priestley was a noted man of science. While his theory of burning or oxidation is not in a class with
Antoine-Laurent Lavoisier's (1743-94), he still has a place in the history of
chemistry (producing "dephlogisticated" air). As a Nonconformist in religion, a republican in politics, and a materialist in philosophy, Priestley
may be best remembered for challenging the alliance of Anglican religion
with Newtonian mechanics and constitutional monarchy. For the first
time in his life Jefferson discovered a thinker who was both intellectually
honest and Christian. From the perspective of rationalism, this would
seem an impossibility. Priestley was Jefferson's discovery of a miracle. It
may well be that Priestley was equally surprised to have found in Jefferson
an honest politician.

Priestley's *History of the Corruptions of Christianity* (1782) became for
Jefferson the "groundwork of my view of this subject," one of the bases "of
my own faith." The Protestant Reformers had of course regarded the practices of Roman Catholics as corruptions, but had not dared to suspect that
the creeds themselves could be so regarded in contrast to the original
preaching of Jesus. Jefferson had little idea of the difficulties of historical
archaeology, or of temptations to project our own ideal and mistaking it for
the original. The quest for the original Jesus was hardly distinguishable
from the search for the highest ideal morality.

If the Platonistic philosophy of one substance and three persons was
invoked to make Christianity acceptable in the third century, then why not
in the eighteenth claim, with the same motive, that Jesus was a reformer
who came to "teach men how to live virtuous lives on earth so that they
would be rewarded rather than punished in the life to come"? Then the
Trinity can be shelved as a historical curiosity, along with original sin, the
atonement, and the whole construction of theology. Jefferson went beyond
Priestley in objecting to the miracles of Jesus (including rising from the
dead) as impossible suspensions of the laws of nature. Otherwise he embraced Priestley's view of true Christianity as a religion based on the unity
of God and the primacy of morality.

In the year following his *Syllabus* Jefferson wrote *The Philosophy of Jesus* (1804). Later came a more ambitious compilation of Gospel verses in Greek, Latin, French, and English, *The Life and Morals of Jesus*. The former was intended to refute the attacks on the president by Federalists and clergy who called him an "infidel." The latter is known as "the Jefferson Bible."

The difficulty with finding a common morality for the new republic by using the morality of Jesus is that believing Christians, such as his friend Benjamin Rush, expected that if he said "I am a Christian," he must also confess that Christ was divine, the Son of God, and Savior of the world by his sacrificial death.

Whether or not Jefferson was a Christian, he developed a concept of order that bears analogy with the Decalogue as seen from the perspective of the natural law tradition. Jefferson himself cited the Pauline identification of the morality of the Gentiles as of divine origin (Rom. 2:14). In some statements Jefferson included three of the Ten Commandments: "Reading, reflection and time have convinced me that the interests of society require the observation of those moral precepts only in which all religions agree, (for all forbid us to *murder, steal, plunder, or bear false witness*)." In sum, if we count Jefferson's acceptance of monotheism, from his *Syllabus* his argument that the idolatry of paganism needed reform, his praise of the benefits of the Sabbath, and his emphasis upon the inner motive as well as the outer act, we can say his morality comprises versions of most of the commandments of the Decalogue.

In fact, if one checks the original ten, only three are missing. Clearly if "taking the Lord's name in vain" is put in civil terms, it provides a reason why he objected on frequent occasions to the calumny and libel to which he had been subjected. As for the first table duties, we have already seen examples of his reverent respect for the Creator. And "Honor thy father and mother" would come under his head of "natural duties." When he proposed being "a good husband and good father" to Elbridge Gerry, he added: "be a good citizen." Finally, among the great virtues he included marital fidelity, keeping promises, and fulfilling duties connected to his station in life. It is no wonder he did not live up to his own high standards.

The question then is, if Jefferson's letters and speeches are filled with moral statements so closely related to applications of the Ten Commandments, why did he not cite this as the code fulfilled in the simple precepts of the Gospels? Was it the association with Moses? He objected to many unspecified laws as irrational; we may suspect that these are ritual ordinances. He also shrank with horror from the penalties of Mosaic civil law, such as stoning to death, as prescribed for more than a score of offenses.

Jefferson could have observed the traditional distinction between moral, ceremonial, and civil law, which allows for detaching from the whole body of the law the Ten Commandments. The ten had often been seen as not only given on tablets of stone on Mount Sinai but also revealed to each person's conscience — with no judicial punishments prescribed. But while Jefferson had the works of Philo Judaeus among his books, there is no evidence that he had read Philo on the Decalogue, which would have reinforced the argument for the necessity of the commands to a good society. He could have stressed that Jesus accepted the Mosaic commandments and amplified them.

The so-called Enlightenment occasioned a certain amount of cultural oblivion.

Jefferson's Quarrel with Moses

Did Jefferson hesitate to subscribe to the commandments because, in conjunction with the creed and the Lord's Prayer, they are part of catechetical training, and, by royal decree, painted on tablets in Anglican churches? But then, in natural law theory only the moral commandments are considered, and Jefferson was committed to the universal law of nature undergirding rights of persons. To use the Decalogue would have completed his scheme by stressing the many "natural duties" he found prescribed.

The moral principle contained in Mosaic law, though not in the Ten Commandments, is "an eye for an eye" (Lev. 24:20; Deut. 19:21). Jefferson was convinced that *lex talionis* was not the morality of civilized persons but that the maxim of Jesus was: "Ye have heard that it hath been said, An eye for an eye, and a tooth for a tooth: but I say unto you, That ye resist not evil: but whosoever shall smite thee on thy right cheek, turn to him the other also."

Jefferson leaves no doubt whatsoever that he regards the Mosaic law as morally defective and a danger to American legal progress. We can see why he thought so. The first table commandments had been applied by the state to punish atheists and polytheists. Witchcraft was considered akin to idolatry and devil worship. The second and third commandments had served as a basis to punish divergence from orthodoxy as blasphemy, and to enforce peculiarly rigorous application of the Sabbath.

Jefferson even denies that the Ten Commandments had rightfully become part of the common law of England. He is then quite consistent in not quoting the Decalogue as God's law. It could not be a part of true religion, for it was the voice of a jealous and angry God. In his most extreme judgment, Jefferson recognized in the theology of Calvin the worship of a devil. For Jefferson to accept divine punishment of children for the sins of the fathers would have been to deny the truth that God is just. Each ought to be judged for his own acts. It was Jesus who rejected divine retribution and relaxed the strict prohibition of work on the Sabbath for acts of mercy and providing food, and who asked of those ready to stone the woman taken in adultery, "Let him that is without sin cast the first stone."

In addition to all these substantive reasons, there was also a matter of taste and style. The Decalogue was part of catechetical recitation, and together with heavy-handed clerical admonition without reason or wit, its use was particularly known from Puritan texts. Not that Jefferson did not want to inculcate certain commandments, such as "Honor thy father and mother." Jefferson argued that works of literary genius, such as Shakespeare's plays, can better create "a lively and lasting sense of filial duty [which] is more effectually impressed on the mind of a son or daughter by reading King Lear, than by all the dry volumes of ethics and divinity that ever were written." The writer of his own age most admired as a good moralist was Laurence Sterne. Just reading about an incident in *A Sentimental Journey* may move the reader, Jefferson believes, to acts of charity.

Jefferson's Morality, Both Classical and Christian

When Jefferson reads the moral teachings of Jesus in the Gospels, he finds "diamonds in the dunghill." Some moral imperatives shine as the authentic innate moral truths implanted in all minds by the Creator. In Jefferson there is a rationalist right reason that recognizes not only the virtues of a good person but the obligations to society and state, which are cited from texts of Cicero. There is also a theistic conscience that finds its pattern of righteousness in a sublime example of obedience to divine command. Jesus was the tragic victim, said Jefferson, of "throne and altar." Jesus' efforts to purify corruptions were misunderstood, and corruptions continued and multiplied.

It may seem arrogant for Jefferson to offer to correct Christian history and theory by constructing his own interpretation of the truth of the Gospels. He admitted often that he lacked adequate "information," particularly about Judaism, out of which Jesus came, Jefferson believed, in the role of a "reformer." Moreover, he accused theologians of constructing a system so complex and sophistical that the laity could not understand it and would need a priesthood to try to explain what it was. One of the difficulties encountered by those with conspiracy theories is that those who are attacked may attribute the attack to another conspiracy; indeed, the polemics of the enlightened and the clergy in the eighteenth century resemble the crossed monologues of communists and capitalists in our own century. By accusing sectarian theologians of disturbing the public peace and dividing society into irreconcilable segments, Jefferson appears to them as an anarchistic rebel against the divine moral order. But he knew that ideological harmony was needed in the new republic.

What, in the end, is Jefferson's particular contribution? Perhaps the least controversial, at least, is the work of his old age, statements of the virtues and duties in which the historical origins are forgotten or are too well blended to be ever identified as either "classical" or "Christian" or possibly some other sort. Jefferson justified the blending of biblical with pagan ethics by citing the same text used by the scholastics and the Protestant Reformers, Romans 2:14: "The Gentiles which have not the law, do by nature the things contained in the law. . . ."

The verse following that one provides a significant clue to understanding him. At heart, Jefferson was a moralist in the best sense. That is, he looked inward, consulting what Saint Paul called "the work of the law written in [our] hearts, [our] conscience also bearing witness, and [our] thoughts . . . accusing or else excusing one another; in the day when God shall judge the secrets of men" (Rom. 2:15-16).

Jefferson wrote out a list of moral rules that has achieved some notoriety as Jefferson's ten commandments. It reminds one of Benjamin Franklin's sometimes deceptively simple advice. If it were all we knew of Jefferson, he would not have been included in this study. And yet it does suggest his personal involvement in the decalogic paradigm. It comes from a letter to the son of a friend who had named his son in the president's honor — Thomas Jefferson Smith. The letter was written a year and a half before Jefferson's death on 4 July 1826:

A Decalogue of Canons for Observation in Practical Life
1. Never put off till to-morrow what you can do to-day.
2. Never trouble another for what you can do for yourself.
3. Never spend your money before you have it.

4. Never buy what you do not want, because it is cheap; it will be dear to you.
5. Pride costs us more than hunger, thirst and cold.
6. We never repent of having eaten too little.
7. Nothing is troublesome that we do willingly.
8. How much pain have cost us the evils which have never happened.
9. Take things always by their smooth handle.
10. When angry, count ten, before you speak; if very angry, an hundred.

These commonsense rules all fall under the virtue of prudential habits that an individual can test by observing good results. They refer to no divine source and omit any reference to Providence and heavenly rewards. Again, if they stood alone as the only decalogue of Jefferson, we should classify him as one who had used the archetype in a secular or humanistic manner. But Jefferson knew that there were "duties to God" or virtues of the first table as well as "duties to man" or virtues of the second table. In the same letter to his namesake comes a sevenfold version that resembles the laws of the sons of Noah. Jefferson might well have considered them "duties of natural religion" — and, like the Noachic commandments, universal and eternal.

1. Adore God.
2. Reverence and cherish your parents.
3. Love your neighbor as yourself, and
4. Your country more than yourself.
5. Be just.
6. Be true.
7. Murmur not at the ways of Providence.
   So shall the life into which you have entered, be the portal to one of eternal and ineffable bliss.

By making central to his code the love of country, Jefferson fitted the commandments to civil use.

Jefferson's Legacy

Jefferson's great contribution to American civil morality is respect for the variety of religious persuasions and evenhanded protection of the rights of diverse faiths, with the appeal to their shared moral principles. Perhaps the best brief coupling of rights with moral duties is in the First Inaugural (4 March 1801).

He addresses citizens of a country dedicated to "our equal right to the use of our own faculties, to the acquisitions of our industry, to honor and confidence from fellow-citizens, resulting not from birth, but from our actions and the sense of them." Then comes the religious basis, the virtues of a people

> enlightened by a benign religion, professed, indeed, and practiced in
> various forms, yet all of them inculcating
>   1. Honesty
>   2. Truth
>   3. Temperance
>   4. Gratitude
>   5. Love of man

People with these five universally accepted virtues can govern themselves. It is a kind of second table. Jefferson was a creative moralist, and one of his most brilliant contributions was to formulate a table of duties that are necessary to protect the rights of fellow citizens.

For a minimal first table linking human happiness to divine Providence there's this expression of hope, which, from a twenty-first-century perspective, may seem a little sanguine but which gives us an insight to Jefferson's inner disposition toward God as revealed here with the author's characteristic emphasis on happiness: "Acknowledging and adoring an overruling Providence, which by all its dispensations proves that it delights in the happiness of man here and his greater happiness hereafter." Perhaps Jefferson's high concept of Providence — notice the categorical optimism of "all its dispensations" — is what gave him the ultimate sanction to dismiss much traditional thinking.

Likewise, the theology of the First Inaugural strips the Mosaic first table of the jealousy and anger of YHWH, along with the punishment visited upon "children of the third and fourth generation," which Jefferson considered immoral. "I have trust in him who made us what we are and know it was not his plan to make us always unerring. He has formed us moral agents. Not that in the perfection of his state he can feel pain or pleasure in anything we do; he is far above our power."

And from a letter dated 1814 we can construct five commandments for Jefferson's second table, "duties to man":

1. Promote the happiness of those with whom he has placed us in society, by
2. Acting honestly toward all,
3. Benevolently to those who fall within our way,
4. Respecting sacredly their rights, bodily and mental, and
5. Cherishing especially their freedom of conscience as we value our own.

To conclude: a citizen has natural rights to (1) the pursuit of happiness; (2) his property and reputation; (3) his claim to good will; (4) "rights, bodily and mental to safety and security from harm and threat"; (5) and his "freedom of conscience." Others' rights are duties to protect and promote. Especially, as coupled with commandments, this is a significant differentiation beyond the better-known but more compact "life, liberty, and the pursuit of happiness."

The above versions of the decalogue show Jefferson the moralist reflecting on the biblical model in ways that draw upon his own private and public experience.

Jefferson Epitomized

The mistake in writing about the so-called Jefferson Bible is to consider only what was left out. What shines, as gems, are the moral maxims. If we arrange these in the order of the Mosaic Decalogue and number them correspondingly, the tables lose their sharp distinction and come out something like this:

1. "Thou shalt love the Lord thy God, and thy neighbour as thyself."
2. "Ye cannot serve God and mammon. Love the one, and hate the other."
3. "Swear not at all. Let your words be yea, yea and nay, nay."
4. "Sabbath is made for man and not man for the Sabbath."
5. "Whosoever shall do the law of God is my sister and my mother."
6. "Love your enemies. Be not angry. . . . Forgive. . . ."
7. "He who lusts commits adultery." "Let him who is without sin cast the first stone."

8.   "Give to him that asketh."
9.   "Judge not that ye be not judged."
10. "Lay not up for yourself treasures on earth."

Jeremy Bentham:
Blunt Critic of the Decalogue

A mong judges who have brought the law of nature and the Mosaic code of law before their judgment seat, arguably none has condemned them more thoroughly than Jeremy Bentham (1748-1832). This alone makes it necessary, to any general study of the Ten Commandments that takes rejection into account, to examine Bentham's argument with care.

Bentham is the founder of the utilitarian movement continued by James Mill (1773-1836) and his son John Stuart Mill (1806-73). The principle of utility was developed in criticism of the previous grounding of obligation in divine command. For Bentham the rightness of actions depends on their utility, and their utility depends on their consequences, specifically with regard to pleasure and pain. Bentham advanced many useful proposals, such as for a Panama canal and the freezing of peas. If he understood people to be seekers after pleasure and avoiders of pain, his idea of pleasure was not individualistic and endures in this formula for the goal of government: the greatest happiness of the greatest number. If he attacked natural right as a "fiction," he also argued that a statement about the intermediate ends of government — which may include equality — assumes an awareness that the perceived utility of a good depends on one's need for that good. There may be nothing "natural" about equality, but it remains an intermediate end of government.

Bentham's goal was to take ethics out of the realm of theology and put it into the realm of science. Whereas the theologian rested his claims on ancient sacred texts, such as the Decalogue revealed to Moses on Mount Sinai, Bentham would rely only on what is evident to the senses. Empirical method includes making inferences from particulars, "gathering," as he calls it, to arrive at general truths. Sensations are either pleasurable or painful: this distinction is the only basis on which we can say what is good and what is bad. Therefore we can use a principle of utility: what ought to be is what conduces to good, that is, to pleasure, and what ought not to be is what conduces to bad, that is, to pain. Considering two acts both of which produce pleasure, do the one that produces the greater pleasure; or, if there is an equal choice as to pleasure, do that which brings the least pain. Pleasures and pains are measurable units: clear decision can be arrived at by calculation. We can compare pleasures and pains as we calculate profits and losses.

It is not that mankind had to wait for this truth to be discovered until Bentham at the end of eighteenth century. Following commandments, according to Moses, leads to blessings, and disobeying brings curses upon one and one's children. But the truth, according to Bentham, had not seen clearly and separated from what is meaningless. His form of ethical judgment detaches the problem of the good and the right from any transcendental or metaphysical basis. It also detaches it from mere personal disapproval. No one is as clear about the assumptions and implications of the traditional view of happiness as is Bentham in his critique of the most famous of Anglo-American legal treatises, Sir William Blackstone's (1723-80) *Commentaries on the Laws of England* (1765-69). Bentham dryly called his piece "A Comment on the Commentaries." According to Bentham, Blackstone stated that articles of his system are founded in the demonstration "that this or that mode of conduct tends to man's real happiness, and that therefore very justly . . . the observance of it ought to be either commanded or allowed of by the law of the country where it has that tendency; or, on the other hand, that this or that mode of conduct is destructive of man's real happiness, and therefore that . . . the law of the country ought to forbid it." For Bentham this is the plain truth, and he accepts it. But Blackstone immediately goes on into the theology of natural law, which is followed by what Bentham designates as the mystery and poetry of theology and metaphysics: "The Law of Nature . . . being co-equal with mankind and dictated by God himself, is of course superior in obligation to any other. It is binding over all the globe, in all countries, and at all times: no human Laws are of any validity, if contrary to this; and such of them as are valid derive all their force, and all their authority, mediately or immediately, from this original." The first statement is clear to anyone who knows pleasure from pain; cause from effect; acts and declarations of one kind, allowed, and another kind, not allowed; laws of one country and laws of another country. But the second statement, about the law of nature, is mysterious. This higher law is without beginning in human history, universally binding, and without end, never enacted by any legislature, but that on which all acts of legislators depend for force and authority, and most mysterious of all, dictated by God.

The two are contrasted as "real" on one hand and "non-entity" on the other — "action and word." Bentham wants no fiction, only fact of "tangible substance." Bentham demands, in his test of making plain sense, that meanings be made as clear as "the nose upon a man's face." Now if Blackstone protests that God is not that kind of thing, then Bentham objects that the theological realm of the "sacred" is protected from inquiry. To "tread upon tender ground" is, as Bentham suggests, to commit blasphemy. The mystery is then wrapped in enigma. Reason is supposed to discover divine and natural laws which are universal and eternal; this is Adam's reason, "clear and perfect, unruffled by passions, unclouded by prejudice, unimpaired by disease or intemperance. . . . We should need no other guide than this."

But every man now finds the contrary in his own experience: that his reason is corrupt and that his understanding is full of ignorance and error. Because of Adam's fall, divine providence has given us a revelation of "divine Law, and [these doctrines] are to be found only in the holy scriptures." Bentham's use of Calvinistic theology shows that he knows the arguments well enough to frame a position against traditional natural law as too much a concession to philosophical reason. But Bentham does not take the problem seriously enough to notice that there are inner contradictions in the tradition of depending solely on "holy scripture" if the tradition also accepts that there is a prophetic interpretation of the law "written on tablets of the heart," and also a Pauline doctrine that "pagans do by nature the things that are of the Law." Finally, if Bentham had read Calvin as we have tried to read him in this book, he would have found that depravity does not exclude some degree of rationality, including the ability to distinguish good from evil.

In any event, Bentham cuts himself off from understanding his opponent and participating in dialogue. Indeed, he uses the standard objection of the twentieth-century logical positivist: all "leading terms, 'reason,' 'discover,' 'Law of Nature' . . . 'clear and perfect' . . . being unmeaning, communicate the same quality to the rest of us." The rationalists, even including John Locke, had always a bridge from mathematics and logic to ethical principles: as there are truths of reason, that A = A, so there are moral truths known analytically: for example, that promises ought to be kept. But

Bentham has pushed empiricism beyond any defense of a law of nature. His empiricism would use induction only, and he renounces deduction.

The blunt truth is, says Bentham, that a chapter of the Bible has no bearing on positive law — such human laws as the laws of England. A historian might object that Alfred the Great prefaced his collection of Saxon laws with the Ten Commandments from Exodus 20, that the monarch of Great Britain takes a sacred oath at coronation to enforce God's laws. But such an objection would only convince Bentham that there has been much nonsense in the past, and that much remains as relics of theology, now to be swept away. The appeal to tradition becomes a way of continuing uncritically the nonsense of the past.

Four Confusions

"Once for all" Bentham is to demonstrate four confusions of the tradition:

1. The impropriety of mixing theology either natural or revealed with jurisprudence;
2. and of natural in particular with either jurisprudence or morality:
3. to shew how absolutely unserviceable and indeed disserviceable the idea of God is for the purpose of solving any political problem,
4. and to represent the absurdity of jumbling, in the manner he [Blackstone] has done, things sacred with profane.

More recently, logical positivists have attacked "metaphysics," when their real target was theology or philosophy maintaining meaningful statements about God. This rejection of the basic belief of the Ten Commandments is most plain in Bentham, who deserves credit for the bluntness of his thoroughgoing secularism.

A few observations are in order. Revealed theology assumes that in setting creation in order the Creator legislates and has, because of his power, supreme legislative authority, which he shares with rulers. Thus the authority of human legislators is derived from that of the Creator, and the ultimate obedience to God requires all humans to honor and obey their rulers. Natural theology, finding from science that the world is orderly, reasons to a first cause of order: thus if man completes his knowledge, he must accept the analogy between physical laws like the law of gravity and the laws of ethics which govern human action. But the analogy has no bearing on what it is to obey a law made by a legislator. To break a law, in the strict sense, is to know that one may be punished for the crime. There is the sanction of hanging for having killed. We scarcely know the theological punishment in this life, and the punishment in another life is another fiction. While revealed theology does provide commandments, these are not properly laws unless the sanction is made clear. In the case of Deism, "What it may furnish is a *sanction.*"

Take someone considering murder. Three motives may contribute to prevent him from committing murder: one, the fear of being *damned* for it; two, the fear of being *hated* for it; and three, the fear of being *hanged* for it. The fear of being hanged proceeds from the human law. The theological sanction is said to add "moral guilt" because of "conscience," but this is something unmeaning, and "obligation" is mysterious, and as we have seen, "God" is a fiction.

The second of the four confusions noted by Bentham is not explained as well as the first. We must suppose that "natural in particular" means physical objects or things, and "jurisprudence and morality" mean the way men seek pleasure and avoid pain; the legislators make laws to sanction what men ought and ought not to do. In the former realm of things we are not studying the pursuit of happiness, and in the latter realm we are not contributing to physics. So it is "chimerical" to engage in the effort to derive by inference "the will of God," of whom we presumably have "no positive command." Such inference would result in nothing that "determines what is politically right and wrong." In contrast to the "natural" is presumably what Bentham notes in the Mosaic law, "the history of transactions from which moral rules may be deduced." What has he in mind? Probably Cain's murder of his brother Abel. The sanction was a mark upon Cain, and he was shunned. Without a statute made by a legislator, the rule is: "Don't murder your brother, unless you want to be hated and banned." This kind of customary sanction of punishment is ascribed to "the Common Law of all nations."

What is the "idea of God" that Bentham argues is irrelevant to the solution of "any political problem"? There is "the Will of God" as represented by the "subordinate human Legislator Moses," and the "Will of Jesus," "himself a part of God." The first, the "Law of Moses . . . had originally, the whole of it, an original binding force of its own over the particular nation to whom it was delivered. . . . It has still a part of it, a binding force, and that over all nations: for example over our own: but this no further than it may have been tacitly adopted by Jesus." It is "the Moral Law" that "is supposed to have been adopted and retained," while "the Ceremonial Law . . . is supposed to have been abolished." But Bentham finds "no division into any such two parcels." What he finds in the New Testament is ambiguity with regard to the law of Moses: "now speaking in favour of it, and now in derogation. . . . [This] would savour . . . of levity and inconsistency. It would seem not to be the discourse of a Legislator, much less a divine one." To make the statements consistent, the statements "in favour of this Law . . . have been thought to speak . . . of the moral: when in derogation . . . of the ceremonial." To resolve such ambiguities in the New Testament, especially with regard to Sabbath and circumcision, theologians have devised their own way of dividing commandments to be observed and commandments to be rejected or left optional. "This mark, say they, is the general or particular utility of the article, of the regulation in question."

The third confusion is that the "will of God" is useless in "solving any political problem" because we can't from Scripture alone find out what it is, and theologians resort to utility, the will of man, to resolve the ambiguities.

The fourth confusion is between things sacred and profane. According to the analysis above, the sacred is the confused, the profane is the clear. To show the confusion Bentham appeals to the judgment of "writers of our own Church [Anglican], the most orthodox and the most distinguished for their attachment to religion." For example, the eminent historian Edmund Burke (1729-97), who in his *Account of the European Settlements in America,* first published in 1759, considered the Puritan imitation of Jewish polity in New England. The Puritans suffered from a "contracted way of thinking and most vigilant enthusiasm. . . . [T]he first laws which they made . . . were grounded upon [the books of Moses] and were *therefore* very ill suited to the customs, genius, or circumstances of that country, and of those times; for which reason they have since fallen into disuse."

Bentham concludes that legislators should not consider theology, God, or anything else sacred when making law. "To act consistently they must take their choice — they must be either Legislators altogether, or Divines altogether. They cannot be both at once. When in the Senate, they must either shut up their Bible or their Statute book. They must either give up the notion of drawing arguments from the scriptures; or that of directing their measures to the temporal felicity of the state." Secularization of the law is further argued on the ground that revealed law could only be redundant. "Whatever Laws have been given by the Author of Revelation were meant by him to be Laws subservient to the happiness of the present life," and this is "an indispensable evidence of the authenticity of . . . such laws." Bentham here is asserting that he knows the will of God, which he had denied could be known. Perhaps he is using this assumption only because it is that of a defender of the old theological order. That is, he may be using the figure of speech prosopopoeia, by which one speaks as or for another person; and his original reader may have understood this tactic. It is then, however indirectly, "argumentation *ad theologium*," to show the theologian's incoherence.

The conclusion then is that "with the dictate of utility" the legislator has the one and only test of authentic law. "If conformable, that consideration is of itself reason sufficient for adopting of the measure; that alone justifies it: and it were lost labour to look for any other."

Rather than saying with the tradition that "municipal Law depends on two foundations," laws of nature and revelation, the utilitarian revolution is that law is a "matter of fact that depends upon experience, and is to be collected by observation."

Although Bentham's argument is now complete, he continues to expand his line of reasoning by pouring contempt on the theological and scriptural approach. By analogy to a Punch-and-Judy puppet show, in which Mr. Andrew "says the good things over again for him," lest any of them escape us, Bentham acts "as Andrew to our Doctor." But actually what is added as repetition enlarges our view of what the rejection of divine law involves about the idea of God, of human nature, and of interpreting Scripture. Each of these three further moves aims to show that the tradition is absurd. Our author invites the "gentle Reader" to stay with "the show." He promises first a more clever conundrum than was ever put in a magazine.

God

So far Bentham has referred to no commandment in particular, but with "Thou shalt not kill" he now invites the reader to think about murder. What is the *true unlawfulness* of murder? Is it that murder "is expressly forbidden by the divine, and demonstrably by the natural Law"?

Suppose, goes the conundrum, that only human law forbids murder and that God has not commanded "Thou shalt not kill," nor can this be discovered in natural law. "This being the case, murder you are to understand is not [truly] unlawful." And so: "The puzzle is, which to give . . . of two answers: that murder is, *when it is not* against *those* Laws: or that it is not, *when it is,* against a human one."

The argument is in pure deductive logic, on the assumption that the same kind of act cannot both be and not be lawful. Bentham shares the common assumption that a self-contradiction — that the same thing both is and is not thus and thus — cannot be true. So he assumes the same in the reader. Will you affirm the statutory illegality of murder, even though there is no metaphysical basis, or affirm the metaphysical legality even though it is against statute law? Obviously to Bentham the first resolution of the dilemma is correct.

But what is not at all obvious is whether it is possible that God and nature together do not prohibit murder. We have observed that Bentham assumes that God wills human happiness, and later we find him stating that the God of Moses is a "God of justice." It is incredible that a beneficent and just God would not express his will as "Thou shalt not murder." Bentham's definition of "murder is the killing of a man without any alleviation, excuse, or justification for it." Killing him is certainly bad by utilitarian standards, because usually very painful, with no pleasure at all in being murdered and cut off from any future pleasure. Therefore the assumption that God and nature will tolerate "murder if you care to" seems theologically frivolous, if not blasphemous.

Therefore Bentham has indeed deduced an absurdity with which to tax the believer in divine and natural law, but the cost of doing so is to make an absurd supposition.

Yet to be fair to Bentham's "conundrum," there are theologians who base their arguments on omnipotence. If God is all-powerful, then his will is unlimited. For God to be limited by what we think justice is and what we think consistency is, has no basis and is insolent presumption. God can do whatever he pleases. Therefore he could contradict all the commandments that we have been given and have arrived at by reason and experience, and the will of God might just as well be "Thou shalt murder, commit adultery, steal, bear false witness, covet." But Bentham is not a serious Scotist, stressing voluntarism, and not a theological Ockhamist, though he has many definite traits of nominalism. Based on his own disappointment in not finding systematic jurisprudence in the teachings of Jesus, Bentham's "conundrum" turns out to be frivolous.

An examination of Bentham on God is disappointing. Perhaps his attacks on false views of human nature show him in a better light.

Man

Confronting human nature, Bentham gives his account of obligation and conscience, or as he quotes Blackstone, *forum conscientiae.* We are therefore led to expect an account of why we are obliged to do what we ought, and why we are constrained not to do what we ought not. The discussion is called for because Blackstone denies that adding the punishment to the designation of a crime adds to the *"moral guilt . . . any fresh obligation in foro conscientiae."* In other words, the crime of murder is just as wrong intrinsically whether there is the sanction of hanging for it or not. We must, on this account, know that the act is wrong independent of the legal restraint.

As to its "superadding any fresh *obligation in foro conscientiae,"* to have such a bone to pick just now is rather hard upon us. I have seen a discourse of a hundred pages written upon this same single word *"obligation,"* to find the sense of it. A work of some repute and not wholly without its merit, except that it is rather of the largest, for what it had to do: being rather more of a Nutshell in an Iliad, than of an Iliad in a Nutshell. To this let me recommend the reader, unless the few words we shall have occasion to say presently will satisfy him.

"*Forum Conscientiae"* is a Latin phrase, shews a man's learning, and comes in very prettily, when he knows what he means by it. If *our Author* does, I give him joy. It's more than *I* do. What I know of the matter is this. If a man's fingers itch to commit murder, there are *three* sorts of motives (or of *restrictives,* if the term please better) proceeding from three different sources, that may contribute to prevent him: the fear of being *damned* for it, (no offence, I hope, to polite ears), the fear of being *hated* for it, and the fear of being *hanged* for it. Now the fear of being hanged for it is a fear that proceeds from the human Law (that is, the Law of the Country) having made it unlawful; having forbidden it under pain of hanging, having declared in short that he shall be hanged for it if he does it. Whether now these other fears only and not this are obligations *in foro conscientiae* is what I shall leave for those to consider further who may think it worth their while. *Obligare,* to oblige, is Latin for to bind. To bind a man to do a thing is to make him do it: to be the occasion of his doing it: to hold him fast in such a manner from doing its contrary, that he does that. As to the word *conscience,* and the use of it upon an occasion like this, we may have something more to say to it, in another place.

The next thing we learn is, as much as comes to this, that if we obey a Law that bids us *do* a thing, commit Murder for example, we disobey a Law that bids us *not* do it.

Bentham's position is then that there is nothing in human nature that motivates us to do good and right and nothing that restrains us from doing bad and wrong. There are only the words "obligation" and "conscience." But we do know the logical relation: "to obey a Law that bids us to *do* a thing . . . is to disobey a Law that bids us *not* do it." All we know then of human motivation is that we are restrained by fear, and the more immediate and the more painful physically — say, hanging — the more effective the restraint.

Is there any positive motivation in keeping with the primary goal of seeking happiness? Murder is prevented by "the fear of being hated . . . and the fear of being damned," but are benevolence and aiding life motivated by hope of salvation, by trust in being loved, and/or by the confidence of being honored as a good citizen? We follow "shalt not's"; and it is just as logical to obey the positive version of the sixth commandment as converted from the prohibition of murder by Calvin and others, "Help your neighbor." What of the important summary of the two tables of the law in Leviticus 19, "Love the Lord thy God with thy heart, mind and strength." (This is best known in the version of Jesus as answer to the question "Which is the great commandment?" with the addition, "And the second is like unto it, 'and thy neighbor as thyself.'") If this is the meaning of the law "in a Nutshell," as Bentham puts it, why is this passed over for many quite secondary and tertiary rules and ceremonial prescriptions?

Quite justly Bentham rebuked "oracles," such as proclamations of the prophets, because they are not applicable to statute law, specifically criminal law. Not to love God and neighbor is no crime. Jurisprudence requires a specific act against another person, which can be factually certified and for which a specific penalty can be prescribed and inflicted. Bentham's empirical method, following as he tells us the methods of Francis Bacon (1561-1626), looks to the material and efficient causes and rejects formal and final causes. It is with the latter that "superior laws" are concerned. "Only when we speak of this Municipal and Statue Law do we descend, from the craggy region of unintelligibles; and . . . get footing in the . . . territory of real and ostensible existence."

In summary, Bentham's methods are appropriate to his specific fields of investigation. But the price he pays is high: the neglect of subjects that require a different method.

Does the picture of human motivation presented in "A Comment on the Commentaries" do justice to the author himself?

Bentham's goal is to advance the utilitarian principle because it is "intelligible, . . . fundamentally important, and unquestionably true." His aim is to state plainly what is "real" as opposed to "conceit" and "notion," and to uncover the verbal trick by which expressing the mere fancy is made to appear as "a *tangible substance*." If we take our author at his word, all he says subsequently presupposes opposing fact stated in prose to imagination expressed in poetry, and this commonsensical pose gives the writer the character of an honest man demanding that others measure up to his higher, or ironically lower, standards. What he finds in Blackstone is "Galimatias," "unmeaning," "absurd . . . jumbling," deviation from "the strict and proper sense of the word Law." Does Bentham's account of human motivation allow a place for these high aims of telling the truth in a straightforward manner, with all that telling the truth involves? There is no statute law that a moralist and legal philosopher must be strictly honest, on pain of forfeiting all books of his library or some such appropriate penalty. There must be some moral principle, then, over and above statute law. There may well be a natural law that truth telling is as such to be preferred to deceiving, or truth telling is good use of language and lying is abuse of speech. Certainly there is the ninth commandment, "Thou shalt not bear false witness." No doubt a utilitarian could show that honesty on the whole tends to contribute to "general happiness." Even those who say there is no moral truth that can be known or communicated become angry and resentful when they discover that they have been deceived. But is it credible that telling the truth is only a matter of producing pleasures and avoiding pains?

Bentham, the man, has an intellectual conscience, even if he professes not to know what the word means. He has brought Blackstone's *Commentaries* into his forum of conscience, and he expresses outrage. Bentham's obligation to his reader and to his subject is not accounted for in what he says of not murdering out of fear of being hanged.

Conclusion: there is such incoherence between Bentham's theory and its own practice that we must conclude that his theory fails to give a credible account of human nature, including his own.

❤ 20 ❤

A Diversity of Rationalists:
Montaigne, Pascal, Spinoza, and Hegel

T he contrast between rationalisms supportive and rationalisms destructive of the Decalogue appears in a spectrum between the seventeenth-
century French mathematician and Christian apologist Pascal and the
nineteenth-century German philosopher Hegel.

As a brilliant mathematician and experimental scientist, Blaise Pascal
(1623-62) knew well the profound attractions of the spirit of geometry
which characterizes modern thought from Hobbes onward. Yet for Pascal
scientific reason was transcended by the reasons of the heart.

Though he became perhaps the most quoted apologist for Christianity of modern times, Pascal was deeply appreciative of Montaigne's fearless
and all-questioning skepticism. To appreciate Pascal's achievement, it helps
to know something about Montaigne. Michel de Montaigne (1533-92) is
now famous for his *Essays,* a book expressing an attitude of detachment
that considers all points of view (Shakespeare learned from him by reading
his book of essays in English translation), but he was no dropout. Contrary
to his wishes to enjoy his family estate as a country gentleman, he served
his region when elected mayor of Bordeaux — twice. He became an adviser
to leaders of the Reformation and Counter-Reformation. His was a time of
civil war fed by politicized religion. In one of his essays (II 19) he comments on the spectacle of warring Catholics and Huguenots and recalls the
anti-Christian emperor Julian: "He had assayed from his experience with
some of the Christians that no beast in the world is more to be feared by
Man than Man." Yet Montaigne also wrote this: "It is not believable that in
all this fabric of the world there should not be some mark printed by the
hand of this great Architect; that there should be no image in the things of
the world referring somehow to the Workman who built them and formed

- 196 -

them. He left within these great works the imprint of his divinity; it is only because of our weakness that we cannot discover it."

That is the Montaigne cherished by Pascal, who could see better than many modern readers of Montaigne how such skepticism served Christian faith. Pascal and Montaigne were quite different personalities. Montaigne's essays reveal a mind preoccupied with its own responses to the flux of circumstances; he accepted the wisdom of experience undogmatically. For his part, Pascal showed astonishing brilliance in mathematics as a youth and collaborated with his father on experiments which resulted in the discovery of the barometer and the syringe. He patented a calculating machine. He also contributed to the foundations of probability theory. He lived well in good society. But in 1654 he had the second of two religious experiences and concluded that his religious attitude had been too intellectual. He turned his astonishing mind toward issues of reason and faith. As in his several scientific interests, he made an enduring contribution, this time to Christian apologetics and eventually existential philosophy.

His most famous single concept is found in his posthumously published *Pensées*. Known as "the wager," it is a direct application of his work on probability. The wager is meant to draw the student into faith by noting that if one believes in God, there are two possible outcomes: if God does exist, one wins eternal life; if he doesn't, there are no winnings for anyone.

Throughout the seemingly fragmentary *Pensées* Pascal shows the interpretive power of Christianity. For him the choice is always between Christianity and unbelief. His *Pensées* raise skeptical arguments to reveal a paradox in human nature: such knowledge as we possess — and firmly believe — is always vulnerable to criticism.

In his thoughts on the Decalogue, Pascal embraces historical fact as well as paradox. "I see," he writes, that "the Christian religion is founded [as a fact] upon a preceding religion." Pass over the miracles reported of Moses and Jesus as unconvincing, especially at first. It is the morality of the Jews that is "the most ancient of all," and contrasted to "changeable and singular variety of morals and beliefs at different times." This great people

> worship one God and guide themselves by a law which they say that they obtained from His own hand. They maintain that they are the only people in the world to whom God has revealed His mysteries; that all men are corrupt and in disguise with God; that they are all abandoned to their senses and their own imagination, whence come the strange er-

rors and continual changes which happen among them, both of religions and of morals, where as they themselves remain firm in their conduct; but that God will not leave other nations in this darkness for ever; that there will come a Savior for all; that they are in the world to announce Him to men; that they are expressly formed to be forerunners and herald of this great event and to summon all nations to join with them in the expectation of this Savior.

What is most worthy of attention in knowing the Jews is their law, by which Pascal means the Ten Commandments:

I look at the law which they boast of having obtained from God, and I find it admirable. It is the first law of all and is of such a kind that, even before the term *law* was in currency among the Greeks, it had, for nearly a thousand years earlier, been uninterruptedly accepted and observed by the Jews. I likewise think it strange that the first law of the world happens to be the most perfect; so that the greatest legislators have borrowed their laws from it, as is apparent from the law of the Twelve tables at Athens, afterwards taken by the Romans, and as it would be easy to prove, if Josephus and others had not sufficiently dealt with this subject.

Pascal was a great polemicist, and he knew his audience in all its variousness (had he not studied his Montaigne?). His conversational style, learned perhaps from Montaigne, allows him to engage the reader's incredulity with expressions such as "I likewise think it strange. . . ."

Pascal interprets history within the framework of the biblical scheme of salvation. The scheme had two dimensions, first of the Jews as God's chosen people, the people of the covenant with God's law, and second of the Christian belief that out of Israel came the Messiah to bring the law to all mankind. Pascal accepts the traditional Christian philosophy of history, most commonly known through Saint Augustine's *City of God* (after 412), and believes we can know a necessary and universal moral code. But as we have seen, the seventeenth century saw a crisis, political as well as religious, of epochal proportions, Hobbes and Locke offering only the most famous political responses. Pascal's response was both more narrow and more profound. Today he presents a unique combination of the scientist and the man of arduous faith. Pascal's grasp of the state of mind shared by some of his readers is eloquently preserved in the anxious exclamation of the nonbeliever: "the eternal silence of these infinite spaces terrifies me." This image of human being engulfed by the immensity of space proved to be of remarkable durability, inspiring in the twentieth century the existentialists.

Hegel

Perhaps Pascal would have tried to arrange his seemingly random but no less profound *pensées* into a (more) systematic work had he lived, but that would not prepare the reader for the systematic though often opaque writings of G. W. F. Hegel (1770-1831), the high rationalist of the nineteenth century. Hegel created a philosophy of history that reduces the Decalogue to a primitive, tribal, and exclusive code of a superstitious Oriental people whose religion is "still very limited and unspiritual in character." His attitude toward Judaism went through several phases. It moved away from mere rejection of the religion of servitude, a position he held for most of his life, to an acceptance of Judaism as the first great religion of freedom. Then, in his dialectical fashion, he settled on Judaism as, yes, a religion of freedom, but one with a fatal contradiction (the divine as a national deity), and the laws of God as no laws of reason but rather prescriptions of the Lord.

The pages of Hegel's *Philosophy of History* (1837) show us a "rationalism" so very different in its judgment of the Ten Commandments that it is of the destructive type in contrast to the constructive type common from Newton to Kant. (This is all the more interesting because it was once common for Christian philosophers and theologians to consider themselves Hegelians or "absolute idealists." The most well-known American examples are Josiah Royce and William Ernest Hocking.) The passage in which Hegel gives his belittling judgment of what Pascal had extolled is written in the now infamous jargon of "absolute" and "concrete." Drawing on Spinoza's *Tractatus Theologico-Politicus* (1670), it is the clearest rejection I know of the view quoted above from Pascal:

> The Jews possess that which makes them what they are, through the *One*: consequently the individual has no freedom for itself. Spinoza regards the code of Moses as having been given by God to the Jews for a punishment — a rod of correction. The individual never comes to the consciousness of independence; on that account we do not find among the Jews any belief in the immortality of the soul; for individuality does

not exist in and for itself. But though in Judaism the *individual* is not respected, the *family* has inherent value; for the worship of Jehovah is attached to the family, and it is consequently viewed as a substantial existence. But the state is an institution not consonant with the Judaistic principle, and it is alien to the legislation of Moses. In the idea of the Jews, Jehovah is the God of Abraham, of Isaac, and Jacob; who commanded them to depart out of Egypt, and gave them the land of Canaan. The accounts of the patriarchs attract our interest. We see in this history the transition from the patriarchal nomad condition to agriculture. On the whole the Jewish history exhibits grand features of character; but it is disfigured by an exclusive bearing (sanctioned in its religion), towards the genius of other nations (the destruction of the inhabitants of Canaan being even commanded), by want of culture generally, and by the superstition arising from the idea of the high value of their peculiar nationality. Miracles, too, form a disturbing feature in this history — as history; for as far as concrete consciousness is not free, concrete perception is also not free; nature is undeified, but not yet understood.

We interrupt Hegel's *Philosophy of History* to note that the author chose to cite Baruch Spinoza (1632-77) rather than Philo Judaeus or Maimonides, who have far more — and more careful — analyses of the Torah. Born into the Jewish community of Amsterdam, Spinoza was excommunicated when he was twenty-four. He kept a low profile for the balance of his forty-five years. Spinoza redefined the study of the Bible as a science, God as nature, prophecy as fantasy, miracles as delusions, Christ as a man. Justice and charity, he said, are all that is required by scriptural writers for salvation; popular religion may well continue this tradition while the philosophically minded will have seen that justice and charity are simply essential to human happiness. Recognized as well versed in the writings of Moses and the prophets (he composed a Hebrew grammar), Spinoza was also widely attacked as an atheist. As a rationalist philosopher, unlike Pascal he attempted to reduce philosophy to the order of geometry. His career and writings offer a convenient turning point after which the philosophical interpretation of the Ten Commandments becomes subject to questions of scientific or historical method.

Perhaps Hegel is following up Spinoza's argument that God is the only substance when he finds in Moses' teaching an excellent beginning point: the "oneness" of God. In the Mosaic tradition this point is stated in the Shema, a Hebrew text consisting of three passages from the Pentateuch and often coupled, as in Jesus' teaching, with the commandments: "Hear, O Israel, thy God, the Lord is One." Hegel writes:

> As among the Zoroastrians, abstract being [became] an object for consciousness, but it was that of sensuous intuition — as light. But the idea of light has at this stage advanced to that of "Jehovah" — the *purely One*. Spirit descends into the depths of its own being, and recognizes the abstract fundamental principle as the spiritual. Nature, which in the East is the primary and fundamental existence, is now depressed to the condition of creature; spirit now occupies the first place. God is known as the creator of all men, as he is of all nature, and as absolute causality generally.

For Hegel, had Moses reasoned correctly — as Hegel himself, of course, does — he would have mediated a covenant between the one spirit and all human spirits, and not merely with a tribe. The fault is the incoherence of "*exclusive* unity." Hegel's first commandment, in Jewish numbering, includes the identification "I am the Lord thy God which brought thee out of Egypt, out of the house of bondage." In Hegel's words, "The God of the Jewish people is the God only of Abraham and his seed: national individuality and a special local worship are involved in such a conception of deity."

Hegel's second commandment follows: "Thou shalt have no other gods before me." Hegel's comment is: "Before him all other gods are false: moreover the distinction between 'true' and 'false' is quite abstract; for as regards the false god, not a ray of the divine is supposed to shine into them." This is most interesting both religiously and philosophically. Let us consider specifically whether Moses erred in rejecting totally the worship of the golden calf. If the bull symbolizes male strength and the cow female fecundity and nurturing flow of milk, can these not convey the idea of creative bounty? To be a good Hegelian, Moses should have explained that the idolatrous Canaanites were not totally wrong. Only that there is more to the absolute spirit than what sexual power and fecundity can convey. Indeed, Moses fails completely to be a sympathetic student of religion of Egypt and Palestine! The iconoclastic prophets, in Moses' train, denied people the use of physical symbols, and Hegel might well claim that his own approach came historically out of the Lutheran continuity from Catholic reconciliation of the worship of the One with an infinity of partial symbols. Hegel asserts that

Every form of spiritual force, and *a fortiori* every religion is of such a nature, that whatever be its peculiar character, an affirmative element is necessarily contained in it. However erroneous a religion may be, it possesses truth, although in a mutilated phase. In every religion there is a divine presence, a divine relation; and a philosophy of history has to seek out the spiritual element even in the most imperfect forms. But it does not follow that because it is a religion, it is therefore *good*. We must not fall into the lax conception that the content is of no importance but only the form. This latitudinarian tolerance the Jewish religion does not admit, being absolutely exclusive.

At this point, if Pascal were allowed the briefest interruption from within the scriptural tradition, he might ask, "How, if Judaism is 'absolutely exclusive,' could the prophet Isaiah foretell a Messiah for all nations?" Hegel interprets from outside the long tradition, and so seems our contemporary.

Does Hegel follow with comments on "Thou shalt not take the name of the Lord thy God in vain"? I think he couples this with Jesus' comments "Swear not at all, neither by God nor his handiwork" and "Let thy yea be yea, and thy nay nay." "In virtue of the prevailing spirituality the sensuous and immoral are no longer privileged, but disparaged as ungodliness. Only the One-Spirit — the nonsensuous — is the truth; Thought exists free for itself, and true morality and righteousness can now make their appearance; for God is honoured by righteousness, and right-doing is 'walking in the way of the Lord.'"

The commandment to "Honor thy father and thy mother" is called *the commandment with promise* because of the happy prospect "that thy days may be long in the land which the Lord thy God giveth thee." Hegel's comment on the reward of righteous "walking in the way of the Lord" is: "with this is conjoined happiness, life, and temporal prosperity as its reward: for it is said: 'that thou mayest live long in the land.' Here too we have the possibility of a *historical* view; for the understanding has become prosaic; putting the limited and circumscribed in its proper place, and comprehending it as the form proper to finite existence: Men are regarded as individuals, not as incarnations of God; sun as sun, mountains as mountains — not as possessing spirit and will."

The fifth commandment, "Remember the Sabbath to keep it holy," is doubtless the "severe religious ceremonial" mentioned in Hegel's remarks on what he thinks Judaism shortchanges: "particular concrete individuality."

We observe among this people a severe religious ceremonial, expressing a relation to pure thought. The individual as concrete does not become free, because the absolute itself is not comprehended as *concrete* spirit; since spirit still appears posited as non-spiritual — destitute of its proper characteristics. It is true that subjective feeling is manifest — the pure heart, repentance, devotion; but the particular concrete individuality has not become objective to itself in the absolute. It therefore remains closely bound to the observance of ceremonies and of the law the basis of which latter is pure freedom in its abstract form.

The sixth commandment, "Thou shalt not commit adultery," is only very generally considered, and possibly coupled with "Thou shalt not covet thy neighbor's wife," the ninth commandment. "[I]n Judaism the *individual* is not respected, the *family* has inherent value; for the worship of Jehovah is attached to the family, and consequently viewed as a substantial existence." And: "The family became a great nation" with heroes, and later kings, such as David, defending independence and even making conquests. Indeed, "Originally the legislation is adapted to a family only."

Hegel may well have thought the careful reader could see that he was providing a running commentary on the commandments, and thinking of "Thou shalt not kill," "Thou shalt not steal," "Thou shalt not bear false witness," and "Thou shalt not covet thy neighbor's house" as providing protection of the lives of family members, together with their property and reputation.

Once again Pascal might interrupt: "If the individual has no respect, why are the commandments addressed to 'thou' rather than to 'you, the family'?"

Since his final objection to the Decalogue is that it was formulated before there came to be a Jewish state, it may be that Hegel was rejecting or simply ignoring the commandment of the Noachite law to set up a system of courts of justice. Hegel does not refer to Moses as a lawgiver who devised a system of judges over divisions of the people. Did he regard these passages from Exodus as written much later and read back into the story to give it the authority of Moses' name?

In considering Kant's relation to his dogmatic predecessors, such as Newton, we used Kant's own metaphor for what had happened in history: a Copernican revolution. The metaphor applies just as well to the contrast between Pascal and Hegel. Should we read history within the divine plan to bring humanity under the Ten Commandments, or read the Ten Commandments as an incident within empirical history? Traditional rationalism had moral standards which are absolute, but for Hegel's dialectical rationalism of spirit, as for its successor, the dialectical materialism of Marx, these moral standards are relative. But this is only a formal difference in the status of a moral judgment. With Pascal we can hope for no moral truth beyond such a command as "Thou shalt not bear false witness." Humanity, with Pascal, is subject to a higher law, not of its own making, and not subject to change; but with Hegel the commandment belongs to a primitive stage of development, and the process is one of human development in which spirit manifests itself. Pascal identifies himself with Israel with whom the Lord made an everlasting covenant, extended by Christ to all humanity. Hegel regards Israel as a tribal people of the Oriental world, with a few glimmerings of the universal conception of the Absolute which our modern world now has discovered thanks to Hegel himself.

When Pascal reads "Thou shalt not bear false witness," it is he who is the "Thou" addressed by deity. When Hegel reads the prohibition, it is some other, Jew or Christian, who believes that "false witness" is taboo in his tribe and culture.

In contrast to Pascal, Hegel has provided us a very fine introduction to various appeals of reason that seem to elevate the reader beyond the reach of the Ten Commandments.

∽ 21 ∽

Nietzsche and After:
The Lastingness of the Ten Commandments

From the seventeenth century onward, the tradition of the Decalogue was challenged by the modern subject or consciousness, thinking, judging, nothing if not *critical*. The Ten Commandments were a lightning rod for modern philosophers. Indeed, a text, as well as a person, is often best known by its enemies. Perhaps the most vociferous rejection of the Ten Commandments comes from Friedrich Nietzsche (1844-1900). The influence of Nietzsche on twentieth-century thought is incalculable.

Nietzsche famously said: "God is dead. God remains dead. And we have killed him." In support of this statement we may now point to the Holocaust, the systematic extermination of six million Jews by the Nazis. Indeed, since the Holocaust took place in Christian Europe, and Christians participated in the murder of millions of Jews at Auschwitz and other death camps, it would indeed appear that the murder of God — and by God Nietzsche meant the God of Moses — had become a reason of state, a Christian, indeed a Lutheran, state.

We have seen how the Ten Commandments influenced Luther's thinking about the role of citizens in the state. The support of the state in the Lutheran tradition was tested by the Holocaust. For Dietrich Bonhoeffer, the German theologian imprisoned and eventually executed for plotting against Hitler, there came a point in history "where the exact observance of a formal law of a state . . . suddenly finds itself in violent conflict with the ineluctable necessities of the lives of men."

Let us turn to Nietzsche as our guide to modern autonomy. He may seem to contradict himself, but he is never dull.

Nietzsche was a prophet of the new scientific culture. In his book *Human, All Too Human* he wrote: "Since the belief that a God directs the fate of the world has disappeared . . . mankind itself must set up oecumenical goals embracing the entire earth . . . if mankind is not to destroy itself through the conscious possession of such universal rule, it must first of all attain to an unprecedented *knowledge of the preconditions of culture* as a scientific standard for oecumenical goals. Herein lies the tremendous task facing the great spirits of the coming century." These words read ironically now. Great spirits of modern times — one need mention only Karl Marx — did indeed endeavor to set up universal "goals" in the absence of God, but precisely because of the refusal to recognize the Judeo-Christian tradition, as embodied in the Decalogue, these goals have not met the test of time.

Once morality lost the interpretive contexts supplied by the exegetical tradition of the Ten Commandments, it was subject to novel interpretive contexts. Nietzsche believed morality served the will to power. In a passage in *The Gay Science* he explores the new conception of virtues as "drives" and the ironic praise bestowed on such virtue by one's associates.

> A person's virtues are called *good,* not with regard to the effects they produce for him himself, but with regard to the effects we suppose they will produce for us and for society — praise of virtue has always been very little "selfless," very little "unegoistic"! For otherwise it must have been seen that virtues (such as industriousness, obedience, chastity, piety, justness) are mostly *injurious* to their possessors, as drives which rule in them too fervently and demandingly and will in no way allow reason to hold them in equilibrium with the other drives. If you possess a virtue, a real whole virtue (and not merely a puny drive towards a virtue!) — you are its *victim!* But that precisely is why your neighbour praises your virtue! . . . Praise of the selfless, sacrificing, virtuous — that is to say, of those who do not expend all their strength and reason on *their own* preservation, evolution, elevation, advancement, amplification of their power, but who live modestly and thoughtlessly, perhaps even indifferently or ironically in regard to themselves — this praise is in any event not a product of the spirit of selflessness! One's "neighbor" praises selflessness because *he derives advantage from it!* . . . Herewith is indicated the fundamental contradiction of that morality which is precisely today held in such high esteem: the *motives* for this morality stand in antithesis to its *principle!* That with which this morality wants to prove itself it refutes by its criterion of the moral!

As a prophet of hypocrisy, such as that which led to the Christian counte-nancing of the Holocaust, Nietzsche is unique. By the scientific spirit of his pronouncements he illustrates the limitations of his own self-criticism. And yet through the art of his style — which makes such passages end-lessly fascinating — he escapes somewhat the horizon of his own scientific point of view. Sometimes the very acuity of his remarks becomes transpar-ent for a truth he could not recognize. From *Human, All Too Human:* "A prohibition whose reason we do not understand or admit is not only for the obstinate man but also for the man thirsty for knowledge almost the in-junction: let us put it to the test, so as to learn *why* this prohibition exists. Moral prohibitions such as those of the Decalogue are suitable only for ages when reason is subjugated: nowadays a prohibition 'thou shalt not kill,' 'thou shalt not commit adultery,' presented without reasons, would pro-duce a harmful rather than a beneficial effect." As we have seen throughout this study, the ongoing interpretation of the Decalogue within the Judeo-Christian tradition, starting with the Pentateuch itself, strips this insight of its power. The "obstinate" and the "thirsty" man have long been welcome in the long conversation that is the tradition of the Decalogue. In the decalogic tradition the prohibitions are not presented "without reasons": the reasons constitute the tradition.

It seems Nietzsche could hit on truths that have great interpretive power of the very phenomena he rejected as passé. In *Beyond Good and Evil* we read:

> The essential thing "in heaven and upon earth" seems, to say it again, to be a protracted *obedience* in *one* direction: from out of that there al-ways emerges and has always emerged in the long run something for the sake of which it is worthwhile to live on earth, for example virtue, art, music, reason, spirituality — something transfiguring, refined, mad and divine. . . . "Thou shalt obey someone and for a long time: *oth-erwise* thou shalt perish and lose all respect for thyself" — this seems to me to be nature's imperative, which is, to be sure, neither "categorical," as old Kant demanded it should be (hence the "otherwise" —), nor ad-dressed to the individual (what do individuals matter to nature), but to peoples, races, ages, classes, and above all to the entire animal "man," to *mankind.*

In such passages Nietzsche speaks truer than he could have possibly known. His contempt for "individuals" must derive from his penetration of the problem of modern autonomy. It's as if he had just said, "In the beginning was the law."

And yet Nietzsche was very much a child of his scientific and optimistic age. In contrast to "life-affirmation" and the will to power, he understood the power of meekness as ressentiment. In *The Antichrist* he wrote of "Judaeo-Christian morality":

> To be able to reject all that represents the *ascending* movement of life, well-constitutedness, power, beauty, self-affirmation on earth, the instinct of *ressentiment* here become genius had to invent *another* world from which that *life-affirmation* would appear evil, reprehensible as such. Considered psychologically, the Jewish nation is a nation of the toughest vital energy which, placed in impossible circumstances, voluntarily, from the profoundest shrewdness in self-preservation, took the side of all *décadence* instincts — *not* as being dominated by them but because it divined in them a power by means of which one can prevail *against* the world.

In the end, it must be said that this great prophet of modernity, Friedrich Nietzsche, formulated as no one else a basic freedom that many now assume to be their inalienable right. This is the freedom to invent for oneself a new morality. "Each one of us should devise *his own* virtue, *his own* categorical imperative. A people perishes if it mistakes *his own* duty for the concept of duty in general."

Nietzsche's aim was to form a morality that was autonomous. Each reasoner prescribes a law for himself. His moral freedom is to be subject to no other will but his own. Nietzsche would not have said that each of us can and should be his own Moses, for the Mosaic Decalogue was part of a covenant in which God commands. According to Nietzsche, for man to obey violates freedom: this is to be subject to another, and this morality must be of the inferior sort, "heteronomous." The contemporary conversation includes some modern Protestant theologians who dispute Kant, and argue that the divine commandments of Moses and of Jesus are "theonomous," and although sanctioned by the divine, are more perfectly suited to the human condition than is Kant's autonomous categorical imperative.

But Nietzsche makes categorical imperatives unique to each individual, while Kant assumed universality; that is, as each mind arrived at the same logic as Aristotle's syllogistic, and at the same geometry as Euclid's system, so it would come to the same moral principle as Kant's ethics.

How is it that Nietzsche can be so contemptuous of the universal, of "duty in general"? Ordinary people are typified as "tradesmen," and general commandments such as "Thou shalt not steal" are formulated to protect the wares of one greedy tradesman from another, or from thieving customers. So, in *The Genealogy of Morals*, Nietzsche condemns the whole of traditional morality as nothing more than the prudence of shopkeepers: "The feeling of 'ought,' of personal obligation . . . has had . . . its origin in the oldest and most original personal relationship that there is, the relation between buyer and seller, creditor and owner: here it was that individual confronted individual, and that individual matched himself against individual. There has not yet been found a grade of civilization so low, as has not manifest some trace of this relationship."

Nietzsche is a great prophet of modernity. He foretold the moral anarchy we now enjoy. By attacking traditional morality he forces us to explore the tradition, and this we have begun to do. At the same time, this book would lack point if the modern "antitradition" had nothing to learn from the decalogic tradition.

The Realism of the Ten Commandments

The traditional decalogic philosophy is based on realism about human nature. Even before the fall of man, the gratitude of the first perfect woman and man, Eve and Adam, was not sufficient to keep them obedient to one single commandment. Why should we expect after the fall and expulsion from Paradise, that a fallen humanity would not be half Cain-like, envious and hateful and murderous? The Abel-like sort, in the story of the first brothers, are wiped out!

Modern views of human nature are very flattering. It is only the illusion of religion, according to Freud, that makes us unnecessarily feel guilty. Or is it only the illusory expectation of a divine judgment, invented by priests to protect private property of landowners, according to Karl Marx, that makes us feel guilty? Or, more basic to Enlightenment, society has enchained us in traditional shackles, and freed from it we can be as we were meant to be: free.

Why not reject the weak sentimentality of rococo views of us humans as innocent children, noble savages, or angels still close to Paradise and ready for utopia (come a revolution), and accept the truths of Scripture and tradition? We should be ashamed of ourselves. We should confess our sins, and we should first seek to be reconciled with those we have sinned against, and then we should beg divine forgiveness.

A Model of Balance

The most remarkable aspect of the Ten Commandments is that they are addressed to the individual, yet they cover all the major relations of a person to others, who are referred to individually as "thy neighbor." A duty obliging the individual cannot be shifted to another; when duty is to an individual, the relation is one-to-one. If it is "thou" who is obliged in these various ways, then there is no other who can either keep or break that commandment. It is the individual who follows his/her own conscience, who bears the responsibility, who is rewarded or condemned. Yet it is acts and words as well as attitudes that are commended or forbidden. And these acts and words are in relations to others, beginning with the most intimate, of children to parents (and by implication parents to children), or husband to wife or wife to husband. Literally the "neighbor" lives in the vicinity, as we commonly say "next-door neighbor," those with whom we are likely to have the most dealings of everyday life. The pertinent question of Jesus is "Who is my neighbor?" (Luke 10:29), and the answer expected of us is "anyone" and "everyone." Hence the Decalogue is not solely a personal morality, it is also essentially social. It is of course the human side of the covenant of people, Israel, made under Moses at Sinai. This gives it a place in human history, and its maker YHWH secures its cosmic side, in the sense of relation of humankind to the Creator.

Moral and political philosophies of the modern world fall into opposites, individual or social, standards of the person or of the group. The Decalogue is the best example of balance, inclusive of both poles. These opposites are best known today in political ideology: "libertarians" defending the rights of the individual, "communitarians" who turn our attention to "the common good." The balance of the Decalogue is a powerful reason for keeping it central. If we accept it, we cannot go to either the extreme of libertarianism or the extreme of communitarianism. In the debates between them we find evidence of the search for balance: libertarians accuse communitarians of oppressing the individual with the burden of the common good, and communitarians accuse libertarians of exaggerating the individual and neglecting the common good.

This is not the only way in which the Decalogue is the model of balance. A significant contrast is between the past and the future. This is in the first table, which can be regarded as tying together a historical past of the ancestors with an anticipated future of the descendants. Specifically, gratitude is expressed to God, "who brought thee out of the land of Egypt, out of the house of bondage" (Exod. 20:2). This identification of the present person with the past ancestor is amplified in the other version: "The Lord our God made a covenant with us. . . . The Lord made not this covenant with our fathers, but with us, even us, who are all of us here alive this day" (Deut. 5:2-3). The children, or children's children, then accepted the commandments, as did their ancestors: the covenant is then the bond between the generations, and descendants take the place of ancestors. The present is a bridge between past and future.

Equally intense is our identification with our descendants. There is both fear and hope as we consider the consequences of the either-or: idolatry or faithfulness to the true God. "Thou shalt not bow down thyself to them [false gods] nor serve them: for I the Lord thy God am a jealous God, visiting the iniquity of the fathers upon the children unto the third and fourth generation of them that hate me: and showing mercy unto those that love me, and keep my commandments" (Exod. 20:5-6). The other version stresses the number of the latter who are blessed: they are "thousands" (Deut. 5:10).

Past and future are linked in remembering the creation of the world on the Sabbath, and in the very next commandment also, "Honour thy father and thy mother, that thy days may be long upon the land which the Lord thy God giveth thee" (Exod. 20:12). The other version, commanding that all servants enjoy the day of rest, the Sabbath, recalls the liberation of freemen from bondage: "Remember that thou wast a servant in the land of Egypt" (Deut. 5:15). Honoring parents ensures that "thy days may be prolonged and that it may go well with thee" (5:16).

Some complain that conservative ideologies glorify a past as ideal, a past that never was except as we wish it had been. Others complain that liberal and radical ideologies are utopian, directed toward a future that can never be. The biblical view expressed in Exodus and Deuteronomy recalls liberation from slavery, recognizing the struggle between good and evil, and looks forward to a future that is possible, a reasonable expectation under the covenant. The Decalogue is a corrective to the exaggerations of a future under a messiah or in a new Jerusalem.

This last consideration leads us to the healthy balance of the

Decalogue between the mundane and the ideal. By the mundane is recognized such ordinary evils as are forbidden by law: murder, theft, false witness, and stated with details that have become quaint for us, the bad motives of envy of what is the neighbor's and desire to take it: "Thou shalt not covet thy neighbor's house, thou shalt not covet thy neighbor's wife, nor his manservant, nor his maidservant, nor his ox, nor his ass, nor anything that is thy neighbor's" (Exod. 20:17). The other version is more explicit about the movement of the heart that may eventually destroy the family: the temptation to breach the faithfulness implied by "Thou shalt not commit adultery" (Exod. 20:14; Deut. 5:18 in a slightly different form): "Neither shalt thou desire thy neighbor's wife" (5:21).

We should not be offended by this sequence of "Thou shalt not's," nor by the fact that these are the wrongs we commonly do to one another. Decalogic morality pertains to everyday life.

Jesus' Sermon on the Mount intensifies the impact of the commandments on the individual heart. With the kingdom of God "at hand," Jesus says: "Ye have heard that it was said by them of old time, Thou shalt not kill . . . but I say unto you, That whosoever is angry with his brother without a cause shall be in danger of the judgment" (Matt. 5:21-22). With the same perspective, Jesus intensifies "Thou shalt not commit adultery" (5:27). And also others such as "Thou shalt not forswear thyself, . . . but I say unto you, Swear not at all" (5:33-34).

Universally Human

In Judaism, earlier than Jesus, we find the maxim "Take heed to thyself, my child, in all thy works, and be discreet in all thy behavior: and what thou thyself hatest, do to no man." The famous Rabbi Hillel, invited to summarize the law while standing on one leg, replied: "Whatsoever thou wouldest that men should not do to thee, do not do that to them."

The Ten Commandments are historically linked to the Golden Rule. One summary preserves the content of the two tables of the law: love of God and love of fellow man. The positive "love" is in biblical language contrasted to the hostile rejection of neighbor, "hate" (Matt. 5:43). But the Golden Rule is purely formal, and is known in both positive and negative forms.

The summary given by Jesus has been often cited as the point at which morally there is a center of agreement with Jewish teaching and that of other world religions, such as that of Confucius and Gotama Buddha, and some say, all religions. One form is "Therefore all things whatsoever ye would that men should do to you, do ye even so to them: for this is the law and the prophets" (Matt. 7:12).

The other quotation from Jesus is, "And as ye would that men should do to you, do ye also to them likewise" (Luke 6:31). The first is in context of the Sermon on the Mount, the second in the Sermon on the Plain (Matt. 5:1 and Luke 6:17). The Golden Rule has great appeal. It can be the first moral rule taught to children: "Would you like it if another did that to you?" It encourages each of us to put himself/herself in the place of another. It is morally wrong when another harms us, hits us unprovoked; and the child is taught to reason in a similar way that he should not hit another unprovoked. The principle of mutuality is the basis of most, and some moralists say all, moral judgment.

The philosophic beauty of the Golden Rule may be compared to Kant's categorical imperative: it isolates the pure form of moral judgment. It is more than thinking mutually, of putting yourself in place of the other; it is also regarding relations between persons from the perspective of an ideal observer. Behind the Kantian formula "So act that the rule of thy act could be made law universal," there seems to be the thought that as a generous and just God has given good gifts to those who ask, so we ought to act toward our neighbor (Matt. 5:45-48; 6:8; 7:11). Both the religious and philosophic versions presume a righteous and beneficent person, and thus there is some content which otherwise would be purely formal. A malevolent person might use the form: "I steal from you as you steal from me" or "I kill you as you kill me." To avoid this cynical interpretation an early Latin version of the passage from Matthew, though not the official Latin version of the church, the Vulgate, qualified "things": "Whatever *good* things, therefore, you wish that others should do unto you, even such do unto them, for this is the law and the prophets."

This is a good example of the ongoing conversation that is the decalogic tradition.

The early Christian church included among its necessary requirements: "Whatsoever ye do not wish should be done unto you . . . do not do to others" (from Codex D, Western Recession of the Council of Jerusalem, Acts 15:29). This became a principle of our common law through King Alfred the Great. He commented: "From this one doom a man may remember that he judge every man righteously; he need no other doom book. Let him remember that he adjudge to no man that which he would not that he adjudge to him, if he sought judgment against him."

Part of the appeal of the Golden Rule in this age when in many areas of life it is said "There are no rules," is that it can scarcely be attacked for explicitly specifying duties to God, as are the Ten Commandments. Confucius is author of the most ancient version, from the sixth century B.C., and so contemporary with other great sages. "What you do not like if done to yourself, do not do to others." Confucius, like Jewish and Christian sages, also states the principle positively as reciprocity, or relation "heart to heart."

The appeal is to what is universally human — to what transcends all differences of sex, language, color, or ethnicity, and all differences of creed. This may well be the root of the democratic affirmation of equality. It both satisfies reason and asserts a natural law that we can affirm without anticipating its decline or obsolescence. It is ideal and so often commonly affirmed but broken in practice that we can regard ourselves as a species of hypocrites.

If it were only an aspect of a particular stage of human culture, the Decalogue should have become as out-of-date and irrelevant as the Code of Hammurabi and the Egyptian Book of the Dead. Why should commandments written down in Hebrew, in what we call the Bronze Age, by a leader of fugitive nomads on their way to primitive agricultural life, have anything to say to us in totally different circumstances? But instead of dying of irrelevance, it survived by constantly being reapplied by prophets and philosophers. It not only survived in the Greco-Roman empire, it became part of the official religion of the empire. It became as well known in Greek among the subjects of Constantine's Byzantium as it had been in Alexandria when Philo showed how a Jewish philosopher could present its prescriptions as necessary to the ancient city life of Egypt as it had been in pastoral and agricultural Palestine.

The Ten Commandments survive because they are well fitted to the human condition and can be adapted to any stage of cultural development. Our sampling of different varying traditions of the ancient text shows how it grows and changes in meaning as it reveals itself to different minds. But only by having a constant central core of moral principles, applied in specific concrete relations, could the text acquire a fund of associated interpretations embodying over three thousand years of experience.

Selected Sources

[Paul Grimley Kuntz did not complete the footnotes to this book, but he left a partial list of sources. — ED.]

Chapter 3
St. John of the Ladder. *The Ladder of Divine Ascent.* Translated by Archimandrate Lazarus Moore. New York: Harper & Row, 1959.

Chapter 5
Lees, Beatrice Adelaide. *Alfred the Great, the Truthteller: Maker of England.* New York: Putnam, 1915.

Chapter 6
Schimmel, Annemarie. "Lull, Ramón (c. 1232-1316)." In *The Encyclopedia of Religion,* edited by Mircea Eliade, 9:52-53. New York: Macmillan, 1987.

Chapter 7
Rickaby, Joseph, S.J. *St. Thomas Aquinas, the Commandments of God: Conferences on the Two Precepts of Charity and the Ten Commandments.* Translated by Laurence Shapcote, O.P. London: Burns, Oates and Washbourne, 1937.

Sorgia, R. Raimondo M., O.P. *Opuscoli Teologico-Spirituali.* Rome: Editioni Paoline, n.d.

Thomas Aquinas. *St. Thomas Aquinas on the Two Commandments of Charity and the Ten Commandments of the Law.* Translated by Father Henry Augustus Rawes, with a letter by Cardinal Archbishop Henry Edward Manning. London: Burnes R. Oates, 1879.

—————. *Basic Writings of Saint Thomas Aquinas,* vol. 2, *Man and the Conduct of Life,* pp. 817-52. Edited by Anton C. Pegis. New York: Random House, 1945.

—————. *Fede E Opere: Testi Ascetici E Mistici.* Translated by Eugenio M. Sonini, S.J. Rome: Città Nova Editrice, 1981.

Torrell, Jean-Pierre, ed. *Les Collationes in Decem Preceptis de Saint Thomas D'Aquin,*

Revue des Sciences Philosophiques et Théologique, tome 69, pp. 229-63. Paris: Librairie Philosophique J. Vrin, 1985.

Chapter 8

Geffkin, Johannes. *Die Zehn Gebote.* 1840.

Iannucce, Remo Joseph. *The Treatment of the Capital Sins and the Decalogue in the Sermons of Berthold Von Rigensburg.* Catholic University of America, Studies in German, vol. 17. 1942. New York: AMS Press, 1970.

Rudolfi, Roberto. "Savonarola, Giralamo." In *Encyclopaedia Britannica, Macropaedia* (1981), 16:289-291.

Weinstein, Donald. "Savonarola, Giralamo." In *Encyclopedia of Religion,* 13:89-90.

Chapter 9

Vaughan, Robert. *Tracts and Treatises of John de Wvcliffe, D.D. with Selections and Translations from His Manuscripts, and Latin Works.* "Expositio Decalogi." London: Blackburn and Pardon, 1845.

Wycliffe, John. *Select English Works of John Wycliffe, Miscellaneous Works,* vol. 3. Edited by Thomas Arnold. Oxford: Clarendon, 1871. "The Ten Commundents."

Chapter 10

Luther, Martin. *The Large and Small Catechisms.* In *The Book of Concord: The Confessions of the Evangelical Lutheran Church.* Translated and edited by Theodore G. Tappert, with Jaroslav Pelikan and others. Philadelphia: Muhlenberg, 1959.

Pelikan, Jaroslav. In *The Encyclopedia of Religion,* edited by Mircea Eliade, 5:250-55. New York: Macmillan, 1987.

Wace, Henry, and C. A. Buchheim. *Luther's Primary Works.* London: Hodder and Stoughton, 1910.

Chapter 11

Aston, Margaret. *England's Iconoclasts.* Vol. 1, *Laws against Images.* Oxford: Clarendon, 1988.

———. "Iconoclasm in England, Official and Clandestine." In *Iconoclasm versus Art and Drama,* edited by Clifford Davidson and Ann Eijenholm Nichols. Kalamazoo, Mich.: Medieval Institute Publications, 1989.

Calvin, John. *A Commentary of the Psalms of David,* vol. 1. Geneva, 1557. On the basis of Arthur Golding's translation (Oxford, 1839; Oxford: Talboys, 1840).

———. *Institutes of the Christian Religion.* Translated by John Allen. Philadelphia, 1926.

———. *Commentaries on the Last Four Books of Moses Arranged in the Form of a Harmony.* Translated by Charles William Bingham. 4 vols. Grand Rapids: Eerdmans, 1950.

———. *Institutes of the Christian Religion.* Edited by John T. McNeill. Translated by

Ford Lewis Battles. Library of Christian Classics, vols. 20-21. Philadelphia: Westminster, 1960.

———. *John Calvin's Sermons on the Ten Commandments*. Edited and translated by Benjamin W. Farley. Grand Rapids: Baker, 1980.

Cranz, F. Edward. *An Essay on the Development of Luther's Thought on Justice, Law and Society*. Harvard Theological Studies, no. 19. Cambridge: Harvard University Press, 1959. "The Three Hierarchies," pp. 173-78.

Earle, Alice Morse. *Sabbath in New England*. London: Hodder and Stoughton, n.d.

Gregory of Nyssa. *The Life of Moses*. Translated by Abraham J. Malherbe and Everett Ferguson. New York: Paulist, 1978.

King, Margaret L., and Albert Rabil, Jr. *Her Immaculate Hand: Selected Works by Ami about the Women Humanists of Ouattrocentro Italy*. Medieval and Renaissance Texts and Studies. Binghamton, N.Y., 1983.

Luther, Martin. "Wie das Paulus und Petrus und vor allen Chistus selbst in Evangelium taten. Diese Dekaloge sid soviel klaer als der Dekaloge des Mose." Thesen 52-54, *De Fide*. Weimar Ausgabe, vol. 39, I.

Wright, David. "The Ethical Use of the Old Testament in Luther and Calvin: A Comparison." *Scottish Journal of Theology* 36: 19.

Chapter 15

Hobbes, Thomas. *Leviathan*. Edited by A. R. Waller. Cambridge: Cambridge University Press, 1904.

Locke, John. *Some Thoughts Concerning Education*. Cambridge: Cambridge University Press, 1880.

———. *Paraphase and Notes on the Epistles of St. Paul*. Edited by Arthur William Wainnright. Critical edition with introduction and notes. 2 vols. Oxford: Clarendon, 1987.

Chapter 18

Jefferson, Thomas. *Jefferson's Extracts from the Gospels*. Edited by Dickinson W. Adams and Ruth W. Lester. Introduction by Eugene B. Sheridan. Princeton: Princeton University Press, 1983.

———. *Literary Commonplace Book*. Edited by Douglas L. Wilson. Princeton: Princeton University Press, 1989.

———. *Thomas Jefferson: Writings*. Edited by Merrill D. Peterson, pp. 762-64. New York: Library of America, 1984.

St. John, Henry, Viscount Bolingbroke. *Philosophical Works*. 5 vols., 1754-77. New York: Garland, 1977.

Chapter 19

Bentham, Jeremy. *A Commentary on the Commentaries* and *A Fragment on Government*. Edited by J. H. Burns and H. L. A. Hart. London: University of London, Athlone Press, 1977.

Index